D1524993

PRAISE FOR

The Unshakeable Faith of an Inventor

Only rarely can one find in English the memoir of a man from Estonia. The life story of Otto G. Lellep will be of great interest to engineers and to others interested in the history of technology. An engineer, inventor, and scientist, Lellep had global impact on the production of steel, nickel, and cement.

HEIKI RAUDLA
FORMER PARLIAMENTARIAN, ESTONIA

Otto Lellep's account of his early life includes a detailed description of life on what was a technologically advanced farm in late 19th century Estonia. He also considers an important political era. With his recollections of his father's life, he provides first and second-hand accounts of two active participants in the Estonian nationalist movement in the late 19th and early 20th century, describing the struggle of Estonian farmers for land ownership, the fight for an education system using the Estonian language, and, finally, the establishment of an independent Estonian state.

BILL J. DARDEN
UNIVERSITY OF CHICAGO PROFESSOR EMERITUS,
DEPARTMENTS OF LINGUISTICS AND SLAVIC
LANGUAGES & LITERATURES

The Unshakeable Faith of an Inventor conveys the life, studies, and work of Otto G. Lellep with vivid detail, wisdom, and charm. The memoir gives us an encyclopedic view of the twentieth century, with the helpful addition of insightful commentary by Dr. Renate Lellep Fernandez.

ALEXANDER SOIFER
PROFESSOR OF INTERDEPARTMENTAL STUDIES
UNIVERSITY OF COLORADO, COLORADO SPRINGS

The Unshakeable Faith of an Inventor

OTTO G. LELLEP

Remembering and Remembered

To a Readership living
or visiting in Montgomery
Place. January 19, 2023
Renate Lellep Fernandez
RL

ANNOTATED BY RENATE LELLEP FERNANDEZ

EDITED BY KESAYA E. NODA

Brandt & Maher Publishing

comments welcome,
or a prospective
reviewer.
Renate
renate.l.fernandez@
gmail.com
312 522-3945

The Unshakeable Faith of an Inventor
Otto G. Lellep, Remembering and Remembered
© 2022 Annotated by Renate Lellep Fernandez
Edited by Kesaya E. Noda
Brandt & Maher Publishing

Published 2022
Brandt & Maher Publishing
Printed in the United States of America
Distributed by Epigraph Books

ISBN: 978-1-954744-83-7
LCCN: 2022909972

Edited by Kesaya E. Noda: Your Life, Your Family Stories.
Cover and interior design by Lisa Carta.

CONTENTS

Interview at Allis Chalmers in Milwaukee
Financial agreement with Allis Chalmers
Successful pelletization of taconite (low-grade iron ore)
Allis Chalmers research and development plant built at Carrollville
Industrial-scale pelletization plant built in Minnesota
Allis Chalmers produces "grate kiln system" (Lepol kiln)

LIST OF MAPS

PHOTOGRAPHS, SKETCHES, AND ADDENDA

Unless listed in brackets (indicating photographs taken from family collections) all photographs and sketches are as included in Otto's manuscript. Sources of addenda are as indicated.

MY FATHER'S WORLD

Maps and Reflections
Renate Lellep Fernandez

The following maps indicate significant countries, cities, and sites relevant to the long life of Otto G. Lellep, as mentioned in his memoirs.

I have also included a few areas I believe are significant, though unmentioned directly in my father's writing. Yekaterinburg, founded in the eighteenth century, had become a major stop on the Trans-Siberian Railway by the time Otto traveled to the Ural iron mining area to investigate nickel deposits there. As a child, I learned at home from my father to romanticize the Sami, a people of far northern Norway, Finland, and Russia through whose tribal lands [Lapland] he, in 1917, may have had to travel on his way to America, as Germany was then blocking the Baltic sea route.

My father did not write of having visited or worked in the Andes, but he had admired, and brought home to us in California, a finely worked drinking container from there for the consumption of sacred *pulque*, an alcoholic drink. And Hibbing, of northern Minnesota, was at the very center of the mining district that includes the Mesabi Range and the North Michigan Peninsula, sources of the low-grade mining ore that Otto's Lepol kiln made economically viable.

Though it hardly appears in his personal story of being and becoming an inventor, land and geography figured keenly in my father's awareness and appreciation. As a parent, he insisted upon his daughters developing spatial knowledge and a sense of orientation: learning first of all the street names in our neighborhood, then the land, lands, and waters on an ever larger scale. Meeting up with us in California in the late summer of 1941, he presented us with a puzzle of the United States—territory we had just crossed by automobile from east to west—and a second puzzle map of the world, whose capital cities we memorized enough to be able to recite at the dinner table for his pleasure.

In this regard, most memorable for me was his insistent requirement that I learn and be able to pronounce in the English I was just beginning to learn, the names of all the streets I had to cross—"Linden," "Utica," "Tilghman"—to go from our residence on Allen Street to Cedar Beach Lake and Pool that hot and moist summer of 1940. Not until I could recite them to him aloud was I allowed to walk alone to that cooling magnet of attraction.

In September, my sense of neighborhood grew to include Muhlenberg Elementary School a few blocks in the opposite direction. Such Germanic names were easy for me. Native-derived words such as "Utica" were a pleasurable exotic turn in my mouth and imagination. Otto did not allow me to run a few blocks away to eagerly fetch him his newspaper, *The Chronicle*, until I could speak and spell out loud for him that improbably unphonetic word, thereby enabling me to purchase it with an Indian nickel.

My father promoted the learning of spatial knowledge, but social, conventional knowledge, like that related to gender, we had to learn on our own. Thus, that first summer, adult women assumed that I was a boy—an eight-year-old clad only in a dark pair of trunks—someone to shoo out of the dressing room at Cedar Beach. I had invaded their women's privacy, they thought.

My father, for all his experience of places and nations, routinely asserted and emphasized that he was a "citizen of the world"—a "cosmopolite," if I remember correctly—that he was neither a nationalist nor patriot of any entity on this planet. Not that I would ever deny that he, an Estonian, had become a naturalized US citizen and I, born of him, was by birth also a citizen of the US. Until I was well into adulthood, however, I always understood him simply as an Estonian, until, when editing his memoir, I was taken aback by the realization that he had actually and officially once been a Russian—an officer of the Russian military! This was a shock to me, as he had presented himself to me only as one who loved his homeland and its language, simultaneously affirming that his allegiance was to nothing but the Cosmos.

My father's response to Gandhi's death has always remained in my memory. He received the news with sudden tears, which rolled down his cheeks. It was the death of a humanitarian cosmopolite, as my father himself had, for all his life, aspired to be.

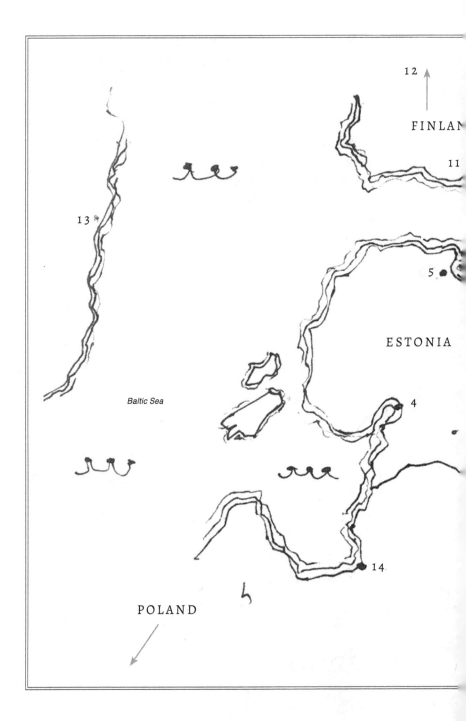

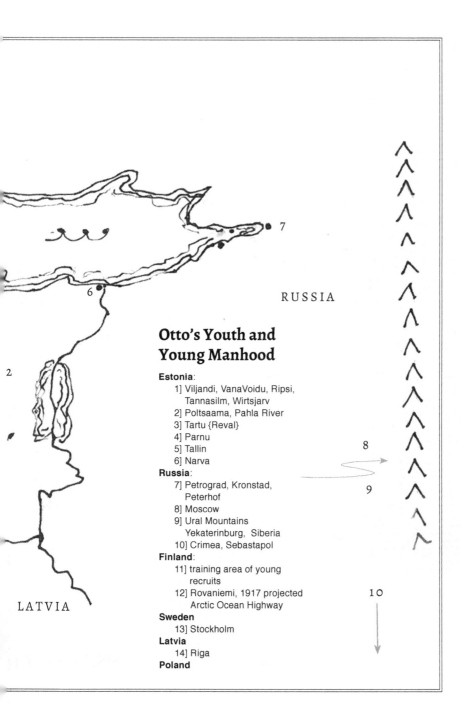

RUSSIA

Otto's Youth and Young Manhood

Estonia:
    1] Viljandi, VanaVoidu, Ripsi,
       Tannasilm, Wirtsjarv
    2] Poltsaama, Pahla River
    3] Tartu {Reval}
    4] Parnu
    5] Tallin
    6] Narva
Russia:
    7] Petrograd, Kronstad,
       Peterhof
    8] Moscow
    9] Ural Mountains
       Yekaterinburg, Siberia
    10] Crimea, Sebastapol
Finland:
    11] training area of young
       recruits
    12] Rovaniemi, 1917 projected
       Arctic Ocean Highway
Sweden
    13] Stockholm
Latvia
    14] Riga
Poland

Work and Study in Estonia and Beyond

Norway: and northwest boundary area with Russia:
1] Kirkenes, Peshengo, Nikel, Murmansk:
2] Tromso
3] Trondheim
4] Bergen, Oslo [The boundary between Norway and Sweden is deliberately uncertain; historically they were one country until early in 20th century]

Finland:
5] Sami country [Lapland], Torneu
6] Finland area in general including Rovaniemi and OGL unspecified troop training ground.

Sweden:
7] Stockholm {Sweden, notably, does not extend to Barent's Sea or the Arctic Ocean, as does Norway bordering Russia}

Russia: center:
8] Petrograd, Kronstad, Peterhof
9] Moscow, Novgorod, Tula, Borodino, Military posting

Russia: east and south:
10] Ural Mountain Chain, Yekaterinenburg, Siberia
11] Crimea, Sebastapol

Estonia: Tallinn, Narva, Poltsaama, Tartu, Viljandi, Parnu [more detailed on map titled OGL's Youth and Young Manhood]

Latvia,
12] Riga

Poland
13] Warsaw
14] Lodz

Germany
15] Ruhrgebiet [Ruhr District], Dusseldorf, Essen, Oberhausen, Dortmund, Bochum, Neubeckum, Hösel
16] Insel Fehmarn, Rostock, Braunschweig, Luneburgerheide, Claustal im Harz, Goslar; Lübeck
17] Berlin, Dessau, Rudersdorf, Dresden, Oberschlesien, Oranienburg, Ore Mountains {Erzgebirge}
18] Bonn, Heidelberg, Leimen, Mannheim, Tubingen, Bodensee, Mainz

Switzerland:
19] Bern, Rieder Alb, Aletsch Glacier, Zurich, Mannerdorf

Belgium:
20] Brussels

Italy:
21] Brenner Pass
22] Mailand {Milan}
23] Genoa, Nervi

France, Spain, Portugal [Iberian Peninsula]:
24] Paris
25] Pyrenees
26] Valencia
27] Gibraltar
28] Cangas de Onis, Bilbao
29] Lisbon

Greece:
30] Athens

Not mapped: Other destinations and bodies mentioned by OGL or in Lellep Family Archive: Beirut, Cairo, India, Japan Hong Kong, Thailand, India, South Korea, South Africa, Chile; Barent's Sea, Atlantic Ocean, Pacific Ocean, Indian Ocean, Mediterranean Sea, Black sea.

Atlantic Ocean

FRAN

SPAIN

28●

●29

25

26 ●

27

Otto's Career, Employment, and Family Life

NORTH AMERICA

CANADA
1. Sudbury, Copper Cliff

MEXICO
2. Acapulco and coastal area
3. Mexico City, Teotihuacan

COSTA RICA
4. Nature Reserve

CUBA
5. Havana
6. Isle of Pines

UNITED STATES
7. New York City
8. Pittsfield, Massachusetts
9. Maine coastal region
10. Bethlehem, Lehigh, Allentown, Egypt, Germansville
11. Pittsburgh and surrounding industrial area
12. Huntington, West Virginia
13. Cleveland, Warren, Ohio
14. Wisconsin: Milwaukee, Wauwatosa, Carrollville
15. Michigan Upper Peninsula, Lake Superior, Mesabi Range
16. Wisconsin: Madison
17. Minnesota: Duluth, Hibben,
18. Minneapolis
19. Golden, Colorado
20. California Bay Area: Berkeley, Muir Woods, Stanford, Los Altos
21. Southern California: San Diego, Los Angeles, Alhambra, Vista, Fontana

SOUTH AMERICA

ECUADOR
22.

ARGENTINA
23. Buenos Aires, Loma Negra

SOUTH AMERICA

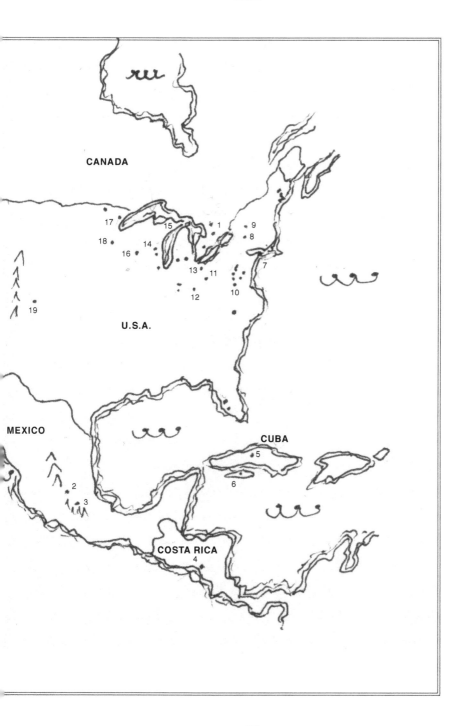

FOREWORD

Ultimate credit for editing belongs with Dr. Renate Lellep Fernandez—though I did all the initial work on the text. We have left to Otto the choice of spelling—sometimes "czar," sometimes "tsar"—and "Wiljandi" rather than "Viljandi," for examples, though we use modern spelling in the endnotes. We have followed the same practice with names: Johann "Kohler" in Otto's manuscript becomes Johann "Köler" in modern texts and in the endnotes; today's Männedorf, Switzerland is "Mannerdorf" in Otto's memories.

Otto's spelling and use of names changed over the course of his writing the manuscript. When referring to his daughters during their time in Germany, he writes "Liisa" and "Renate." In the United States, "Liisa" becomes "Lisa" (or "Lee" in his letters) and "Renate becomes "Nate." To avoid confusion, we have used "Liisa" and "Renate" until the daughters appear in descriptions of the family's life in the United States.

Some of Otto's choices probably reflect his schooling ("fibre" versus "fiber"). Others are signs of the context of his memories (life in Germany, where his daughter was "Liisa" versus life in the United States, where she was "Lisa"). Still others are more significant. A passionate inhabitant of Estonia and student of matters Estonian recently observed in a note to me that "Viljandi" is the Estonian spelling of the city's name. There is no "w" sound in Estonian. "Wiljandi" is German spelling. He believes Otto's spelling is a manifestation of "Russification"—the attempt when Otto was a child, and even more violently and massively later, to suppress and destroy Estonian language, history, heritage, culture, and any possibility of Estonian autonomy or nationhood. According to him, the Russian powers of Otto's time preferred even German to Estonian spelling.

As the initial editor, I have been privileged to work on Otto's manuscript and have tried always to remain faithful to his intent and language. Because the text often lacked transitions, I added them, indicating my additions in brackets. As mentioned, the original work contained many sections that were repetitive or out of chronological order. I re-ordered the text, increased the number of chapters, eliminated repetitive descriptions, occasionally found alternatives for frequently used adjectives, and smoothed the language for clarity and readability.

Otto enriched his text with many photographs, most of which he took himself. We have added even more from the Lellep Family Archive, indicating these additions by enclosing their captions within brackets.

Otto was in his mid-eighties when he wrote this book. It would surely have been a very different piece had he written it five or ten years earlier. His age caused him to err occasionally in details related to dates, places, and chemical formulas, but in essence—in all that matters—I believe we can trust that we are reading, in his typescript, a true account.

In the endnotes (written by me unless otherwise indicated as the work of Renate), I have noted discrepancies in details and have employed modern American and current Estonian spellings. I have not cited each source I used in the individual notes, trusting that for an informal memoir such as Otto's, edited as it is by a non-academic, non-scientist, and intended as it is for family and general readers, a selected bibliography will suffice.

My short endnotes cannot even begin to do justice to the complexities of Estonian history: the power shifts between the Estonians, Baltic Germans, and Russians; and the conflicting, evolving visions and alliances of such leading Estonians as Jakob Hurt, Konstantin Päts, Jaan Tönisson, Otto Strandman, and others mentioned by Otto in his memoir. I offer the notes with apologies for their inevitable simplicity, and I encourage readers to explore further and more deeply on their own.

My deepest thanks to Dr. Roger Soderberg, professor emeritus of Dartmouth College, for many long conversations and emails regarding Otto's descriptions of his experiments and furnaces. He was most generous with his time and expertise. Dr. Eric Suuberg and Mr. Dylan Moore also assisted with basic explanations. B. J. Bernard, president of Surface Combustion, Inc. (where Otto once worked), offered a helpful discussion of surface combustion.

Dr. Ainsley Morse and Dr. Richard Morse provided translations of Russian terms and comments on literary references. Mr. Reinhart Sonnenburg helped with the translation of the speech given when Otto was presented with the Carl Lueg Memorial Medal, and Mr. R. Paul Firnhaber provided invaluable discussion of many matters Estonian. My husband, Christopher Dye, has my gratitude for his encouragement and help throughout my work on the manuscript. Above all, I salute and deeply thank Renate Lellep Fernandez, Otto's youngest daughter, whose vision, commitment, financial support, and involvement made the editing and publication of Otto's memoir possible. Her comments will deepen any reader's view of her father.

I apologize for any errors I may have inadvertently introduced. Responsibility for them is mine.

Kesaya E. Noda
August 2020

INTRODUCTION

Otto G. Lellep and His Memoir
Kesaya E. Noda

When Otto G. Lellep was in his mid-eighties, after a long and successful career as an inventor, he mentioned several times to his daughter Renate Lellep Fernandez that he thought his work was done. He had assessed the facts. He was too old to serve as a consultant, traveling across the United States and internationally to sites using the Lepol kiln, the high-temperature system he had created for burning cement or iron ore pellets.[1] Nor was it possible for him to initiate or continue his past experiments with steel, iron ore, cement, magnesium, or nickel. If he could not work, she understood, Otto wanted to bring an end to his life.

Renate, and particularly her husband, James Fernandez, suggested a different door for Otto to open. "Your work isn't done," Jim said. "You haven't yet written your memoir." Otto agreed, took up a pencil, and began to write his manuscript in 1968.[2]

Otto Lellep was born in Estonia (then a guberniya of tsarist Russia), but Estonian was only one of his languages. He also spoke English, German, Russian, Spanish, and some French. Intending this memoir for his children (raised in the United States), grandchildren (born here), and friends from various countries of origin, he chose to write in English, giving his handwritten pages to his niece, Alice Veinbergs, to type.

Otto had a native English speaker correct the language of his memoir, but when he believed it done, Alice and other family members nonetheless suggested that he have it edited. After years of working and living in the United States, Otto had a good grasp of English, but by the time he was writing, age had narrowed his vocabulary and diminished his ability to sequence events. The text contained many repetitions, and the story jumped back and forth in time. Most problematic for general readers, Otto offered little background for or explanation of his many references to chemical reactions, metallurgy, high-temperature furnaces, and the properties of nickel, steel, iron ore, cement, and taconite.

Otto's response to the suggestion that he seek an editor did not surprise his children. One morning, in 1972, before anyone involved could further pressure him to have the manuscript worked on, he quietly put all the pages under his arm and strode to a local copy shop. Some days later he picked up twenty copies of his book. Each was hard bound with a green cover and included 272 pages of typed text, double spaced; reproductions of photographs he'd taken and developed; sketches of the layout of his family's Estonian farm; and diagrams of several of his earliest and later experimental prototypes and inventions. The memoir was his, and his alone. He triumphantly mailed the copies to his family and friends.

Almost forty years later, when Otto's daughter Renate asked me to edit his book, we agreed that we wished above all to preserve and honor Otto's voice—that of an Estonian man writing in one of his several languages.

Otto tells what is by any measure an extraordinary story. He was born in 1884. His family was relatively prosperous compared to the Estonian farmers around them, but their lives were ruled by work. When he was young, everything his family wore or ate came from their farm, the sea, or the forest and river nearby. At meals, the Lelleps and their few workers sat at a long wooden table and ate with wooden spoons, cutting both bread and meat with their pocketknives. Otto later remembers the first time he was exposed to "cutlery," so the family must not have had forks. Linen pants and shirts were made from flax grown and processed on the farm, then spun into thread by Otto's sisters. Horses pulled plows, and all power came from a water wheel and turbine running off a millpond, dammed not by concrete, but by wooden timbers that rotted and had to be periodically replaced.

From these beginnings on an almost pre-industrial farm, Otto became a professional inventor and metallurgist. Finding his own funding, he worked in Europe, South America, and the United States, ultimately specializing in large-scale, high-temperature, industrial furnaces. He created a revolutionary, oxygen-blown furnace for the production of steel and, through his Lepol kilns and traveling grate systems, radically improved the efficiency and possibilities for iron and cement production in the United States and Europe, South America, Jordan, India, South Korea, Japan, and South Africa.

In writing his memoir, Otto assumed that his readers would share his knowledge of cement, steel, industrial furnaces, and metallurgy. For non-specialists, a discussion of terms and a brief look at the background of his work will be useful. The political, historical, and cultural context of his life is also vital, so a few comments on the Estonia of his time will, I hope, provide a broader perspective on his story.

CEMENT AND STEEL

Otto had his first success working with cement, the powdery mixture that forms concrete when it is mixed with water, sand, and rock. Portland cement is manufactured in four stages. First, raw materials such as limestone, sea shells, and chalk are crushed, ground, and milled with binding materials such as clay, iron ore, and sand. This fine powder is loaded into a high-temperature kiln, or, in the words of Otto and other engineers, "charged" into it. When "burned" at a high temperature, the mixture is "sintered," that is, formed into solid lumps or nodules. These are called "clinker." Ground and mixed with gypsum, clinker becomes Portland cement.

Over time, producers had developed two methods for processing their raw materials into clinker. In the "wet-method," the mix was ground wet and fed into the kiln as a slurry. In the "dry-method," it was fed in as a powder. In the 1920s, drawing on the memories of his family farm in Estonia and driven by an innate thriftiness, Otto invented a brilliant and now commonly accepted means to save cement producers millions of dollars in energy costs. Understanding that the powdered raw mix tended to blow back, out of the kiln, and reasoning that it was a waste of heat to create a slurry then burn off its liquid, he invented an effective technique for pelletizing the powdered raw mix: the first step in a semi-dry process. He then created a system utilizing a traveling grate and the otherwise wasted, hot exhaust gas of the kiln in order to burn the pellets into clinker. Otto's system, developed on an industrial scale through collaboration with the Polysius Company in Germany, was and is sold internationally as "Lepol kilns" (a compound created from the combination of LEllep and POLysius).

Otto's invention of the Lepol kiln greatly increased the fortunes of the Polysius Company and brought welcome income to its inventor. Otto then turned his attention to steel, an alloy that begins as iron ore (an oxide of iron containing various quantities of other elements). When heated in a charcoal fire, the iron ore releases some of its oxygen to form a relatively pure form of iron. Hammered by a blacksmith, this can be worked into and shaped as "wrought iron." At very high temperatures, iron melts and begins to absorb carbon, forming "cast iron." As it was first produced in the West, cast iron came to be called "pig iron," because the troughs into which the molten metal flowed for hardening resembled piglets nursing at a large sow. Wrought iron (carbon content .02–.08 percent) is malleable but for some functions too soft; cast iron or pig iron (carbon content

3.0–4.5 percent) is hard but for some functions too brittle. Steel (carbon content .2–1.5 percent) is between the two: harder than wrought iron yet more flexible and malleable than cast iron.

In his memoir, Otto references various methods of steel production. The Bessemer converter process, invented by Sir Henry Bessemer in 1856, first made possible the mass production of the metal. In Bessemer converters, compressed air is blown through molten pig iron, emptying it of some carbon and silicone, leaving steel. However, because the presence of phosphorous makes for an unwelcome brittleness in the steel, the process could only be used on pig iron made from phosphorous-free ores, which were rare.

In 1876, Sidney Gilchrist Thomas, a Welshman, discovered that phosphorous could be drawn from the pig iron in the converter by the addition of a chemically basic material such as limestone. Called the basic Bessemer process or the Thomas basic process, this revolutionary discovery made it possible for manufacturers to use iron ore mined from many regions in the world. The price of production fell and the output of steel skyrocketed, but in the meanwhile, other inventors had been seeking further improvements.

During the 1860s, Karl Wilhelm Siemens, a German engineer, developed an alternative means of production. His open-hearth process used coal gas (and later natural gas) to heat a broad, shallow, open-hearth furnace. Siemens passed exhaust gases through refractory (non-flammable) bricks ("regenerators") that were set in an open pattern. Incoming cold gases were then channeled through the hot bricks, preheating the air and gases before they entered the furnace. This allowed for the efficient attainment of extremely high temperatures.

By adding wrought iron or iron oxide, Siemens was able to reduce the carbon content in the molten pig iron through dilution and oxidation. In contrast to the Bessemer process, which created steel in what has been described as a "volcanic rush," the open-hearth method was slow, allowing time for laboratory testing and fine control over the chemical composition of the metal. In addition, it made possible the production of steel in larger batches and the use of scrap metal in the production process, advantages that resulted in the widespread domination of the open-hearth process by 1900.

Otto turned his attention to the steel industry while he was in Germany, during the 1930s.[3] It was then possible to produce pure oxygen in large quantities, and he reasoned that the use of blown oxygen, rather than air, would vastly improve the production process first envisioned by Bessemer. Through a series of experiments, Otto succeeded in creating an oxygen-blown furnace for steel—almost surely the first in the world. Unfortunately, he was never able to fully develop and market his idea. In the 1940s in Switzerland, Robert Durrer independently invented a technique for using oxygen, and he is commonly given credit for discovering the process.

Otto realized his final contribution to metallurgy during his employment with Allis Chalmers, in Milwaukee. By the 1950s, stores of high-grade iron ore had greatly decreased in Michigan and Minnesota. Means had been found to separate iron ore from taconite—a low grade of ore previously considered waste rock—but the resulting powder was impossible to process. Drawing on his past experience, Otto was able to invent an energy efficient system for creating pellets from the powder.

On its website, the Minnesota Department of Natural Resources writes, "Taconite saved Minnesota's iron ore industry." It credits Dr. E. W. Davis of the University of Minnesota for playing a large role in the discovery of the extraction process but remains disappointingly silent regarding the inventor of the pelletizing process, noting only that pelletization was achieved after "many years of hard work."[4]

Under the best of circumstances, aspirants have steep hills to climb if they wish to become inventors and support themselves through their work. Otto's challenges were far greater than the usual, however, for though he always had a homeland, he did not have a country.

HISTORICAL BACKGROUND

For centuries, European conquerors oppressed the people of Estonia culturally, economically, politically, and socially. Bordering on Russia, the Baltic Sea, and the Gulf of Finland, the small territory that became the country of Estonia was beset by centuries of wars, famines, and plagues. By the early thirteenth century, Germans or Danes dominated nearly all of the continental lands of the Estonian people. In the centuries following, the Germans and Danes; the Russians, Danes, and Swedes; the Swedes and Poles; and the Russians and Swedes battled for control. In the early 1600s, after five years of war, Russia ceded to Sweden all of Estonia; a little more than three decades later, after another war and a Russian victory, the balance of power in the area shifted, and Estonia eventually came under Russian rule. Other than the nineteen years of its existence as the republic of Estonia in the 1920s and 1930s, Estonia remained under Russian/Soviet control until 1991, when the Soviets recognized the independence of the country.

In many of the early pages of his memoir, Otto refers to the "German land barons" and mentions how long and powerfully their domination had lasted. As early as the end of the tenth century, German movement eastward had reached the Baltic region and by the end of the thirteenth century, its merchants and crusaders had mastered the area. In the century before Otto's birth, the vast majority of Estonians existed as serfs or peasants on lands owned by the German elites, who imposed their language, customs, and religion.

German domination continued under Sweden and in the transition to Russian rule. At the end of the Great Northern War, in the 1721 Peace of Uusikaupunki, Sweden conceded to Russia the loss of Livland (the Polish/Swedish/Russian province in the southern part of the Baltic littoral that included Viljandi, an important city for Otto and his family) and Estland (the Swedish/Russian province in the northern Baltics that included Tallinn). Tsar Peter I, however, agreed not to interfere with German power in both areas.

With the accession of Tsar Alexander I in 1801, a small window began to open. Initial agrarian reforms granting peasants some rights were followed by increasingly significant changes, particularly under the more liberal Alexander II. In 1849 (in Livland) and 1856 (in Estland) some land was made available to Estonian peasants for rent or purchase. By 1882, over 50 percent of the land available to peasants in Livland had been sold. Otto's father, an impoverished schoolteacher, was able to buy their family farm in 1883.

Remembering his childhood, Otto refers frequently to "Russification" and often describes his father as a leader and "patriot." The juxtaposition highlights two opposing forces in the Estonia of his time: attempts by Russia to bring the outer regions of its empire more closely under its control (particularly through the forceful imposition of the Russian language) and a growing awareness and assertion of Estonian cultural identity—commonly called its "National Awakening."

Otto attained an education with only the most arduous effort. Neither the Germans nor the Russians wished to make any more than a minimal education available to the Estonian peasants—if that. Under Tsar Alexander III, Russian was forcibly imposed as the language of all education and public administration. This policy of "Russification" thwarted country-wide Estonian efforts to establish what would have been the first secondary school to use Estonian as the language of instruction: the "Alexander School," named in honor of Alexander I.

Otto mentions his father's attempts to help establish the Alexander School and his deep disappointment when he enrolled Otto and discovered that it offered a lower level of curriculum, taught almost entirely in Russian. Even so, the ethos of the "National Awakening" continued to envelop both father and son. Estonian historian Toivo U. Raun describes "rural intelligentsia"—certainly including Otto's father—as taking a lead in the National Awakening, "the attempt to raise the national consciousness of the Estonian people." This period saw the creation of a written grammar of Estonian, the writing of *Kalevipoeg* (a national epic), the formation of an Estonian literary society, the publication of Estonian newspapers, and the celebration of national song fests that attracted thousands of Estonians and that, in the end, primarily featured stirring works by Estonian composers. Otto met or mentions many well-known leaders of the period: Johann Köler, Jakob Hurt, Carl Robert Jakobson, and Konstantin Päts, the man who became head of the independent nation of Estonia in 1918 (for the Estonian Provisional Government) and ruled periodically in the 1920s and early 1930s.

THE INVENTOR

In the book that follows, Otto traces the course of his education in Estonia and Germany, as well as his work in Europe, Argentina, Mexico, and the United States, referencing events in Estonia, as well as the outbreak of World War I, the Russian revolution, the Depression and market crash of 1929, and Hitler's rise to power. Still, his story unfolds from and around one central choice: his decision to become an inventor. In one account, he describes the decision in practical terms. Elsewhere, he links it to an idealistic wish to help "humankind."

In a letter to his wife, Frieda Aina, written in 1944 when Otto was looking for work in the area of Pittsburgh, Pennsylvania, he offered a more introspective view of his decisions, however.

> Usually my letters describe my doings or events in professional or business life. Everything in my letters has been usually and mostly concerned my own person. I have neglected you and children so often, yes, most of my life. I am and have been a selfcentered, typically introvert (as the psychologist say) person. . . .
> Selfcentered is not exactly the same as a narrow minded selfish person. I have not cared much for selfglorification, the pettier personal comforts and smallish social vanity. But I have deified always my work . . . I have neglected you,

children and my professional friends for the sake of my
technical dreams and inventions.

In these inventions I saw human progress and benefit.
Sure my inventive work has benefited humanity, the Lepol
kiln saves the cement industry 2 million dollars yearly. I
certainly am proud of this benefit. . . . But I am not ashamed
to confess to you that chasing ardently after inventions and
thus endeavoring to better our more material standard of
living and especially the material standard of humanity I have
missed practically entirely the intimate family life with you
and children. Even my best friend Klaas wrote me sometime
ago: "Why do you write all the time about yourself. Tell me
also something about your family."[5]

There is little such self-reflection in Otto's memoir. He presents
his story almost entirely through the lens of his inventing: how he
was drawn to it and what he needed to accomplish it. Readers are left
to ponder some obvious questions for themselves. How was he able
to become an inventor and to support himself and his family? What
inner resources buoyed him through his many disappointments and
the blows he sustained from people and world events?

Though Otto's tone is matter-of-fact, I find his story poignant, as
did his daughter—but only upon a later reading. Here is a man who
grew up in a farm family of relative prosperity, in which, nonetheless, life was so dominated by labor that he remembers only a few
moments of tenderness. He describes and cherishes each of them: a
short time with an aunt and uncle, two precious moments of attention from his mother, one from his father, and one from his sisters. To
complete his education and find work, he had to learn five languages.
To undertake his experiments, he had to create the space for them in
basements and garden sheds—or ask to borrow the laboratories of
university professors who did not know him. And he had to be bold
enough, to believe in his ideas enough, to ask businessmen to back
him for thousands or even millions of dollars.

There is a cost for a family living with a man possessed of a singular focus on his vocation, as Otto acknowledged at least once. But I am left wondering: did Otto decide to invent or did he have to invent? In *The Psychology of Being*, Abraham Maslow seems to be describing the man we meet in this book. He writes:

> People with intelligence must use their intelligence, people with eyes must use their eyes, people with the capacity to love have the *impulse* to love and the *need* to love in order to feel healthy. Capacities clamor to be used, and cease in their clamor only when they *are* used sufficiently. That is to say, capacities are needs, and therefore are intrinsic values as well. To the extent that capacities differ, so will values also differ.[6]

Otto was a man with genius or near-genius level abilities: an inventor who, when he was impressed into military service, secretly built one furnace in his battalion's bathroom and later constructed another using what seems to have been a tuna fish can. Does such a man have a choice about fulfilling his abilities or are they needs that must be met? And what must it have been like to live with such a man?

THROUGH A DAUGHTER'S EYES

After I first spoke with Otto's younger daughter Renate and agreed to work on his memoir, I telephoned her to try to orient myself. Who was her father? What did she know of him?

In response to my questions, Renate shared only a few small memories. She remembered swimming in Lake Anza in Berkeley. The raft where her sister played was beyond Renate's reach, so Otto offered to help her, urging her to hold his shoulders and float behind him as he swam her to the raft. "He was so pale and bony! All I could feel was his bones. He seemed to have no flesh!" she said. She remembered a time before then, when she was playing with her sister Lisa downstairs, below Otto's study in their house in Hösel, Germany. Their games were too noisy for Otto, who banged on the floor for silence. And she vividly recalled the last weeks and months in Hösel at the outset of World War II, observing, especially painfully, that in the memoir Otto remembered himself as being in Germany with his family, when in fact he was in the United States, and her mother, valiant and alone, had to make a way for them to flee. Though she did not say so, this experience and Otto's mistaken memory must have felt akin to a betrayal.

When trying to remember her father, Renate often spoke movingly of herself. "I was trying to be American!" she explained. "I was trying so hard to fit in." A young refugee in Berkeley, California in the midst of World War II, the daughter of an obviously German mother and a German-seeming father, and still learning to speak English herself, she of course wished to fit in. Like most children of immigrants, she was fiercely focused on learning a new language and adjusting to her US school and classmates. She had little time for her father, just as he rarely had time for her.

Now eighty-seven, Renate read her father's memoir as none of us could. Otto wrote to describe himself as an inventor; Renate read his text looking for the man. Most powerfully and immediately, she noticed how Otto positioned himself. She knew her father, incontrovertibly, as Estonian. And yet, early in his memoir, when recalling his efforts to go abroad for advanced technical study, Otto acknowledges the realities of his political context and refers to himself as a "citizen of Russia," a "citizen of the Baltic provinces," and even as a "true citizen of Russia." To Renate's greater surprise, in a May 1940 letter written from the United States to Aina (his German wife), his eyes turn toward Germany. At the time, Aina was billeting German officers in their home and felt vulnerably stateless, given her marriage to a non-German. Nonetheless, Otto writes, "In the event Germany wins and brings about an early peace and reorganizes Europe, Germany will be the best country in which to proceed with my research and inventions. Indeed, we are rooted in Germany. You would begin to feel that upon living here a while."

Given his esteem for his father, his frequent work with Jewish engineers, and his explicit sense of himself as a "patriotic Estonian," one would expect Otto's emotional loyalty to lie with Estonia. Nonetheless, he easily divorces "Germany" from the realities of Nazi power and seems to pay little heed to the fate of his "beloved homeland," failing, in his memoir, to even mention Estonia's hard-won independence or the bloody invasions by the Nazis and the Soviets in the 1940s.

Who is this man, with such contradictory loyalties? Tracing Otto's travels between nations and continents, as he worked and lived in Estonia, Germany, Argentina, Mexico, and cities scattered from the East to the West Coast of the United States, Renate came to see her father as a man without a sense of home in any nation. He became a "citizen of the world," she believed, and found his home in his work.

In reading Otto's manuscript, Renate was also led to reflect upon her father's attitudes toward women and men. She recalled his respect for his niece Alice Veinbergs and family friend Elfriede Friese.[7] Otto openly admired "capable" women, yet his text reveals his belief in women's limits: yes, women spin and weave, for example, but only men are inventors. Men create the machines that far surpass any woman's capacity for production, and, for Otto, the value of labor is measured in terms of what men can accomplish—not women. Further, the realms of men are separate from the realms of women, as Renate learned when she wanted to enroll in a high school drafting class. Otto did not prevent her, but he led her to understand that no drafting room could ever include a woman.

Otto's views of the rightful roles for women made him a man of his times and of his Estonian/German/Russian cultures, but he was in other ways a radical. Certainly, he was determined to marry and waited many years until he was sure he could support a wife and children, but once he approached marriage with Frieda Aina Brandt, his views were surprisingly progressive. In the memoir, he notes that both he and Frieda Aina were "experienced people," writing, "I did not claim to have lived as a holy man, and Aina, too, had some excusable experiences in friendships with men." Renate evinced no surprise at the text. She had long known that before their marriage, her parents had themselves medically examined for any diseases related to prior intimacies and that they signed a contract vowing to release one another without recrimination if no children were born to them. Aina asked if Otto had other children, offering to raise them if so. Her joy in motherhood was so deep that she later urged Renate, "If you don't marry, do become a mother nonetheless."

Without Renate, I would not have known the story of the wedding contract. (Otto never mentions it in his book), but I did notice his repeated descriptions of food and his frequent allusions to severe problems with his stomach. Paging through the memoir, Renate noticed them too. She highlighted the monotony of the food and the intense labor required to obtain it when Otto was a child. She also remembered the lifelong discipline her father brought to his eating. He cooked and ate his own food, often prepared in a small pressure cooker that stayed on the stove in her family's kitchen. His staple was chicken, which he suspended in gelatin to make a solid, aspic-like block that he could cut into slices—always in the measured amount he deemed optimum for his health.

Renate observed the connection between her father's work and his ailments. Although his inventions were promising, or even patented, Otto nonetheless repeatedly lost or could not find funding. These rejections imperiled his ability to support his family and thwarted his passionate wish to develop his ideas. The anxiety and disappointment that followed were blows that he experienced physically: a "somatization" of his feelings, in Renate's words.

As Renate and I went through the edited memoir together, page by page, I was struck by how her reading of it shifted my perspective on her father, and, perhaps more significantly, how it seemed to shift hers. Was the gift of the Primus stove Otto sent to Africa after she and Jim married there, simply a practical present from an engineer? It seemed more than that, when she read of the Primus stove that Otto found at his family's farm and took to one of the schools where he boarded when he was a boy. That stove was a piece of equipment that had belonged to his brother Jaan, and it made Otto's difficult, critically important task of feeding himself exponentially simpler. Otto's later choice of a Primus stove as a wedding gift was no accident.

Realizing this, Renate then remembered, too, the blue Volkswagen Bug Otto gave to her and her husband when they returned to the US from anthropological fieldwork in Africa—as well as the metal bicycle seat (probably German) for them to attach to the horizontal bar of Jim's bicycle. This gift came when their daughter Lisa could sit sturdily upright, so that she could ride with Jim—not behind him but within his embrace. Otto's interest in family and his concern for them "manifested itself in these ways," Renate observed.

The children of immigrants often feel a tension between themselves and their parents, between their current culture and the culture of the family's past. Understandably, Renate's mention of this tension centered most on her absent father. In all the stories she told as we read and re-read the memoir, her mother was always and ever "Mutti" (the tender, German word for "mother"). In contrast, her father was "Otto," until, towards the end of the four years we worked together, her view and understanding having broadened with each rereading of the manuscript and the discovery of new letters to add to the family archive, she began to refer to him as "my father."

Renate's accounts of both her parents and of her journeys as a child and woman will find their way into the memoir she plans to write herself. This will happen soon, I hope, for she has her own story to tell. In the meantime, her perspectives, memories, and questions enliven and provide a broader perspective on Otto's story. They are captured in endnotes that I encourage everyone to read.

1.   For a view of the kiln's significance, search "Lepol Thyssen-Krupp."
2.   Otto's letters in the Lellep Family Archive reveal that in his old age, he himself

vacillated regarding the dates he began and finished his memoirs. We find first mention in the extant letters to his daughter Lisa in 1969. "52 pages of handwriting are ready," he writes, "but I am only at my 9th year of age on my father's farm." In 1971, he tells her, "Have finished the story of my long life."

3. See Appendix 2, "The Inventor" ("Der Erfinder"), by Werner Oellers for a literary account of Otto's work with steel.

4. Website of the Minnesota Department of Natural Resources: http://www.dnr.state.mn.us/education/geology/digging/taconite.htm (Accessed July 28, 2015.)

5. For the full text of the letter, see Appendix 1.

6. Abraham J. Maslow. *Toward a Psychology of Being*, third edition. (New York: John Wiley & Sons, Inc. 1999), 168.

7. Born about 1905, Elfriede Friese was a close family friend who served as a social worker in Philadelphia and internationally. See Appendix 14 for Renate's tribute to her.

ALICE [LELLEP] VEINBERGS

In a letter to Lisa and Renate, found in the Lellep Family Archives and dated November 15, 1971, Otto wrote that he had presented a typewriter to Alice, whom he described as knowing German, Russian, Estonian, English, French, and Swedish. Born in St. Petersburg, Alice left Russia for Narva in 1917, at the time of the revolution. She graduated from the university in Tartu and thereafter completed her studies in French at the Sorbonne. Otto:

> Returning from France, Alice served as the correspondence secretary at the Presidential Chancery of Konstantin Päts, the last Estonian president in Tallinn, who, with other Estonian leading persons, was deported by Russian Bolshevics to Siberia. When the Bolshevics invaded Estonia, Alice and her mother escaped to Sweden. There, Alice learned Swedish and was employed over nine years as a secretary at the Telfon Company in Stockholm. Her mother died in Sweden while waiting for her visa to immigrate to the United States, and Alice came to the United Sates alone. She worked as a medical secretary at the University Hospital in New York and married a capable Latvian real estate man, Eric Veinbergs, who lives most of the year in New York. They liked the warmer climate of Florida and built a modern two-family house in Cape Coral.

ACKNOWLEDGEMENT

I thank my talented niece, Alice Veinbergs, born Lellep,
daughter of my brother, Jüri Lellep, who worked as a botanist in the
Imperial Botanical Garden of Peter the Great
in St. Petersburg, the capital of tsarist Russia.
Alice graduated from the University of Tartu in Estonia, and
thereafter completed her studies at the Sorbonne, in Paris.
She speaks six languages. I am grateful to Alice for
improving and typing the text of this book.

Otto G. Lellep

CHAPTER 1

My Parents and My People

1700s and 1800s

*The lands of the Estonian people, particularly Livland,
a guberniya—a territorial subdivision of
pre-revolutionary Russia—where Otto's parents
were born and later had their farm.*

As I write this memoir, I am remembering our history. Seven hundred fifty years ago, all the land of Estonia belonged to the Estonian people. By using advanced weapons, invading Germans conquered the Estonians, enslaved the people, and took all the land. Later, for a short period in the seventeenth century, the country was governed by Sweden, which supported the Estonian people and founded the University of Tartu (known in German as Dorpat).

In 1700, Czar Peter the First conquered the Swedes, and Estonia fell to the Russians.[1] The Russian czars mainly married German princesses, and for many centuries, the Estonians were exploited by German land barons, who owned most of Estonia's land. When my father was born in 1841, and during his youth, Estonia was still part of Russia, but practically speaking, the German landowners governed the country. The pastors of the Lutheran churches, also mostly

Germans, politically supported the land barons and controlled the Estonian schools. They spoke Estonian poorly, but they exerted their influence over pupils and church-goers, warning Estonian peasants of hellfire from their pulpits. There was little interest in the education of the Estonian people. It was easier to handle and punish the poor, subordinated peasants if they remained uneducated.

During Father's lifetime, the Russian government in St. Petersburg began to displace German influence and "Russify" Estonia. This commenced with Czar Alexander the First, who issued regulations compelling the land barons to sell their property to Estonian farmers and permitted long-term payment of the debt.[2] Russification was particularly strong during the reign of Czar Alexander the Third.

My father, Jüri Lellep, and my mother, Liisa Pender, were both born in the county of Tännasilm, near Lake Wirtsjärv. Travel from this area to the nearest city of Wiljandi required a four-hour journey in a horse-drawn wagon over poorly maintained roads.

I know that my father married my mother when he was at an early age and that she was a year older than he. I know very little of my mother. Her last name, Pender, means "bookbinder" in Estonian. It is possible that mother's father was able to bind books, a trade feasible in Wiljandi.

My lack of knowledge about my mother does not mean that she did not care about me. My mother was overburdened. In her time and during my childhood, formal rights for women did not yet exist in England or Germany, let alone in Russia and Estonia. There was no talk about women's rights anywhere in the world. The man was considered the boss of the household. According to the thinking of 1971, we could accuse Father of overburdening Mother, but I am writing of a situation [that occurred] eighty years ago.[3]

[Between her birth] in 1840 and her death in 1893,[4] my mother bore nine children. Living on a large Estonian farm, she had to feed thirteen to twenty people, supervise the work of the girl servants and my sisters, and take responsibility for both the creation of clothing and the laundry of all the members of our family. My mother had a very difficult life.

My father was born [in 1841] in the village of Walma, when there were few schools in Estonia [or in the United States]. Remember that a large part of the United States was prairie then, especially in the northwest, where buffalo ran on the plains, the Indians hunted, and there was little by way of education for children.

My father learned from his mother, who was able to read. Born into a family named Kool ("school," in English), she was employed as a servant by a German storekeeper in the district city when she was young.[5] The Bible was the only book available to her. She is alleged to have taught my father to read when he was five, sitting on her bed. Father attended the parochial school in Paistu for just a few weeks and then educated himself by reading a patriotic Estonian newspaper. At nineteen, he was selected to serve as the teacher of the Tännasilm school.[6]

Until my father was thirty-nine, he and my mother lived and worked in a miserable, old, wooden school building, just eleven meters long and six meters wide. They were provided one room. The pupils used the rest of the building. In their single room, my mother brought five sons and three daughters into the world. I, the youngest, was born later, on our farm, Ripsi. Mother's nine children all grew up without medical help from doctors or hospitals.

Father worked for a negligible salary. Normally, school started at the beginning of October and ended in April, because the children were otherwise needed as herdsmen on the farms. Due to the great distances they had to travel, pupils remained at the school five-and-a-half days each week, spending only Saturday afternoon and Sunday at home. Each child brought a bag of the food needed weekly and drank from a pail of cold water made available inside the schoolhouse. We do not presently think such limited nourishment—one large loaf of coarse rye bread, a small container of pork, and an even smaller one of butter—produces healthy children.

3

Father served as a popular teacher for twenty years, from 1863 to 1883. He was a leader. Earnestly committed to public education for Estonians, he did his best to improve the school. Esteemed by the many hundreds of his former pupils, he was also known as an active Estonian patriot striving to win greater rights for our people.

At one point, though the German land barons in the three Baltic governments of Kurland, Livland, and Estland maintained influence in their sections of Russia, Father sought justice for our people in Riga. He found no help from the government of the German land barons there. "I was so angered by their injustice, I would have dynamited their offices if I'd had some explosives," he told me. Instead, though it was winter, father journeyed to the capital city of St. Petersburg. There being no telephones and no railroad connecting St. Petersburg to Riga, Tallinn, or Tännasilm, he rode for over a week in a horse-drawn sleigh.

Father intended to find influential Estonian friends in the capital city, people who could help improve the miserable and unjust living conditions of many Estonian farmers in his area. In my time, though this was many years later, I remember the poverty. Farmers who had horses and wagons drove to church with their wives, but poor farm workers, men as well as women, walked most of the way barefoot. They didn't want to wear out their expensive shoes, so they put them on only before entering the church, or the city, if they were going there.

After his long trip, Father did meet some influential Estonians in St. Petersburg. [During his and my time], there were important Estonians in the Russian capital, such as the famous painter Köhler, who had friends among the czar's nobles, and Hurt, the pastor of the Estonian Lutheran Church, who collected Estonian fairy tales and original folk songs.[7]

The people Father met sent him by train to the peninsula of Crimea, many thousand kilometers south, near the Black Sea. They wanted him to inspect a large tract of governmental land that Russia

4

1.1   My father Jüri, age 40

was offering for free to landless Estonian farmers. After Father's inspection and positive findings, the farmers obtained the land.[8]

Father was very active politically, giving speeches advocating for freedom for Estonian farmers. He enthusiastically supported Carl Robert Jacobson, the founder, editor, and owner of the weekly periodical *Sakala* in the nearby city Wiljandi. Jacobson was the first to risk claiming full and equal human rights for Estonians.[9]

As a teacher, my father was supervised by the pastor of the church in the nearest city of Wiljandi—Pastor Doll. Father said that some Lutheran pastors were well educated, and in the spirit of true Christian love, they invited Estonian teachers to their homes after church services for friendly conversations and the sharing of general information. Pastor Doll, however, sympathized with the German landowners and did not like poor Estonian farmers.

Father's political fight for the Estonian people displeased Pastor Doll, who fired him, partly under the pretext that he was neglecting his work as a teacher. Father's salary had been insufficient to support the family, so he had earned extra money by buying forest land and converting its trees into firewood. This enabled Father to give my two older brothers a higher education, but Pastor Doll disapproved.

When he was fired, my father had no savings, but fortunately, he was a trusted person with good credit in the local loan society. In 1883, he was able to obtain a long-term loan from the German Credit Bank in Wiljandi, making it possible for him to buy a fairly large farm just seven kilometers from the city.

Father's firing proved to be an indirect blessing. From the time when he bought the farm, the political life and self-respect of the Estonian people began to rise gradually against the power of the German land barons. Father became a capable and progressive famer and industrialist—the owner of a water-powered mill and a successful businessman in the firewood trade.

1. Peter the Great, also known as Peter I, reigned from 1682–1725.

2. In its outline, Otto's characterization of the political and social power wielded by the German nobility in Estonia and the government of the tsars is well confirmed by historical facts. He has, however, telescoped the process by which Estonian peasants at last gained some land and rights. Changes

actually stretched over the course of the reign of four tsars: Alexander I (1801-1825), Nicholas I (1825-1855), Alexander II (1855-1881), and Alexander III (1881-1894).

Under Tsar Alexander I, serfdom was formally abolished in Estland (the northern Estonian lands) in 1816. It was abolished in Livland (the southern Estonian lands, where the Lelleps had their farm) in 1819. These were steps forward, but according to Toivo U. Raun (Estonia and the Estonians), they had little effect on the economics of peasant life. Under Tsar Nicholas I, from 1849, for a period of six years in Livland, noble landowners were required to rent or sell some land to the peasants for a period of six years. A similar law was adopted in Estland in 1856, under Tsar Alexander II. The provisional land agrarian law in Livland was made permanent in 1860. It was only with the accession of Tsar Alexander III and the decision to change the agrarian system within the interior of the Russian empire, however, that the Baltic nobility were pressured sufficiently to allow for substantial, actual reforms. Otto dates his father's purchase of the Ripsi farm as 1883, which would have placed it during the reign of Tsar Alexander III.

While admitting that both terms lack precision, Raun dates the period of "national awakening" and Russification from the 1860s to 1900, spanning the reigns of Alexander II and Alexander III, as well as the lives of Otto's parents and Otto's early years.

3. Otto describes his mother as "overburdened" many times in his memoir.

4. Otto's mother was born in 1839 according to the single tombstone marking the grave of "Jüri Lellep," "Liisu Lellep," and "Mari Lellep."

5. The "district city" would have been today's Viljandi.

6. Today, schools still exist in Tännasilm and outside of the town of Paistu. Otto comments elsewhere that after his father left teaching, Tännasilm built a modern, larger schoolhouse made of brick, which he credits to his father's influence.

7. Johann Köler (1826-1899) was a famous Estonian artist and leader who painted and studied in Europe, then taught at the St. Petersburg Art Development School and the Imperial Academy of Art. A portraitist in demand among those in the highest levels of St. Petersburg society, Köler also taught art to the tsar's family. These positions gave him access to the elites of the Russian empire, allowing him to provide a valuable link between tsarist authorities and the Estonian nationalist movement. Köler strongly advocated for peasants, arguing against the power and privileges of the nobility, and particularly focused on the peasants' struggle for land. From 1904–1905, Otto lived in Tallinn with a man who, from his description, seems to be the uncle of the famous painter. (See Chapter 9.)

A poet and activist, Jakob Hurt (1839-1907) gained a theological degree from the University of Tartu and a Ph.D. from the University of Helsinki. In 1880,

Hurt became pastor of the St. John's Estonian Congregation in St. Petersburg, where Otto first met him. (See Chapter 5.) Hurt viewed every nation as unique, given its differing traits of character, culture, and language. Because of Estonia's small size, he believed its mission lay in the cultural realm. At one point simultaneously serving as president of the Estonian Alexander School Committee, the Tartu Farmers' Society, and the Society of Estonian Literati, Hurt also advocated for the importance of the Estonian language and played a critical role in the collection of Estonian folklore and poetry. Politically, Hurt called for conciliation in the relationship between Estonians and Baltic Germans, effectively accepting German leadership.

8. According to Raun (*Estonia and the Estonians*), in the late 1850s, "Maltsvet the Prophet" sought permission for two hundred to three hundred families among his followers—Estonian peasants probably motivated more by socioeconomic than religious concerns—to emigrate to the Crimea. Raun describes the attempt to depart as at least partially successful. In Miljan (*Historical Dictionary of Estonia*), the move is dated 1861 and the prophet is named "Maltsev." Perhaps Otto's father's travel to the Crimea was related to this immigration.

CHAPTER 2

Our Family

1800s–early 1900s
Ripsi; Tartu; Kronstad; St. Petersburg; Tännasilm;
Tallinn; Mannerdorf, Switzerland

We were a large family. Not all of my siblings lived at Ripsi when I was a child, since some of them had already left for work or marriage, but I will here write more about my parents and introduce all of my brothers and sisters in the order of their births: Hans (1862), Liina and Jaan (1864), Juuli (1867), Jüri (1869), Anna (1871), Willem (1878), and Peter (1880). I was the last-born (1884).[1]

Hans, my eldest brother, was twenty-two years older than I. He studied to become a teacher at the teacher's seminary in Tartu, the university city of Estonia.[2] Hans later taught at a school in Kronstad, near St. Petersburg, and during the time of Estonian

2.1   My brother, Hans Lellep

9

*2.2 My brother, Jaan Lellep, who served as pastor
in St. Petersburg and Teshkova.*

independence [1920–1939] he served as headmaster of the largest public school in Tallinn.[3]

I saw my next-oldest brother, Jaan, only a few times in my life. Jaan attended high school in Tartu, intending to go on to study philosophy and theology at the university. He wanted to become a Lutheran pastor. [While I was still young, he succeeded and was chosen as] pastor of a poor Estonian community near St. Petersburg.

I met Jaan once when he and Hans came home to Ripsi for Christmas, and I saw him later [when I was a child] in St. Petersburg. [In the end], he developed leukemia and moved to Mannerdorf, Switzerland, on Lake Zurich, where he hoped to cure himself. The

2.3 Jaan's grave

well-known Estonian poetess Anna Haava had loved Jaan since he
was a student at Tartu, and she was there, as well. Jaan died in Switzerland and is buried there.

Jaan's twin, Liina, was my oldest sister. Father chose the husbands for his daughters, and [he had] Liina marry a young farmer
in Tännasilm, where Father had taught for twenty years. Liina had
three children, none of whom could receive a university education
because of the small income from [the couple's family] farm.

ANNA HAAVA

Otto says nothing more of the relationship between Jaan Lellep and Anna Rosalie Haavakivi, a well-known poet who wrote under the pseudonym Anna Haava. The only poem of hers I have found in English translation is below.

ONCE ONLY
Once only shall the heart's true passion
Know the pure ecstasy of love,
Once only this miraculous flower
Mirror the mystery from above.

The love that fails, the love that withers
Beyond the reach of eye and mind,
And changes with the changing passions
Differs not in degree, but kind.

Once only shall the heart's true passion
Know love, and then eternity
Draw limits, for there is no power
To alter love's divine decree.

From W.K. Matthews, compiler and translator, *Modern Estonian Poetry* (Gainesville: University of Florida Press, 1953), p. 6.) The translated text is as above. It could be read as "Once only [shall] this miraculous flower/Mirror the mystery from above" or as "Once only this miraculous flower/Mirrors the mystery from above."

Juuli, [who was next in the family], was capable and energetic. She was eighteen years older than I. She received a public school education while Father was a teacher, then married a man named Hasenbusch, whom Father selected for her. Hasenbusch was the tenant of the Ripsi mill. After a year of marriage, they had a daughter, Helene, but unfortunately, Hasenbusch soon died of tuberculosis. Juuli then moved with Helene to the home of our brother, Pastor Jaan, near St. Petersburg. She kept house for Jaan and then accompanied him to Switzerland. After his death, she gave five-year-old Helene into the keeping of the child's grandparents at Ripsi. When the daughter grew up, she studied at a high school for girls.

Juuli remained a widow all her life. She first tried her luck with a little store selling food in St. Petersburg. This venture proved to be unprofitable. In 1902, she moved to Tallinn and took over a small shop that sold ladies' clothing and accessories in a location with busy traffic. She had gained life experience and had learned to speak and write Russian, Estonian, and German while helping brother Jaan. Benefiting from bitter experience, she was successful [at the new venture]. In the beginning, she worked alone, but later she had to engage one, and then two, assistants.

My brother Jüri was a serious and quiet person who especially liked gardening and beautifying our home with flowers, fruit trees, and decorative plants. As he had to do the same jobs as the farmhands, he was able to devote himself to his beloved work only on holidays or late in the evening and early in the morning. Jüri worked many hours while others slept.

[After our first house burned down and was rebuilt], Jüri put a flowerbed in front of the veranda of our new home. One-and-a-half meters in diameter, it was laid out with tall plants in the center and shorter flowers of different kinds around them. Nearby he planted a special ash tree, whose branches grew downward, not upward. He planned the entire garden on the southeast end of the house, planting red and black currants, raspberries, gooseberries, and many varieties of apples on both sides of the sanded walkways.

In order to protect the garden from the strong western wind, Jüri put in a tight row of fir trees that later towered over us. He reserved a large area on the eastern side of the garden for our annual plantings of cabbage and kohlrabi, but he also kept a section for vegetables and a bed of flowers.

Fortunately, Jaan later found a suitable occupation for Jüri as a botanist in the Imperial Botanical Garden of Peter the Great in St. Petersburg, a position Jüri kept almost his entire life.

My sister Anna, [born just after Jüri], had studied in the public school where Father taught. She, too, was married to a farmer in Tännasilm. They had three children, none of whom were able to receive a university education. Anna's husband later became a partner in Father's lumber business.

Willem, [born after] Anna, had no interest in science as it was taught in the schools, but he was gifted with tools and liked handicrafts. As a young boy, he built a small cupboard and painted it himself. When Willem was fifteen, Father gave him as an apprentice to a well-managed, large watermill forty kilometers away. It had facilities for preparing wool for spinning. [Later], for a year or longer, Willem also assisted Father in the forest products business.

After Willem completed compulsory military service, he organized the first steam-driven plant in Tallinn, using woodworking machines for manufacturing doors and window frames. He earned some money at this enterprise and built a modern, comfortable house near the central section of the city. He lived there with his wife and three sons, two of whom became engineers.[4]

My brother Peter was born between Willem and me. Peter was physically strong and intellectually especially able. Among the brothers, he had the highest mental capabilities. He made friends easily with men and women, and he was popular in our community singing group. Peter could dance and play the piano, violin, and guitar, and he liked sports.

Peter stayed in St. Petersburg to attend high school under the supervision of our older brother, Pastor Jaan, but he did not devote himself to his duties consistently and he spent his money too easily in the company of his many friends. Jaan observed Peter's character and decided it was not worthwhile to give him a higher education, so in 1896, he sent Peter back to Ripsi. Father needed someone to manage the farm in his older years.

One year later, I remember, Peter had the luck to win a bicycle in a lottery. Manufactured bicycles were not yet used on farms at that time. This one was made by a village smith, with wheels of steel, and it was heavy. Any boy wanting to ride this bicycle monstrosity ten kilometers on a poor road required athletic ability and strength. It took me two weeks to learn how to ride it. A factory-manufactured bicycle with rubber tires requires only an hour [for practice].

Peter spent a few years on Father's farm as a common worker. There, he became friends with a young co-worker at Ripsi who exercised a harmful influence on him. His companion, an uneducated, coarse young farmhand, was Peter's age. When they reached eighteen years, their natural interest in girls awakened.

In some Estonian villages, the farms were close to each other, but near Ripsi, the farm properties were separated by a half a kilometer to a kilometer. It was a bad practice, but it was common for boys eighteen or older to spend Saturday nights visiting girls on other farms. Young, unmarried men were looking for unmarried girls. They would go during the warm season of the year, when people slept not only in the narrow rooms of the main farm building, but also in unheated storerooms on the property.

Unfortunately, other than at night, there were no convenient opportunities to get acquainted. Boys and girls organized for singing gathered in village schoolhouses, but those times, and the individual meetings that happened on the way to church, were seldom suitable for establishing personal relationships. Church pastors found the weekend nights to be immoral because they led to the birth of children outside of marriage, but natural attraction was sometimes stronger than moral law.

Once, Peter and his crude friend attempted to arrange a night meeting with an attractive girl who lived on a neighboring farm. The girl refused to talk to them, and Peter's comrade persuaded him to write a poem that could be recited, or even sung, as revenge for her prudery. Deplorably, this pseudo-poem was spread to other boys in the community.

Peter's friendship with his uncivilized companion contributed to the spoiling of his relationship with our respected father. At Ripsi, Peter had to obey Father just like everyone else. This did not suit Peter. I remember a nasty conflict he had with Father, in which he not only contradicted Father but also offended him in an unjust and shameful way.

[I was the last of Mother's and Father's nine children.] I guess my birth may have occurred without planning. When I was young, my father and mother; four brothers [Jüri, Willem, Peter, and myself]; two sisters [Juuli and Anna], an aunt, and at least four hired hands lived on the farm. Two older brothers [Hans and Jaan] lived in or near St. Petersburg and one older sister [Liina] was married. Thus, we had thirteen persons in Ripsi during the normal three seasons. This number almost doubled during the harvest time.

My father was strict with us, but his actions remained just. He expected us to do our work willingly, always fulfilling our duties and giving our best efforts. He was the boss of the house. We had no easy, friendly means to approach him. Frivolous talk from us did not please him, and there was no place for tenderness or love. In his opinion, such qualities would have spoiled us.

Father believed in physical punishment for serious misdeeds. He administered this by beating our bottoms with a small bundle of leafless birch twigs. I heard from my older brothers that as the last and youngest child, I received the least of this "education," but I remember one time when I was about three, I was stubborn. For some reason, I was crying, and I would not stop. Father tried to teach me to stop crying by beating me with a bundle of twigs. This did not work, and I began crying more loudly. My stubbornness caused my father to beat me harder, and my skin began to bleed. Increased beating could have been dangerous. The next morning I was swollen and had to be treated with some kind of ointment or oil.

By wearing simple clothing, Father wished to proudly express himself as a farmer. The farmer is responsible for feeding the world, he said. Father's overcoat, suit, and underwear were all homemade. The wool of our own sheep, spun in our textile mill and woven into cloth by my sisters, was used for his overcoat and suit. His shirt and underwear were made of home-grown flax, also spun and woven on the farm by my sisters, then cut and made into clothing by a tailor and his helper, who came to us each year. This clothing was undoubtedly of a more substantial and lasting quality than that sold in the city.

Father did not like stiff, starched white collars. Instead, he wore a clean white kerchief around his neck when he went to town. He didn't care whether or not the shape of his clothing matched the latest Parisian fashions. This was of no interest to him because in his opinion the people of Estonia were morally superior to the French.

Father had considerably broader and deeper knowledge and experience than the average farmer. He had good reason not to pay particular attention to his outer appearance. He was an outstanding person as a teacher, a farmer, a trusted and dependable businessman, and a brave fighter for the political rights of the Estonian nation.

Father's hard behavior disappeared when he drank a glass of beer from time to time with the friendly owners of other farms or co-workers in business. Sitting on a carpet laid on top of a tightly filled sack of hay, farm owners often drove their simple, painted, horse-pulled wagons to a guesthouse in the district city of Wiljandi. They put both horses and wagons next door, in a shed that had a trough filled partially with water and partially with hay, clover, or oats. Inside the guesthouse, the host stood behind a long counter from which he sold bottles of beer and other alcoholic drinks.

After he finished his business, Father liked to sit with one or more friends conversing and drinking in Wiljandi. He avoided strong alcohol, but he liked beer, and he could drink it all day long without getting drunk. The beer made him talkative and he could converse for hours with his friends or acquaintances. He knew a great many people.

One time in my childhood, my usually very strict "papa" took particular care of my wellbeing. On a cold, partly rainy autumn day, I drove the pigs to a faraway field where the harvest of potatoes had been completed. A small percentage of the potato crop always remained lost in the soil, and the pigs could smell and dig out the tasty food.

I saw my father come toward me that cold day, walking across the field. He brought dry paper and matches in the pocket of his overcoat, and he showed me where I could find things to burn nearby. We built a fire and sat down by its warmth. Father helped me bake fresh potatoes in the ashes, and we ate them with butter. My strict father was actually an agreeable, helpful comrade! My entire life, I've remembered this day and his friendly attitude.

My father was known as a good organizer who put everyone to work, but Mother herself was not an organizer. She attempted to do all the work herself. Father seemed not to notice that Mother was overworked taking care of the children, feeding everyone, and having responsibility for clothing and laundry.

One might wonder if our parents liked having the large number of children in our family. The word "love" was not used at that early time on our farm. Being constantly overloaded with work and duties, no one had time for this delicate concept. However, I remember one exception when I was eight years old and not yet attending school.

One quiet, sunny summer afternoon, I was herding pigs on the shore of the small pond near the mill.[5] The pigs were feeding on the juicy grass growing between the rye field and the water. I was relaxed. My eyes wandered. And there came my mother! She was carrying something delicious to eat—a bottle filled with hot coffee and the cream usually made only for important visitors, as well as a few tasty sandwiches on special wheat bread. We sat on the grass and she took the time to talk with her lastborn son and "nest egg" Otto. I remember this exceptional incident with tears in my eyes, even in my old age.

With all her household duties, my good mother had little time to take care of her last, small child. Thanks be to God, it was decided to give me to the care of my kind, wise aunt, the married sister of my father. She and my uncle also lived on the crowded Ripsi farm. They treated me with love.

Sometimes, my uncle played with me. When I was three or four years old, he built me a little cart. He nailed two axles underneath a wooden box in which I could sit, supported by the cart's four wheels. I thoroughly enjoyed him pulling me around the courtyard of the farm. To make me feel more important, he created a cigarette from a piece of newspaper filled with dried leaves from the cherry tree. He would ignite the cigarette, and I would pull the smoke into my mouth. Now when people ask me whether I smoked as a child, I can certainly say yes.

I owe my aunt my sincere gratitude. As a small child, I slept in her bed with her. A friend had given my aunt a tin can filled with coffee powder, a big luxury at the time, and a box of sugar in square pieces. My aunt kept these precious objects under her mattress because the room was so crowded there was no other place to put them. Sometimes, she gave me a cup of sweet coffee, which was considered a special treat.

I remember a comical talk I had with my aunt during the last years of her life. I noticed one day that the small finger-long part of my body between my legs had grown harder. I informed my aunt of this fact. "Dear me," she said, "the cat has put a piece of bone into it."

1. Genealogical records we have researched give the names more strictly Estonian spellings and include a son named Johan among the Lellep children, though a "Johan" is never mentioned by Otto. I, not Otto, have ordered the discussion of the siblings, using the birthdates given in various records. Using traditional Estonian spellings , the children of the Lellep family were: Hans (1862), Liina Kõll (1864), Jaan (1864), Juula Hasenbusch (1867), Jüri (1869), Anna Katharina (1871), Johan (1876), Villem (1878), and Peeter (1880).

2. Tartu is and was widely identified with its university, which was first established in 1632 under the Swedish king, Gustavus Adolphus. The university closed after Sweden's defeat and Estonia's transfer to Russia in 1721, but it re-opened in 1802. It was the only German-language university in the Russian empire. With the onset of Russification, instruction in Russian was mandated there.

3. Estonia's declaration of independence was announced on February 24, 1918 in the Manifesto to the Peoples of Estonia. Two years later, on February 2, 1920, Soviet Russia renounced claims to the territory, and a century later, February 2, 2020, was marked the 100th Anniversary of the Tartu Peace Treaty. Independence lasted almost two decades until, in 1939, the USSR and Germany signed the Molotov-Ribbentrop Pact, secretly dividing Europe into spheres of influence. The USSR invaded Estonia one year later.

4. When Willem's son Endel was young and Otto was beginning to develop one of the fundamental processes he later used in the Lepol kiln, Endel helped with an important experiment. (See Chapter 20.) In 1946, when Endel was a soon-to-be-released prisoner of war, Otto tried to send money to Europe for his support. (Lellep Family Archives, letters of February 22 and March 1, 1946)

5. In the manuscript, Otto writes "small lake," but given that he makes no other references to a "lake," we can probably safely guess that he was near the mill pond.

CHAPTER 3

Ripsi: The Farm, the Mill, the Machinery

Late 1800s

The Ripsi farm in Livland, near the city of Viljandi

My uncle died first, but my aunt lived until I was about six-and-a-half or seven years old. After her death, I was left to the care of my two sisters, Anna and Juuli, who were not yet married. They watched over me from when I was seven until I was nine. [While in their care, and with my aunt], I had many opportunities [to learn about] the farm and my father's mill.

"Ripsi," the farm my father bought, was located in the community of Wanawoidu.[1] Only seven kilometers from Wiljandi, Ripsi sat between the Nuia River and a creek that powered my father's watermill. It took us less than two minutes to run down to the river to swim during the hot days of summer. The Nuia was not yet polluted, and two men using a triangular net could catch a bag full of fresh fish from there in an hour or two.

During my long life, farming and industry have changed in Estonia [and other countries]. Today, in the late 1960s, only about ten percent of the people in the United States are farmers living in the country. Approximately 90 percent are in cities, working in industrial plants, businesses, or other occupations. In 1884, when I was born, about 90 percent of the Estonians lived on farms. Families bought only a few things from the city: petroleum, salt, and steel, for examples. Father handled the money in the city. Money was scarce on the farm.

[During my childhood], a typical Estonian farm was organized to produce most of the necessities of existence. At Ripsi, we grew rye, wheat, barley and oats, potatoes, cabbage, kohlrabi, and rutabagas. Our cows provided us with milk and meat, our sheep gave us wool, and our horses pulled our plows. We raised pigs, too, and we planted flax to use in making our clothes.

The soil of Father's farm varied. Some fields had thick, rich, black soil containing humus. Others consisted of a clayish soil that hardened when the weather was dry and stuck to our feet when it rained. We had a hard time breaking the lumps of clay with the harrow, but it had to be done somehow for us to raise our crops. Some fields were sandy—easy to plow and cultivate, but unsuitable for a rich crop. Others were filled with small and large pebbles of granite or limestone.

Father's farm was unusual. Other farms near Ripsi were smaller, and life was simpler there. Our farm was big, and it was busy year round. In addition to his income from forest products, which allowed him to educate three sons, Father worked hard on his fields. He had ditches dug to drain superfluous water and improved the areas for growing hay, even converting one bog into a hayfield. The sandy, less fertile areas were treated with compost made of peat and dung from the stables. He built a lime-burning kiln on a field that had sufficient limestone[2] and spent much money enlarging the textile section of the mill with English-made spinning machines. The farm buildings were modernized, too, as special workers constructed new ones or improved the old ones throughout many months of the year.

Much of the work of the farm was done in my father's large farmhouse, in which we also lived. In addition to the small, warm room where we processed milk products, the farm building included the *tare* and *rehealune*, places to dry and thresh our crops.[3]

*3.1   The surface of the pond glitters like a mirror and reflects the roof of
the mill. An old-fashioned well with the equipment to haul a pail of water
from a depth of three meters is visible on the right. The mill tenant, his wife,
and two helpers lived on the right end of the building in two rooms. On
its left side, two-thirds of the building consisted of three stories. The water
wheel and turbine were in the cellar; the belt-driven drums for cleaning and
carding sheep's wool were on the ground floor, and the expensive, English
spinning machine was on the [upper] third floor.*

Because of the relatively moist summer and fall seasons, the ripe
crops of rye, wheat, barley, and oats could not normally be left in the
fields where they grew. The threshing process to recover the grains
from the straw required a prior drying process. This was done in the
spacious *tare*, where, in the corner, we had a very large furnace.[4] It
was especially designed to dry our crops and prevent the release of
any sparks that could cause a fire. Built with thick walls and a vault of
brick, the furnace included a structure of wooden bars, five feet from
the floor. Upon the bars, which were spaced apart from one another,
we laid a layer one meter thick of moist straw and bundles of our

crops. The gases of the furnace's hot fire, diluted with air, passed through a thick layer of round fieldstones. Spark-free, they then rose under and through the layer of straw and grains, after which, much cooled, the gases escaped into the chimney stack.

The slow fire in the furnace of the *tare* had to be kept burning for at least two days. Then the bundles of the crop had to be beaten against inclined tables to separate the grain from the straw and the ears. This was very hard work for two or three men working in the heat of the *tare*.

Further threshing occurred in the larger, separate *rehealune*.[5] On a windy day, with the doors opened on both sides of the room, the impure mixture of grain and straw was put through a suspended screen high above the floor. The heavy, pure grain fell through, while the lighter straw and chaff was blown outdoors by the wind. Workmen then shoveled the grain into sacks and carried it into the granary.

In addition to the grains we grew for food, flax was an important agricultural commodity during my youth. Some of the Estonian farmers in the district near the city of Wiljandi earned substantial money from production of this fibre, and a few grew quite rich.

Flax is in some respects superior to cotton. It has a fibre about forty centimeters long, while cotton's is only about five centimeters in length. The flax fields looked lovely when the young plants were covered with shiny, blue blossoms, and the buds that followed were filled with valuable flax seed oil.

During the harvest, women pulled up the ripe, thin flax stalks from the field and bound them into bundles the width of a hand. Men drew the top end of these bundles through a row of sharp knives, separating the buds containing the seeds of flax from the flax stalks. Each stalk had a useless, brittle substance in its center. The fine, strong, long flax fibre lay along the outside.

Separating the flax fibre from the brittle substance in the center of the stalk required a series of complicated processes. First, the flax bundles were immersed for a week or longer in the water of a pond or river. As some fermentation took place, the fibre on the periphery of each stalk loosened from the inner substance.

After they had fermented in water, the bundles were spread on the field to dry. Once ready, they were stored until winter in a room covered by a roof. Final drying was done in the *tare*, but further work was necessary. Workers erected a special machine in the *rehealune*. It consisted of three strong wooden rolls with teeth four centimeters long. A horse pulled a radial beam to rotate the rolls. The unclean flax, now thoroughly dried, passed between them. This broke the inner, brittle material in each stalk and somewhat loosened it from the valuable fibre.

The next operation required time-consuming work by hand in the dust and cold of the *rehealune*. For light, workers each had a very small petroleum lamp, carefully kept in a lantern to shield it from the flammable material filling the room. The workers beat each flax bundle by hand with a wooden "sword," freeing the brittle material from the flexible fibre. This was a dusty, hard, twelve-hour-long, daily job in the winter. At the end, the clean bundles of flax fibre were bound into larger bundles and the daily output of each worker was weighed and registered.

Farming methods of ninety years ago didn't depend upon steam- or gasoline-powered machinery. Much of our equipment was made of wood, but some was of metal and needed occasional repair or renewal. Blacksmithing work was done at the smithy that stood near the mill. It was equipped with a pair of leather bellows, operated by hand. They produced a high-velocity stream of air for the small forge's very hot fire, made of a special coal imported from England.

Father hired a professional blacksmith from time to time, for example, when he needed horseshoes or the new steel rings to cover the wooden wheel of a wagon. For the latter, the blacksmith took a piece of steel about five centimeters wide and two-fifths of a centimeter thick and bent it into a ring. Then he raised the temperature of the fire close to the melting point of steel and heated the two ends of the metal.

When they were sparkling white, he laid them on the anvil, where his helper hit them with a heavy hammer to weld them together.

The blacksmith's trade had to be acquired, but my brothers Willem and Peter learned some skills. Peter could make horseshoes himself. Both of them liked to "harden" the cutting blade of their pocketknives. Wrapping the wooden handle of the knife in a wet rag, they heated the blade carefully to a precise temperature, then plunged it into cold water. They believed the blades were otherwise too soft and that they could thus improve their cutting quality.

I enjoyed watching the work in our smithy, but I especially liked going to my father's mill, five minutes walk away. The general work on the farm intrigued me only partially. I was much more interested in following the doings of different craftsmen who built or repaired equipment near the farm or at the watermill. I wanted to know the purpose of each thing and of what it was made.

Father leased the mill to a competent operator for an agreed-upon, yearly payment. This was no primitive watermill driving a single small grinding wheel, as seen in some mountains in the European Alps. Instead, it had a watermill and a turbine. At a maximum, running water falling over a turbine or water wheel supplied the mill with the equivalent of about fourteen horsepower.[6]

Our good-sized water wheel was located in the cellar, in a mysterious, almost dark room that was hardly accessible. Its air was saturated with microscopic droplets of falling water. As a small boy, I was not permitted to enter this room because of the danger that I'd fall off the narrow board leading to it and drown. Forbidden things are the most interesting, however, and even as a five-year-old, I knew the location of the lever that was pushed down so the water could run on the wheel and start the grinding stone in its rotation.

The other source of power, a turbine, was invisible inside a sheet steel cylinder. As far as I could tell, it produced only noise when it was operating, because I was unable to observe the details of its design.

Sometimes, when the millpond was overfilled with water because of rain, the operator ran both the waterwheel and the turbine.

There were two grindstones in the mill. The simple one produced a coarse rye flour for the bread that was usually consumed on the farms. The other was driven by the turbine. It yielded a fine flour that was sifted through a silken screen. This more expensive flour could be ground from rye or wheat grain, and the bread baked from it was eaten only during holidays.

Known even in ancient Rome, grinding wheels were one of the first inventions of humanity. I watched our mill's heavy stones grind hard grain into flour. We had two wheels of about ninety centimeters in diameter, one placed over the other. The upper wheel rotated, the lower one remained immovable, and the grain fell between the two. It was held first in a container suspended above the wheels. From there it spilled into a small box that shook noisily, ensuring a steady flow.

Father paid for all the repairs and replacement of equipment in the mill. From time to time, in order to keep the grinding stones efficient, the surfaces of both wheels had to be attended to. We called this the "sharpening" of the millstones. First, the container holding the grain was removed and the top stone with the hole in its middle was turned upside down, so the grinding surfaces of both stones were made accessible. The miller's helper had a hammer-like chisel made of hardened steel. He hammered on the smooth surface of the stones to make them rough. He also cleared the stones' small grooves to facilitate the movement of flour and cooling air.

At one point, we had to replace the grinding wheel. Father hired a skilled mason to chip out a new one from a big piece of granite. Such intense, special work took the man all summer.

Any part of the mill made of wood had to be continually replaced or rebuilt, of course, because it rotted in the moist air. Newer equipment made of cast iron could have been bought much more cheaply, but this was available only in far-away cities such as Riga or Tallinn, and when I was young, the railroad to these cities did not exist.

Instead, for some of the equipment, Father hired a specialist. This master of mill building came from the nearby county town and could speak German and Estonian.

Father gave the master mill builder a farm hand as a helper, and he and his helper made the necessary parts of the waterwheel and the very intricate gear wheels. The gears, with their teeth, had to be formed accurately because they had to drive the heavy grinding wheel, which consumed about five horsepower of energy. Over the course of an entire winter, a specialist once built us the large water wheel and the main wooden gear.

The textile section of the mill had much more expensive equipment than the grinding stones and turbine. It held the machinery for the production of fine woolen thread, made from the big bundles of sheep's wool that the farm owners' wives brought to the mill in wagons. Five complicated machines stood on the ground floor, each with a rotating drum covered like a brush with hair-thin steel pins of wire. These drums cleaned the farmers' wool and in the final process, converted it into a uniformly thick wool strand. This in turn was formed automatically into a number of spiral-shaped bundles weighing about one-fifth of a kilogram. The farmers' daughters or servants took the bundles and transformed them into woolen yarn, which they wove into perfect woolen cloth.

Later, my father bought an expensive spinning machine from England and installed it on the second floor of the textile section of the mill building. It had eighty spindles rotating at about 1,200 revolutions per minute. I tremendously enjoyed seeing and hearing this wonderful machine converting fifty kilograms of wool into fine yarn in a short time. Observing it operating a hundred times faster than my sisters using the spinning wheels, I became convinced of the superiority of machines and the men who invented them.[7]

I have remembered two events from childhood all my life. The first involved the pond near the Ripsi mill. The creek that ran through Ripsi's farmland was collected behind a wooden dam, which raised the water to the level of about two-and-a-half meters. The pond's running water powered our mill, but on a quiet day, its surface glittered like a mirror.

It would have been much more efficient to build the mill pond's dam out of cement, but this excellent material was not yet available in the small, nearby city of Wiljandi. Instead, the wooden dam rotted and had to be rebuilt every few years at father's expense.

One day, when the water was released to prepare for a rebuilding, I saw that only a shallow, small creek remained. Poisonous laundry detergents weren't used then, so the many fish that lived in the clean water of the pond were left behind. Imagine, we could catch them by hand! What a joy! We filled a wooden container full of the fish and two men slung it through a rod and carried it to the farm kitchen. For a few days all of us ate delicious, fresh fish.

My second memory is from my earliest childhood. One day in May, in 1887, when I was three, I remember hearing the terrible words, "Fire! Fire!" My great aunt, who was taking care of me, grabbed me and ran from our burning farmhouse into the small storage room standing in the old orchard, about two hundred meters away. Farm roofs were made of straw during this period, and as the flames and sparks rose high, our roof was rapidly consumed by fire. Fortunately, we were far enough from it to escape the heat.

My father's old farmhouse burned down that day in May. The horses and cattle escaped the fire because they were in other buildings. Fortunately, our grain, meat, potatoes, sauerkraut, flour, hulled barley, and homemade cloth of wool and flax were kept in the cellar of a separate storeroom, so they too survived. Still, we had to rebuild.

For those born in cities, it is hard to imagine how difficult this situation was for my father and mother. Suppose you had to live in a barn for several months with a family of ten and about four to six hired hands, all without any permanent quarters.

I admired my father's energy, talent, and way of handling people. Immediately after the fire, he began to figure out how to build a new farmhouse, bigger than the old one and with many added improvements. He sketched out an unusually large building and resolved to have its roof on by September. The *tare* had to be ready before the cold, rainy autumn spoiled our crops in the fields.

At that time, fire insurance as we know it today did not exist among farmers. Father was known in the nearest city of Wiljandi as a dependable person, so he was able to obtain a loan from the German Savings and Loan Bank.

[In addition], it was touching to observe how the kindly neighbors came with much help and many presents. Among them, the feeling of mutual help [bonds] was very strong. Most farmers around Ripsi had their own forests, and they gave us logs for the walls of the new farmhouse. They also brought indispensable furniture such as beds, tables, and benches, as well as containers for the cooking, eating, and preparation of food.

Father planned a building that was fifty meters long and ten meters wide.[8] The southern section, consisting of the rooms we lived in and the *tare*, was to be constructed of lumber. The northern section, for the *rehealune* and the stable for the horses, was to be built of granite stones that were found in the fields.[9] Father wanted the new roof made of wood, not straw, which was dangerously flammable.

Even as a three-year-old, I liked to observe the work of the masons, carpenters, and painters during the construction of our new farm building. Masons built the walls of the northern part of the farmhouse to a height of three meters. They cemented the granite fieldstones with a mortar made of hydraulic lime and an admixture of sand.

Workmen mounted horizontal wooden beams on the side walls of the living rooms to support the ceiling and put on the roof. Its shingles were cut by a simple machine driven by water power at Father's own mill. A number of men nailed the shingles to the supporting rods below.

The walls of the southern half of the house consisted of thick fir logs, which carpenters cut with wide, sharp axes to a uniform, straight thickness of fourteen centimeters. They fitted the straightened logs to the lower layers of the building and tightly filled the space between them with moss. The outside surface of the wooden walls was covered with planed boards that were produced on the farm. They were arranged so that the rain could not enter and wet the inside logs.

Two strong workmen sawed the wooden boards used on the inside floor and ceiling. For each one, they took a thick, straight trunk of pine or fir about four meters long and raised it upon two trestles, two-and-a-half meters high. Each man held the end of a broad saw blade, one standing on the trestle and the other below, on the floor. The one above pulled the saw up, while the other pulled it down. They kept the cutting line straight by following a line drawn on the tree with a chalked string. This primitive work required much manpower, which was cheap in those days, and it saved the time and money required for

3.2   *Father's farmhouse at Ripsi as seen from the southeast. The large room for his three educated sons is on the southern end. The stable for six horses is on the northern end. We were proud of the veranda, with its big windows of colored glass, on the southeastern corner of the building.*

3.3   Ripsi's buildings, seen from the east

buying and transporting lumber from a distant sawmill.

By September, Father was happy to have a modern, better farm-house under a roof. The new house, together with the *tare, rehealune,* and stable for the horses, was approximately equal in size to eight, small, one-family American houses. Its very top stood nine meters above the floor line.

Father had spent many weeks planning the construction of this modern building. He provided it with a deep well and a hand-oper-ated pump. Water was guided through wooden channels to different animals and to the kitchen, where potatoes and other food could be cooked for fattening the hogs.

I have made a sketch of the plans and layout of the Ripsi farm. The farmhouse included a room for my father and mother, one for their sons and daughters, one for the hired hands, the *tare,* the *rehealune,* a storage room for our daily food, and two entrances. Also included were a stable for seven horses at the far end and the room in which we stored food for our cattle and pigs.

Room 6 served as the living and eating room for the farm's

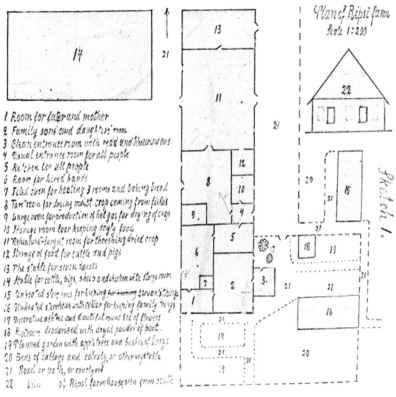

3.4   *My sketch of the house*

permanent inhabitants. It held three wide beds with room for two persons each. In my youth, the members of the family—ten persons—sat together with four hired hands at one long table in Room 6 if there was space, or in the kitchen closer to the cooking equipment and food supply if not. The table could seat up to fourteen at long benches on either side, though twelve sat more comfortably. When the crops from the field had to be harvested during the summer time, the hired hands brought their food outside to eat.

Several buildings stood near the farmhouse: an unheated storehouse and cellar for the family's things; a separate storehouse for the servants' belongings; and an outhouse deodorized with dried, powdered peat. After the farmhouse, the largest building was the stable for cattle, calves, hogs, sheep, and chickens. An inclined road at its eastern end made the top floor accessible to horse-driven wagons delivering hay.

As I was growing up, I felt proud of Father's new farmhouse, which was larger, more modern, and better built than others in our community. Our neighbors' houses had old-fashioned roofs of straw, but ours was shingled. They had only two chimneys—one for the baking oven and the other for the large stove in the *tare*. We had three. One was built between the three rooms in which we lived. It was for the stove that had Dutch tiles and that was used for bread baking and the warming of our quarters. The second vented the gases of the drying furnace in the *tare*. The third served to ventilate the stable for the six or seven horses that did the work of the farm.

We were proud of the veranda, which served as a special decoration for our new house. Located on the southeastern corner of the building, its big windows were made of blue and red glass. It was used as an entrance for us—the educated children of our family.

1. Older land records in the area mention the farm of a "Rip" or "Rips" family. In Estonian, "Ripsi" is the possessive form of "Rip," i.e. "that belonging to Rip," but there has been no record found positively proving that Otto's father bought the farm of the Rip family. Wanawoidu is now "Vana-Võidu," a settlement, or parish, of Viljandi County in southern Estonia.

2. In Estonia, lime could be burned to produce mortar, cement, and paint. Traditionally, limestone has also played a critical role in agriculture. When burned in a kiln, limestone leaves behind calcium oxide, commonly called quicklime. Spread on the ground and hydrated by rain, the lime could be used to sweeten acid soils, turning even bog land into productive fields. Farmers had an ongoing need for the kilns, since the lime had to be periodically reapplied to their land or processed as more material for building projects.

3. The word *tare* is apparently not used in modern Estonian. Today, *rehetuba* refers to the threshing room, including the kiln room; *rehetare* is sometimes used to designate the threshing barn as a whole. Perhaps *tare* is a local or family abbreviation.

4. Otto refers to the drying structure as a "podium." Though he never explicitly alludes to the *tare* of his childhood in his later accounts of the Lepol kiln, his most significant invention, the kiln harkens back to it. By passing hot exit gases over rock-like pellets in the production of concrete before they are expelled, the Lepol kiln system efficiently utilizes heat that would otherwise be lost.

5. Otto calls the second threshing room a *rehealune*, but *rehealune* or *rehielamu* can also indicate the entire barn-dwelling, traditional in Estonia since before the thirteenth century and consisting of the threshing room, drying room, and living chambers. (Raun, *Estonia and the Estonians*)

6. Otto elsewhere describes the water wheel as producing about eight horsepower.

7. Renate:

    In Estonian—Otto's first language—nouns and pronouns are not assigned grammatical genders, and yet this sentence reflects a very gendered, hierarchical vision of life. Women sit at spinning wheels. Men invent the machines that spin "a hundred times faster." Machine labor is superior to hand labor. Men's labor is superior to women's labor. And inventors are superior to other men.

8. At another point in the text, Otto describes the structure as thirty meters by ten meters.

9. Renate:

    Because bedrock in Livland is largely of limestone, any granite available for construction in the area had to have come from far away, dropped by glaciers into the fields. Such boulders are known as *Findlings* in German ("foundlings," in English). Geologists call them "erratics."

    During my visit to the Ripsi farm in 1994, I admired the north foundation wall of one of the original buildings. It had survived as a communal livestock barn throughout the decades of collectivization under Soviet rule. The farm had been returned to the family that had purchased it from a Lellep descendant in the late 1920s. On a return trip in 2018, I was not able to locate the farm again, though I inquired using historic and familial names. A later internet search led me to the image of a beautiful foundation of pink granite—perhaps Ripsi's—that may have been claimed by officialdom as part of an agricultural college or cultural center.

CHAPTER 4

The Seasons, Work, and Food at Ripsi

c. 1888–1893
Otto age 4–9: Ripsi

The fields at Ripsi were cultivated in a five-year sequence. During the first year, a field was left at rest. The little grass growing there was eaten by pigs. The second year, the field was enriched with dung from our stable, which was ploughed in during the summer. In September, it was planted with rye, or sometimes wheat. Father liked to sow the seeds himself. They grew to a maximum of ten centimeters high, until the frost in late autumn hindered further growth. In the third year, the rye or wheat, which had been frozen during the winter, started to grow as soon as the frost disappeared, and a little clover seed was sown between the plants. The fourth year, clover was grown on the rich soil—a nourishing food for our animals. It was harvested as hay, dried in the field, and given to the cattle, or particularly to the horses, since they worked hard all year long. In the fifth year, a crop of barley, oats, or flax was sown and harvested. And then the cycle was repeated from the beginning.

During my childhood, two kinds of ploughs were used. The more primitive one was made of wood. The only steel parts were the two lower ends. They were twelve centimeters apart and were used to break the surface of the field. The more modern plough (still used in many places in the world) was entirely fashioned of steel and was bought in the city. Pulled by a single horse and guided by a man, it cut and turned over a strip of soil about thirteen centimeters wide.

Once the surface of the field was broken, the soil was fragmented into smaller pieces by a horse-drawn harrow: twenty or thirty hardwood blocks held together by three horizontal, long steel rods. Vertical steel scratchers, each two by two centimeters in cross-section and about thirty centimeters long, extended about fifteen centimeters beneath the blocks. Both blocks and steel scratchers adjusted to the surface of the field as the horse-drawn harrow passed over it repeatedly until the lumps of soil were broken. Afterward, the ploughed field, sown with grain, was sometimes smoothed by a wooden roller.

During haying season, the grass in the meadow was cut by a scythe, dried, and stored in sheds, as was the clover grown in cultivated fields. Barley and oats were also mowed by scythe, then dried and collected in high heaps in the fields.

The rye crop was cut with a sharp sickle, shaped like a semicircle. Workers had to lean over in a tiring stoop to the cut the plants, which, when full grown, stood as high as a man. Bundles of rye were heaped in the field to protect them against rain until threshing time. Each stem of the plant had near its top an ear full of rye grains, the substance of which formed the most essential daily nourishment of the common people in northern Russia and Estonia: brown-colored rye bread. In 1940, Russian soldiers in Moscow received a daily ration of three pounds of this kind of bread.[1]

It is remarkable how much physical labor a farmer could withstand. The summer harvest required heavy work each day for about twelve hours, with two periods for rest and eating in the midmorning and afternoon. A typical day began at 6:00 am. At 8:00 am, breakfast was served, and a rest period was granted until 10:00. From 10:00 am until 2:00 pm came another four-hour working period. Dinner and the next rest followed, from 2:00 pm to 4:00 pm. A third working period began at 4:00, lasting almost until the sun went down.[2]

After ten or twelve hours of hard work, the tired people came home, had supper, and dropped exhausted into bed. Today, when machines have replaced human labor, it is hard to believe a farmhand had to swing a scythe without protest for ten or twelve hours at a time. Without complaints, my sisters Anna and Juuli and my brother Jüri did this hard work with the hired hands.

The long Estonian winter required other work, as well. Father's main source of income came from the sale of forest products. Only in the winter, when all the fields, meadows, bogs, rivers, and lakes were frozen and covered with snow, was there time available to transport hay and firewood for the farm and to take heavy logs to the sawmill.

Three workmen and up to six horses did the winter work. The workmen loaded the forest products onto horse-drawn sleighs. They had a hard life. They left early in the [dark] morning, around six o'clock, taking food for breakfast and dinner with them. In the evening, the tired, hungry men returned to have a warm supper and rest for the night. I remember one worker who lost his patience and angrily cursed while carrying the horse's harness from the courtyard.

During the long winter evenings, people on the farm sat in the workroom of the house. Anna and Juuli, my unmarried sisters, did their work there. They, and girls like them, were skilled at producing textiles. Young men would sit nearby for friendly conversations as the girls worked. Anna and Juuli used foot-driven spinning wheels to produce threads of flax or wool. The coarse linen and wool cloth that resulted was durable and of high quality. Father or mother invited a tailor and his helper to come to our farm, and they made suits and overcoats for the whole family. Such clothing was undoubtedly of substantial and long-lasting quality when compared with the clothing sold in the city.

Gradually, the kind of natural life and industry in the home [that I've described] disappeared and necessities were mostly bought in

4.1   This is one of the most important of my photos. My father, as the main partner in forest products, is on the right; his partner Lorup sits in the center; Father's son-in-law, the youngest and minor partner, is at the left end of the table. The partners met at Ripsi at least twice a year to clarify and settle the business accounts related to income, cost, and profit. [This occurred through] friendly discussion and the leadership of the main partner—my father. We mainly see notebooks on the table, but there is also a bottle of beer, there only to satisfy thirst since the thinking of the partners had to be kept clear.

In the background, the wall of the large Ripsi oven is visible. It was used for baking bread for up to twenty people and for keeping the three living rooms of the farm warm. There was a small, rectangular cavity in the center of the oven wall, where I, as a small boy of eight, could sit and see and hear all the proceedings.

the city. But such life and industry existed during my childhood until I went away to school when I was nine. Years later, when I was a student in Germany, I [still] had the economic benefit of wearing clothing made in my Ripsi home.

In the old days, it was a custom on the farm to let the younger children start to perform some light tasks when they were seven. At that age, my job was to herd a flock of thirty sheep—in other words, I became a shepherd. My task was to drive the flock to a particular field, keeping them out of the neighboring fields where young plants of rye, wheat, or barley grew. This was not difficult. Sheep are easy to handle, peaceful animals. They like to stay together and feed on the pasture grass.

When I was eight, I was promoted to taking care of the pigs. A swineherd has a much more difficult time. Pigs are individualists. Every one of them looks out for its own personal advantage. They like to stuff their bellies with the best food they can find, and their sense of smell is very well developed. Pigs prefer potatoes, and my pigs knew where to find them.

Our potatoes grew hand-deep in the earth and to get at them, the pigs wanted to dig holes with their snouts. If this were to happen, Father would see the obvious damage to a potato field, and he would make me, the herdsman, responsible. Obviously, the undisciplined pigs had to be punished. For this, I needed a whip. From flax fibres available at home, I made a very strong string that I fastened to the end of a willow stick. Any pig who strayed illegally into the potato field and ate the precious vegetables received a few painful strokes from my whip.

Once I had a pet pig I named Kutta. I had trained him, and when I called "Kutta! Kutta!" he came to me. I rewarded him with pieces of bread or potato. One day, Kutta and I were in a field with particularly desirable clover. Clover was mostly reserved for feeding the horses, but I wanted to give my dear Kutta a special treat, so I tied a string to a stick and looped the other end over his head. For a while my plan succeeded, but then, against all expectations, I suddenly heard a shrill cry. Wishing to eat more of the tasty food, Kutta had pulled the noose around his neck tighter and tighter, and he was in danger of suffocating.

People on the nearby farm heard the desperate screaming and came running to save Kutta's life. In my excitement and fear, I had forgotten to pull out the stick to loosen the string. I could have been accused of endangering my own pet pig, and I might have faced punishment from my strict father. My explanation that I'd intended to do Kutta a favor was not heard, and I thought Father might hit me on my naked bottom with birch twigs. Fortunately, no punishment followed. As the youngest child, I did receive less punishment than my brothers.

In the mornings, while I herded pigs, my brothers Willem and Peter herded the cattle. The herdsmen for the cattle had to be awakened earlier than the guardian of the pigs because the cows had to be milked before they were driven into the pasture.

I was awakened at about six o'clock. My mother handed me my breakfast, which I later ate in the field. Out of a broad loaf of rye bread, she cut a piece thick on one end and thin on the other. Then she took a conically shaped section out of the middle, filled it with butter, and capped it with bread. A three-quarter-litre bottle of sour milk served as a nourishing drink. I grabbed whatever else I needed, and my dog and I drove the pigs to the field, where we remained from 7:30 to 11:00 am.

Food at Ripsi was quite simple and monotonous. The staple for us was brown, coarse-grained, rye bread, accompanied by sour milk. This was served twice daily at our long table.

We had about fifteen cows. Naturally, there was more milk in the spring and summer when the cows were well fed with fresh grown grass, and not as much in the winter when they ate less nourishing hay. The birth of [their] calves was so regulated by the girl manager of the animals, that, fortunately, the cows delivered milk the whole year round.[3]

We kept the fresh milk from our cows in flat dishes of glass or pottery for many days. As the lighter cream rose to the top, the milk soured and the cream was used to make butter, which we sold in the nearby city of Wiljandi. The combination of the bread and the protein in the milk provided an almost balanced food for workers on the farm. Imperfect separation of milk and cream undoubtedly left a small portion of fat in the sour milk, but it was probably a little scant in fat content. Twice a week only, everyone at the table received a piece of fat pork consisting mostly of bacon.[4] This was based upon sound human instinct, not scientific calculation.

We needed a large area for growing cabbage, our most important vegetable. We ate the cabbage fresh for only a short period during August. Year round, we kept it available as sauerkraut. Modern science has shown that sauerkraut and its liquid provide a good source of vitamin C, but we did not know about the importance of vitamins in my childhood.

At Ripsi, we made sauerkraut by cutting the cabbage into thin strips and pounding it in big wooden containers in the cellar, where it fermented. This sour, healthy food was cooked with crushed grains of barley for many hours in a huge cast iron kettle in our kitchen. It was served as a porridge with sour milk and bread. Such porridge was also popular in neighboring Scandinavian countries.

In addition to the sauerkraut and barley porridge—or the alternative, consisting of wheat flour served with a hole in the middle filled with molten fat from bacon—our diet included soups made of potatoes, peas, or beans and a little sweet milk. Potatoes were served many different ways and, as on any Estonian farm during my childhood, we had *taar* to drink.

At Ripsi, we made *taar* in a process similar to that used in the brewing of beer. We began by keeping a layer of barley grain moist, in a warm room. When the grain started to germinate and a large part of the starch was transformed into sugar, we poured the sweet, moist mixture into flat pans and baked it in a hot oven. In the kitchen, we kept a large wooden container, about 0.75 meters in diameter and 1.2 meters high, with a layer of clean straw at the bottom to provide a filter. We spread the baked, sweet germinated barley on top of the straw and filled the container with clean water. After a week of brewing, with the water replenished from time to time, this rich mixture was removed. In the meantime, it had been transformed, not into alcohol, but into a refreshingly sweet-sour beverage that we obtained by opening the cock at the bottom of the container and filling a pitcher.

Silk provided an additional source of protein on my father's farm.[5] Members of the herring family, *silk* are silver colored fish about fifteen centimeters long. They were salted and kept all year in a large container in the cellar of our farm, but the delivery of the fresh *silk* always made people happy. Once a year, in the spring, each farm sent a farmhand in a horse-drawn wagon to a bay of the Baltic Sea not far from the city of Pärnu. There, fishermen brought loads of the fish, which were sold at low cost. They were immediately cleaned by local working girls, salted, and loaded onto the farmers' wagons.

I remember a wagon arriving at Ripsi one day, loaded with about 1,500 kilograms of *silk*. We gave a pail full of fresh fish to those living in the farmhouse next to ours. All of my long life, I have remembered the excellent taste of this seldom seen food, equal in quality to Portuguese sardines. When fresh, the *silk's* delicate taste provided an appreciated contrast to the monotonous food we ate daily.

[We had a few other treats.] Round-shaped rutabagas weighing up to several pounds each were stored in our cellar until Christmas time. When they were covered with ashes in the bottom of our big stove and baked for hours, they were transformed into a sweet tasting delicacy. Yeasted wheat bread, not the daily, coarse rye bread, was also baked, mainly for holidays such as Easter and Christmas. Well-fed bulls, cows, and horses were sold during special fairs announced ahead of time on the calendar, and from time to time a sheep or calf was slaughtered to feed us.

[I should describe how our food was served.] During the summer harvest, the hired workmen brought their own food and ate outside, but in my youth, all the members of the family—ten persons—and four regular farmhands, sat at the same table. It accommodated the fourteen of us sitting on long benches, with Mother and Father at the head. I remember when I was a small child, I was unable to reach the food if I dangled my feet below the bench, so I sat on my knees.

We functioned well with this democratic way of life. No one in the family had privileges over the workers. Food was served in a few large pottery dishes. Plates with knives and forks weren't yet used at tables in Russia and Estonia. Everyone had his own wooden spoon, and we each had a pocket folding knife for cutting bread or meat. My civilized eating habits with table service came gradually after I entered my brother's school in Kronstad, near the Russian capital city of St. Petersburg.

1. Otto does not elaborate on the significance of this date—the year that Soviet forces crossed the border and occupied Estonia. A puppet government and undemocratically elected Riigoku (parliament) then proclaimed the country the "Estonian Soviet Socialist Republic." The year before, in August of 1939, Vyacheslav Molotov and Joachim von Ribbentrop had signed the German-Soviet Nonagression Pact (or the Molotov Ribbentrop Pact). A secret protocol also signed then—and two successive secret agreements—divided Eastern Europe between the two countries. The Soviets were assigned Lithuania, Latvia, Estonia, Finland, and parts of Poland, and in June of 1941, over 10,000 Estonians were arrested and deported to Russia. German forces drove the Soviets out of mainland Estonia later in the summer, but the Red Army re-occupied Estonia in August and September of 1944.

2. On June 24, 2018 in Estonia, the sun rose at 4:11 am and set at 10:29 pm.

3. Renate:
     The skillful management of reproduction was critically important to ensuring a year-round supply of milk, which provided both nourishment and income. The knowledge of breeding implemented by Otto's sisters and their female help has since developed into an important branch of animal science at agricultural universities.

4. "Fat pork" today is a cut having little meat or none at all. It is still available in Estonian supermarkets. Never smoked, it is eaten raw. Otto's use of the term is unclear. Perhaps "fat pork" to him meant fat with bacon, the whole having been smoked. Elsewhere, he writes that only the farmhands received the fat pork.

5. Karin Annus Kärner (*Estonian Tastes and Traditions*) translates Baltic herring as *räimed* and refers to salted *räimed* as *silk*. In North America, smelt are said to be the closest cousins to the Baltic herring (Clupea harengus membrus) or European sprat. Renate: "Baltic Smelt": Sprattus europea.

CHAPTER 5

Some Special Memories

c. 1888–1893

Otto age 5–9: Ripsi

As I have said, food at Ripsi was mostly monotonous and work was hard, but I have one special memory of a very cheerful Christmas celebration when I was about six years old. My oldest brothers, Hans and Jaan, had come home for the holiday. Jüri brought in a tall fir tree from the forest and took it into the biggest room in the farm. I was temporarily forbidden to enter that room because sisters Juuli and Anna were busy decorating the tree.

Special bread made from refined rye and small buns created from imported, white "Moscow flour" were baked in the oven. Later, the buns were cut in half and covered with an especially delicious mixture of eggs, cream, cottage cheese, and butter. The smells of the blood sausages, pork, and hulled barley frying in the large oven promised appetizing food. All the living rooms and the kitchen were thoroughly cleaned and the floors were covered with fresh sawdust that smelled of resin. Everyone bathed in the sauna and put on clean clothes.

After some time, my sisters opened the door that had been kept closed and invited us all to enter. There before us stood the huge Christmas tree, topped by a large shining star. It was incredibly beautiful, lit with dozens of candles and decorated with apples and presents and strings of silver and gold that glittered in the candlelight. My heart beat hard, and my happy feelings brought tears to my eyes.[1]

Father gave a speech about the Christmas holidays. We were celebrating the birthday of God's son, Jesus Christ, who delivered us from sin, he said. Then he and my brothers and sisters started singing cherished Christmas carols in harmony—soprano, bass, and tenor.

The presents for six boys and two girls (the third was married and not at home with us), as well as those for the hired hands, hung from the tree or lay on the floor beneath it. Later, the gifts were distributed. Everyone received something. When I opened my package, I found a brand new pocketknife made by a Swedish firm called Fiskars. It had a blade of the famous, hardened, Swedish steel.

I was the very happy owner of such a practical gift. Boys on the farm when I was growing up had to learn to use the pocket knife as a universal tool, not only for eating at the table, but also for making toys and many other useful items. When sharp, my knife could cut food, wood, or paper. I turned its dangerous, sharp blade 180 degrees to fit it into the handle so I could safely carry it in my pocket, and I tied it to my jacket with a string to prevent myself from losing it.

Later, I learned to sharpen my knife myself, just as we sharpened the axes and other cutting or drilling tools that belonged to the men on the farm. I did the coarser grinding on a wet, rotating grinding stone. The finer sharpening I did by rubbing my knife blade against a very fine-grained, wet, honing stone.

I have another special memory from the time when Anna and Juuli were caring for me. I always enjoyed spring as the best season of the year. I loved to walk or run in the delightfully warm weather when the first green grass and little blossoms appeared on the fields and meadows. During Whitsuntide,[2] life in the fields, meadows, and forests awakened fully.

One year, Anna and Juuli made me a new suit. During the first day of Whitsuntide, they washed and combed me, dressed me, and took me for a long walk on a quiet path through our pasture near the forest. It was a sunny day. The first grass had grown and the birch trees, with their young leaves, gave off a fresh aroma. Bees buzzed around the blossoms and we heard some birds singing. The large fir trees revealed the beginning of young cones on their higher branches, and we even saw a lively squirrel leap from one branch to another.

How beautiful and good life was! My sisters and I picked some flowers, and all of us felt festive. During Father's younger years, there was very little chance to be friendly and loving with each other. We were always kept so busy that we had practically no time for pleasant walks to observe the beauty of the blossoming meadows and trees or the young green rye, wheat, or barley swaying to and fro with the wind. Our father was strict, and he trained the younger generation to work hard. For this I am very thankful. But I will never forget this exceptional occasion with my sisters.

[I have memories of times I spent with Peter and Willem, as well]. One spring when I was seven, there was a short period when the cattle and pigs could be driven to one pasture. Peter and Willem drove out the twenty cows, and I followed with the twenty pigs. We were in a pasture partly covered with alder bushes and fir trees, near a pit between Fox Mountain and a lower mountain. There, neighboring farmers loaded wagons full of the sand they needed for the lime mortar used in buildings. Together, the three of us had many possibilities for particularly interesting activities. Peter was about two years older than I, and Willem about four years older. They had much more practical experience than I.

[On the day I am remembering], Willem had his pocketknife, as usual, but he had taken along a small hand axe, as well. We did not want to be idle while herding our cattle and pigs, so we decided to build a "summer castle." Willem used his axe to cut alder tree sticks as tall as a man. He sharpened the lower ends and hammered the sticks into the ground to create the four solid corners of a building. On top of the corners, Willem somehow fixed four strong alder beams.

It was easy to fill in the side walls and the ceiling of the castle with thin twigs of alder, which we cut with sharp pocketknives and bound to the solid frame of the structure using the flexible and strong roots of the fir trees growing near the pasture. We left an opening on one side for an imaginary entrance. When the summer castle was ready, it was two meters long by two meters high on each side, and all three of us could lie down inside and admire our own handiwork.

The companionship of three brothers guarding the cattle and pigs together on a relatively small area with juicy grass lasted only a few days. The cattle ate up the grass and my twenty pigs had to go back to the field closer to the farm building, but we brothers sometimes had other chances to be together.

When he was an adult, Willem had the skill to build all kinds of things with his hands, and this was true even when we were young. Once, in the ditch of running water between the pasture and the area for growing hay, Willem built a watermill using only his pocketknife. First, he made a dam by driving strong sticks into the floor of the ditch and laying horizontal sticks against them. He made this wall watertight by spreading it with a mixture of grass and clayish mud. Next, Willem shaped a channel from the bark of an aspen tree and fixed it on the top of the twenty-five-centimeter high dam. Water ran nicely over the channel and formed a waterfall below.

To utilize his waterfall, Willem built a simplified watermill, about twenty centimeters in diameter. It consisted of a straight central shaft, which had a centrally located nail on each end. The nails rested in grooves on the top of two supporting sticks. Twelve pieces of wood for paddles or shovels, each about 30 x 25 x 3 millimeters, were fixed on the perimeter of the shaft. He fastened the inner end of the paddles into symmetrically spaced slots on the periphery of the round, straight shaft.

I observed with satisfaction how the little watermill kept running smoothly, even overnight, but unfortunately, there was a heavy rain one night. The ditch into which Willem had built the watermill temporarily received about twenty times the normal flow of water. This destroyed the dam and his creation. I tried to build a watermill too, when I was seven, but because of my unskilled hands, mine soon fell apart.

When I was about eight, I had a conflict with Willem and Peter, who were then twelve and fifteen years old. The river Nuia and the creek flowed with clean water then, and they were rich with fish. One warm summer day, Willem and Peter used a *liiv*, a fishing net, with good luck. They caught some fish, which they cleaned and cooked with potatoes and fresh milk to make a particularly tasty soup.

I watched them, and the aroma whetted my appetite, but unfortunately, my older brothers denied me any of the delicacy. I wept bitterly over their stinginess and told them: "I will study diligently. Someday, I'll become a doctor, and I'll avenge this insult." The grandiose idea of a doctoral title seems to have inspired me very early in life.

In September, after the harvest of the rye, the cattle and pigs could again be driven together onto the field, and the three herdsmen—brothers Willem, Peter, and Otto—became friendly once more. The season gave us the opportunity to partake of something unusual and enjoyable. A big granite [boulder] stood in the middle of the large field where the cattle and pigs were feeding. It had probably traveled from Sweden to Estonia during the ice age. Without consulting our mother—who probably would not have allowed it—we decided to build a baking oven behind it and to secretly make pancakes. Our activities could not be observed from home.

Drawing on my previous experience, I built the oven. We smuggled wheat flour, butter, a mixing dish for the dough, and a pan from the house. The baking proceeded perfectly, and we ate the butter-covered pancakes until our bellies were overfilled.

Shortly after that, Willem, age fifteen years, decided to build a small plant for manufacturing bricks. From clay, we formed small bricks about 6 x 3 x 1 1/2 centimeters. These seemed sufficiently dry after being left for one day on the large stone. Willem then made a huge fire of dried firewood on the stone and put the dried bricks into the hot coals below the fire. To our regret, the insufficiently dried bricks burst and split during the heating and our brick factory failed.

After I grew up and studied in Germany, I made a useful invention that saved many companies millions of dollars, but I also lived in harmony with my older brothers. [Despite my earlier vow], I had no desire for vengeance.

1. Renate:
    Our last Christmas in Hösel (our home in Germany), Otto took Lii and me walking in the dark forest. When we came in and took off our wraps, we stood before double doors that probably led to a parlor. When the doors were opened, there was the tree, lit by real candlelight. My heart beat hard, and my feelings brought tears to my eyes. Reading the passage above brought tears to my eyes, again. We didn't know then that that would be our last Christmas together as a family until we were able to be a family again some time later in the United States. And I didn't realize until now, in reading his memoir, that I was feeling what my father felt in his childhood.

2. Whitsuntide is celebrated during the three days—or week—following Whitsunday (the seventh Sunday after Easter, when the Holy Spirit is said to have descended upon Jesus' disciples).

CHAPTER 6

I Begin Inventing

c. 1887–1893

Otto age 3–almost 9: Ripsi

When I was a swineherd, I had a dog as my helper, but he wasn't very useful. Instead of training him, I preferred to produce something with my own hands or to plan and think. From the time of my youngest years, I'd begun inventing toys and useful articles.

Father had no time to spoil us children, so we had to find our own toys. When my father's old farmhouse burned down, I discovered the steel crank of a spinning wheel in the ashes. I pushed its straight axis into the gravel and rotated the crank by hand, claiming this as my own grinding mill.

At age seven, I found a tube-shaped, crooked blade of onion in our garden. [I took it to] our courtyard, where there was a well with a water pump, and next to it, a trough filled with water. Playing with the onion in the trough, I discovered that I could make the water run through its tube, and I joyfully claimed to have invented the siphon.

[Clay provided me with many possibilities.] When I found it on the side of a ditch near the field where I was herding pigs, I discovered I could make it uniformly malleable by adding some water and kneading it with my thumb or a stick. Once I'd worked with the clay, I could easily form it into egg-size balls or any other shape I wanted. It was simple to build walls, towers, steeples, and even castles.

Once, I made a small, round cooking stove. On the windward side, I left a hole into which I could push kindling. The smoke escaped from the opposite end through an open slot. On a sunny day, the thin wall of my fireplace dried hard as a stone. I brought some butter and an egg from home, which I fried and ate with pleasure. I was pleased and somewhat proud of my homemade kitchen equipment. Now, as an inventor who has specialized in the construction of economical industrial furnaces many thousand times larger than the one I built in my childhood, I think that the play of an eight-year-old boy foreshadowed the work of the engineer of forty years later.

To pass the time while I was a herder in my father's fields, I also made two kinds of whistles. I knew Estonian children played with a duck-shaped toy that made a few sounds when they blew into a hole in its tail. I decided to improve the toy so it would whistle.

Using the clay I'd found, I was able to create a hollow duck that made some sounds, but it was so soft it was liable to break in my pocket. I discovered that if I put a well-dried duck into the glowing coals below the large cooking kettle in the Ripsi kitchen, it became stone hard. Later, I drilled two holes in the back of my toy. Blowing into the tail of the duck and closing and opening the holes let me produce three different sounds, which satisfied me for a time.

I created a different kind of whistle from the branches of alder trees. When the warm weather made the sap in the trees start to move and the buds began to develop, the bark of the willows and alder trees loosened from the inner substance of the stems, especially in the smaller branches of the trees. That was the time to make a whistle. First, I cut off a piece of alder as long as my hand. By hammering on the bark, I was able to loosen it and pull it off. I built my instrument from the tube-shaped bark and two sticks of bark-free alder. What fun I had blowing it!

When I was a little older, my brother Hans presented me with a primitive musical instrument called an ocarino.[1] It was made of clay that had been hardened in a fire. My ocarino had ten holes, one for each finger, and it produced eleven musical notes somewhat similar to the tones of a flute. After a while, I learned to play a few simple melodies on it. I carried it in my pocket while I was guarding the pigs, and during quiet evenings I used to impress people on the neighboring farm with some simple songs.

One day, my ocarino fell on the stone floor and broke. The loss grieved me, and I decided to make one for myself. This was an ambitious task, since I had only my ten fingers and a sharp pocketknife. I did not succeed immediately, but after a few trials, I was able to improve my technique.

In order to shape the interior of the ocarino, I used my knife to cut a stick about two-and-a-half centimeters in diameter and about eleven centimeters long. Next, I pressed a layer of clay about four millimeters thick around it. The inside of the ocarino was formed when the clay dried and I pulled out the stick. On the side of the instrument, I attached a thumb-thick piece of clay and made a hole into which I could blow. Without diminishing the inner volume of the ocarino, I carefully closed off the open end with clay. Much patience was required when I shaped the blowhole and the ten openings needed for the musically correct eleven tones.

After the instrument was thoroughly dry, I took it to the kitchen fireplace. Underneath Mother's huge kettle, I heated it very gradually between red-hot charcoal pieces until it reached a bright red temperature and became hard. I was about twelve years old when I perfected my homemade ocarino, and I was happy to be able to sell one or two to my schoolmates and other friends.

In my youth, children did not receive pocket money from their parents, so I had to find some way to earn spending money. I wanted so much to order sweet raisins from the city. The thought came that I could make the straw hats that most people wore in the

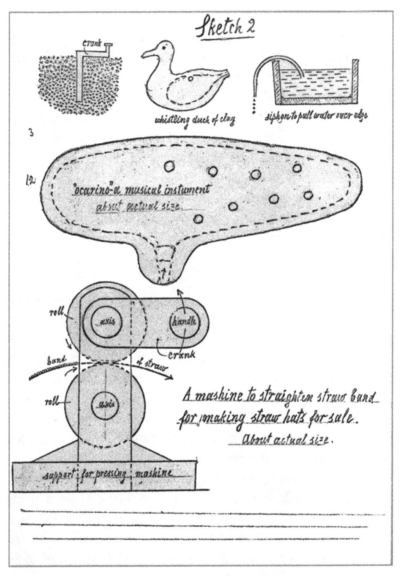

6.1 Ocarino and hat press

summer to protect their faces from the sun and the rain. I knew that the children on neighboring farms had learned to make them.

The production of straw hats required long hours of diligent work. First, I had to select stalks of a uniform size from bundles of rye straw. I moistened them to make them pliable, and then braided them into long, uniform bands, one-and-a-half centimeters wide and about sixty meters long—the length required for one hat. I could roll the band as I braided and comfortably carry the roll while I was standing or walking slowly with the pigs. Braiding straw became automatic, a sideline activity while I continued my main job of guarding the pigs and preventing them from running into the potato field.

Before I could sew a hat, the braided band had to be smoothed and straightened, so I decided to make a pressing device. I used two rolls, each of which had an axis. The axis of the upper roll was pressed against the lower one by two heavy stones. I attached a crank to the upper axis and ran the moistened straw band between the rolls as I turned the crank.

My final task was to use a needle and thread to sew the band into a hat, which I sold for twenty Russian kopecs. *Only twenty kopecs,* you might think, but this would buy me two pounds of raisins. I ate them with great pleasure!

My life on the farm continued as I've described until late in the summer of 1893. When I was almost nine years old, my dear mother fell seriously ill. The lower part of her body grew swollen, and she was unable to walk. During her fifty-four years of life, Mother had never consulted a medical doctor. Less serious ailments or sufferings had been cured according to *Hausdoctor,* a textbook written by a competent doctor.

Because of the seriousness of Mother's ailment, my oldest brother Hans came back to Ripsi from Kronstad to see her. Hans was by then a university graduate and Jaan was a Lutheran priest. They recommended that Mother be immediately taken to the lazaret, a kind of substitute for a hospital. It was located in the nearest city of Wiljandi. Father consented to their plan.

In preparation for the journey, Father's painted wagon was

filled with soft hay. Packed in blankets, Mother was placed on the wagon bed. I was called to her, to speak with her for the last time. Neither Mother nor I could articulate a word. With deep, sad feelings and tears in our eyes, we looked at each other and held hands.

Mother died shortly thereafter in the *lazaret*, which eighty years ago had no trained doctors. I did not attend her burial ceremonies, but Father, Hans, and Jüri did. Hans had his work as a teacher and an assistant to the pastor at the Estonian parochial school in Kronstad, so he had to return there. When he left, I went with him. At the time, I was almost nine, and because Hans was twenty-two years older than I, he assumed my father's duties toward me.

1. Now commonly known as "ocarina." Often shaped like birds or animals, ocarina-like instruments are associated with ancient Mayan, Aztec, and Inca cultures.

CHAPTER 7

The Kronstad Years

c. 1893–1895

Otto age 9–11: Kronstad

Hans and I traveled to Kronstad by train and ship.[1] Because we had no railroad in the nearby city of Wiljandi, we first rode in a horse-drawn wagon to a faraway station. It took us about seven hours, and I got tired.

The passenger train arrived during the dark night. To see and feel the operation of the famous, grand train was for me an entirely new experience. The noisy locomotive puffed smoke and white vapor, and the large cars, each as big as a small house, held benches for many passengers. At one point, for some reason, I stepped out of the car and the train started to move. Fortunately, Hans found me in time and pulled me back inside. During the journey, being quite tired, I slept part of the time on the wooden shelf above the seats.

The next morning, we arrived in Russia's famous capital city of St. Petersburg. Hans and I took a taxi to the Estonian colony, to the big house and Lutheran church of Pastor Hurt.[2] He was a well-known collector of Estonian folklore, fairy tales, and old Estonian songs, idioms, and folk sayings.

My brother Jaan served as an assistant pastor to Pastor Hurt. Unfortunately, Jaan and the pastor were both out. For some reason, Hans had to leave as well, so I was left alone in the reception room until the kind and friendly Mrs. Hurt came in. She was French, but she was easily able to talk with me in Estonian.

Mrs. Hurt first fed me. She brought a large glass of sweetened, hot tea and two slices of Estonian coarse wheat bread, still warm and covered with melted butter. Then she inspected my home-woven and home-tailored clothing, made by my sisters at Ripsi. The quality of cloth was no doubt very good, but the tailoring was perhaps not quite suitable for the capital city. She left the room, and when she returned, she presented me with a warm, winter overcoat, beautifully tailored and formerly worn by her own son, who had outgrown it. The overcoat fit me perfectly.

After a while, when my brother Hans returned, he hired a taxi and we rode to the harbor, where we boarded a small steamship for Kronstad, which was about twenty-five kilometers away. St. Petersburg and Kronstad were founded 190 years ago by the famous czar Peter the Great, who had defeated the Swedish king after a long war and won for Russia all of Estonia. Kronstad was a fortification on a small island and was intended to protect the capital city against foreign invasion. A Russian military fleet floated in its harbor.

The majority of the inhabitants of Kronstad were Russians, but a colony of Finns and Estonians together built a Lutheran church there.[3] The German Lutheran church stood opposite the Estonian-Finnish one, and the two, with their auxiliary buildings, formed a small cultural center where young people came together for choir singing or other festivities.

The Estonian-Finnish church had a garden and a house for the Estonian pastor, Pastor Eisen, as well as a house with living quarters for my brother Hans and the teacher of the Finnish community. Hans was the senior teacher in the Estonian school.

Inside, the church's layout was well adapted to the needs of the two small communities. The altar was located at the west end of the building, with rooms in each of the four corners separated by walls from the main, central space. The corner rooms on the western end were classrooms for the children of the Estonian and Finnish communities. The upper story rooms were for the younger pupils, and the lower ones for the older children. The man who cleaned and took care of the church lived in the room in the third corner, and the fourth was usually unoccupied, though a coffin was kept there occasionally.

The Finnish and Estonian schools each had two teachers. I did not see much of the Finnish children, probably because there were only a few of them. About fifty children, eight to twelve years old, studied in the Estonian school. Hans taught in the upper classroom and Mr. Ronimois in the lower.

I began as a pupil in the class for the younger children. I did not enter as an outstanding student. My sisters had taught me the ABCs while I was at Ripsi, but I learned to read in a short time when I became nine years old [on September 29, 1893].

In our class, the teaching was done in Estonian and Russian. Religion was important, and only Estonian was spoken during the hour of that instruction. School began in the morning with a prayer.

At school, our minor misdeeds were punished with light discipline. Children had to extend their hands to the teacher, who hit them with a flat, wooden ruler. A more serious punishment called for pupils to sit on their knees on the bare floor in the corner of the classroom. In order to please the teacher, the children, particularly the girls, gave him a little gift from time to time. "Here is a picture for you, our teacher!" they called, holding up a little colored picture on a carton.[4]

We students also had time for fun at school. During recess, boys and girls ran about in the roomy courtyard around the church. In the Estonian school, we boys also discovered a special, daring sport we enjoyed between lessons when it was too cold outside for us to play in the courtyard. Sitting on the polished, wooden banister next to the stairs connecting the upper and lower classrooms, we glided to the bottom from the second floor. This was forbidden as a dangerous sport because we could have broken our bones, but most forbidden activities give a special pleasure, [including this one]!

I lived in a four-room apartment with Hans. We had two bedrooms and a kitchen, which were very small, and a larger room with a piano, a violin, and numerous sheets of music. Hans taught me how to cook many meals on his small kitchen range, which was heated by firewood. I boiled the water for morning and evening tea, and we ate bread and butter. For dinner, I cooked meat with potatoes and vegetables such as cabbage or carrots. The cooking water served as a soup. Our bread was usually brown rye bread purchased from a store, but we had plain white bread sometimes, too. The smallest monetary unit, one Russian kopec, could buy us four pieces of sweet *zwiebak*, a kind of biscuit toasted in slices. We seldom had this luxury.

Hans served as an organist and assistant to the pastor and was in charge of the adult Estonian singing choir. He was a man willing to become a friend to many, and he knew all the leading Estonians in Kronstad. The postmaster, Mr. Rotberg, was his friend.[5]

Mr. Rotberg was an outstanding man with numerous desirable qualities and talents. He could play the symphonies of world-famous composers on the piano, but he could also compose or improvise music that pleased his listeners. He often visited my brother so that they could play together, Rotberg at the piano and Hans on the violin. I listened to their playing, made tea, and prepared something for them to eat during their breaks.

During the winter, Hans and Mr. Rotberg traveled by sleigh to St. Petersburg. In the summer, they took a small steamship to nearby Oranienburg and from there boarded a train to St. Petersburg.[6] Whenever they returned to Kronstad, they talked about the theatrical productions they had seen or the fine restaurants where they had eaten. They did not have much money to spend on these trips, as their salaries were modest.

Sometimes the parents of the [Estonian] school children invited Hans and me, his little brother, for Sunday dinner. The Russian habit was to be generous to the guests.[7] Although these hosts were usually poor, their table was richly covered. Often they served us Russian soup, *borshtch*, consisting of red beets, cabbage, celery, and carrots. Next came oven-baked meat or pork with potatoes, followed by a sweet dish of fruit for dessert.

Pastor Eisen, who was Hans' supervisor at the Estonian school, invited Hans and me to see the Christmas tree in his home one Christmas vacation. On the green branches, a few dozen candles glittered beautifully between shining silver balls, tasty reddish apples, and thin bands of silver and gold strings.

Pastor Eisen had edited and published a collection of old Estonian folk tales concerning the doings of the devil and smart Hans. He gave me his booklet as a Christmas present. It was my ninth year of life, and this was the first book I [ever] read. I admired it and was particularly happy that smart Hans was always wiser and more clever than the devil. Hans found ways to cause the devil trouble.

In the days of my childhood, religion was more important than it is today. At home, each day during the Eastern holidays between Palm Sunday and Easter,[8] Hans let me read from the Bible the stories of what happened to Christ, and I was induced to follow his doings in my thoughts.

On the streets, I remember a popular and esteemed Greek Catholic monk who was usually called "the Holy Ivan."[9] Holy Ivan normally lived in St. Petersburg, but sometimes he visited Kronstad. When the street boys saw him riding by, they ran behind his taxi shouting loudly, "Have pity on us! Have pity on us!"[10] The pockets of Holy Ivan's overcoat were stuffed with kopecs, and he would fill his hands with the small copper coins and throw them onto the street for the Russian boys.

The Russians went to the Greek Orthodox Church, the highest authority of which was the almighty Russian czar.[11] They strictly observed the practice of fasting during Easter's holy week, and they celebrated Christ's resurrection with all the more joy and pleasure.

According to tradition, the celebration started exactly after midnight on the first Easter holiday.[12]

One night, before midnight, I went with some of Hans' friends to a place near the Russian cathedral to watch the ceremonies. About a thousand people were gathered there in calm and happy expectation. Precisely at midnight, the large bells in the tower of the cathedral began to ring, first the big ones—the low basses—and then the medium and smaller bells—the tenors and sopranos. They tolled together, sending forth an overpowering, joyful sound.

The friendly Russians, men and women, began to kiss each other. The men kissed the ladies first on the forehead, then on the right and the left cheeks, and at last on the chin, saying "Christ is risen." The ladies answered: "Indeed, He is risen." The main doors of the cathedral opened and out came a parade of priests, clad in vestments glittering with gold and silk embroidery and wearing crowns decorated with jewels.

Carrying crosses and holy icons, the priests marched three times around the cathedral, singing of the Holy Son of God, Christ, now risen, who through his suffering on the cross had redeemed us sinners and brought us salvation.

The sad fasting was done. A crowd of women had brought all kinds of tasty food—roasted ham, covered with dough and baked; rich cakes stuffed with a mixture of whipped butter, cream, sugar, and cottage cheese; a Russian specialty known as *pascha*; small, decorative, pyramid-shaped cakes called *kulitch*, which were delicately spiced treats made of white flour, eggs, and raisins;[13] and heaps of colored hard boiled eggs. The festival foods had been placed on tables along the cathedral wall and were sprinkled with holy water and blessed by the priests as they marched by.

During the three Easter holidays, when people customarily visited their friends and neighbors, the tables in prosperous homes remained covered with tasty food day and night. After entering, a guest would approach the lady of the house and kiss her face four times, as I described above, on the forehead, on each cheek, and on her chin, and say joyfully, "Christ is risen!" Then the guest had to drink vodka or wine and eat some of the nicely arranged, rich foods on the table.

While prosperous people could feast, the common people of Kronstad were living in very poor, miserable, unhygienic housing. Eighty years ago, when I was there, a long house with two floors usually had a large hall on each floor. Family units were fashioned on both sides of the hall, each about three meters long and three meters wide. The "walls" between the little rooms and the middle hallway were only made of cotton cloth. A strip that could be pushed aside when one entered served as a door. The top of these cell-like rooms opened to the two-and-a-half meter height of the hall.

Families with a number of children lived in these narrow cells. There were about forty units off a large hall, and they all shared a common kitchen and one toilet. The water used in Kronstad came from the polluted Neva River, which flows through St. Petersburg. People had to boil it before they used it for cooking or drinking, as it often caused cholera.

The Russians went to the Greek Orthodox Church, the highest authority of which was the almighty Russian czar. At the time, there was no talk about the rights of the people. The common man found his usual amusement in drinking vodka with a high content of alcohol. Drunken people sometimes had quarrels and fights causing injuries.

I didn't like to leave the courtyard of the church for shopping or other reasons. Hostile Russian boys, stronger than me, housed feelings of national superiority. They insulted me, shouting, "You are a despised *chuhna*!" a word for people who were unable to speak Russian.[14] They meant new immigrants, such as Estonians and Finns.

I wanted to beat up those boys, with their sense of national superiority, but being smaller and weaker, I was somewhat afraid. My brother Peter was two years older and much stronger than me and the evil street boys. From time to time, he visited Hans and me from St. Petersburg, where he attended school under the supervision of our brother, Pastor Jaan. Then he and I could walk safely onto the streets together.

During summer vacations, the schools in Kronstad and St. Petersburg closed, so Peter and I returned to Estonia by train. According to a prearranged agreement, we would find a horse-drawn wagon and driver from Ripsi waiting for us at the railway station.

The ride to Ripsi on unpaved roads took about seven hours. I felt very happy to leave the strange customs of Russia and come back to my cherished homeland, Estonia. Arriving in the courtyard of Ripsi, I saw again my dog Muri, who recognized me after the seven months of my absence.

The green grass on the fields had begun to grow. A herdsman was required to guard the pigs, so I took up my usual summer employment, but life at Ripsi was not the same as it had been. After my mother died, the farm needed a woman to direct the household; supervise the handling of the cattle, sheep, and pigs; work in the garden; and feed everyone. In addition to the usual farm hands, Father also hired skilled men who built new buildings on the farm or machinery for the mill, and they had to be fed too.

For a while, Mary, the daughter of a farmer, lived at Ripsi. Mary was a very capable girl. She was in charge of the cattle, the pigs, and the sheep, and she was wise and able to handle people. Mary's memory was phenomenal. She remembered exactly what had happened on the farm—when a member of the family visited or a calf was born. On Sundays, she read the Bible, and she knew all of its stories. Mary's salary was small, though, and she could not buy nice clothes. Father somehow neglected her.

Apparently, at some point, my father consulted my oldest married sister Liina concerning his possible re-marriage. As I have mentioned, Liina was the wife of a farmer and lived not far from the school where Father had been a teacher for twenty years. As I heard later, she expressed her opinion that Father should not marry a girl who could bear him more children, given that we already had six boys and three girls in our family.[15] Liina and my other sisters were well acquainted with an older girl in the neighborhood. Father could marry her without increasing the number of his children, and they suggested Liina's friend to be his second wife.

Father accepted the family's proposal and the marriage ceremony was performed on the Ripsi farm in June 1894. About forty guests came to the celebration because Father had many friends near Ripsi, Wiljandi, and the school where he had taught. In preparation, beer was brewed and special foods known on the farms were cooked. Pork was fried in a half a dozen large rectangular pans, and Estonian sausages were made. Three different kinds of bread were baked from coarse-ground and fine-ground rye, and also from wheat. A large number of small wheat buns were baked and cut in two. Each half was covered with a rich mix of cottage cheese, cream, eggs, and butter. Wine and stronger alcoholic drinks were bought in the city.

A pastor invited from Wiljandi directed the religious ceremony, which was accompanied by choral singing. I helped serve the numerous guests who remained in Ripsi for two or three days. As they started to leave, some ladies came to console me, since I now had only a stepmother and no real mother. They gave me some spending money.

The first few weeks in Ripsi with my new stepmother were dramatic. I had been friendly with Mary, who had taken care of us and the farm. I felt indifferent toward my new stepmother. She tried to be good to me, but she was not able to win my friendship. Mary, however, remained my real friend.

Mary did not dare speak directly against my stepmother, but indirectly, she let me know that she was better able to mother me. She was an orderly person who had grown up on a small farm with only a few people. At Ripsi, she had taken care of many more. I felt that in general, Mary was the more capable.

Feelings were somewhat strained, though fortunately they didn't rise to open conflict between Mary, my stepmother, and me. Gradually, Mary came to the conclusion that it would be easier for herself and others if she cultivated a friendly relationship with my stepmother. A wise and intelligent person, she eventually became a friend and assistant to my stepmother, and life at Ripsi stabilized.

At the end of August, Peter and I traveled back to our respective schools, he to St. Petersburg and I to Kronstad, where I learned to read and write elementary Russian. I bought a Russian fairy tale book called *The Czar's Son and the Gold-Colored Cock,* which I read with interest.

My life with Hans continued much as it had the previous year. I made some friends. A skilled master electrician named Watto lived on the second floor of our apartment house. He was an Estonian and was employed as a foreman in Kronstad in an electrical repair shop of the Russian navy. Watto had a wife, a daughter, and a son named Jonny, who was a little older than I. Jonny and I became friends, and we played cards together from time to time. He advanced through the Russian schools in Kronstad and later studied in St. Petersburg to become a graduate electrical engineer.

I also became friendly with the man who cleaned the church and the Estonian school. With his permission, I used to creep into the narrow space between the sheet steel roof and the wooden roof of the church. The room was populated by pigeons, who filled the bottom of the small space with their droppings. I could also climb up the narrow stairs leading to the tower of the church where the bells hung. From that high point, I could look over all of Kronstad, the ocean around it, and the warships floating in the harbor.

As a senior teacher, assistant to the pastor, and conductor of the Estonian choir, Hans was a prominent man among the Estonians in Kronstad. As I've described, he was often asked to dinner on Sundays, and I was welcomed, as well. An Estonian widow named Mrs. Kana invited us repeatedly. She made her living by providing room and board to single Russian marine officers, and her abundant, well-prepared food was as good as that served in the best restaurants in Kronstad. At Mrs. Kana's, I ate fresh lettuce salad with powdered sugar and lemon juice for the first time in my life.

Mrs. Kana had two pretty, young daughters, who cooked as well as their mother. Hans fell in love with the older daughter, Juuli. The younger one was taller, and being pretty, she kept a reserved and dignified manner. With her musical talent and excellent voice, she could have become a professional concert singer. Mr. Rotberg fell in love with the younger sister. Hans and Mr. Rotberg intended to marry those pretty girls.

In May, when the Estonian school closed, I had to return to Father's farm in Estonia to take up my job as a swineherd. Hans, Mrs. Kana's oldest daughter, and I traveled together to St. Petersburg by ship and from there by train to Estonia, where a driver from Father's farm was waiting to transport us in a horse-drawn wagon to Ripsi. Hans wanted to introduce his intended bride to Father. I sat with the driver in the front seat, Hans with his girl in the back seat. The seven-hour ride on the poor road tired me.

Hans, Mrs. Kana's daughter, and Maria, the six-year-old daughter of my sister Liina, had a good time in the garden at Ripsi. The strawberries and [black] currants had begun to ripen. The guests picked and ate them, and little Maria started to learn Russian from Hans' girlfriend. The strange and difficult pronunciation of certain Russian words amused the berry pickers and Maria.

Hans had brought a present for Father from Kronstad: an electrical bell with a battery, insulated wiring, and a contact button for our entrance door. Eighty years ago, electricity was an almost unbelievable wonder on Estonian farms. When someone pushed the button near our door, the bell twenty meters away in the living room began to ring, even though the insulated wires did not move! This signaled to us that a stranger had approached the house. Hans also gave me a present, the cherished ocarino that broke on our stone floor.

Father found Hans' girlfriend suitable to become his wife. Once the two of them married, there would be no room for me in the apartment, so they returned to Kronstad without me.[16] I was eleven-and-a-half years old at the time.

During my two years in school, I had learned to read and write in both Russian and Estonian. Father's financial standing and the income he could expect from forest products were not yet clear, but he wanted to see how my abilities and character would develop, so he let me continue my education.

1. Today, commonly known as "Kronstadt" or "Kronshtadt," the town is located on the island of Kotlin, west of St. Petersburg proper.

2. See note on Pastor Hurt at the end of Chapter 1.

3. Here, by "Russian," Otto must mean ethnic Russians, in contrast to "Estonians," who were part of the Russian empire by fate—not choice—and who were distinct from ethnic Russians in terms of their language, culture, and, often, their sense of identity.

4. By "carton," Otto perhaps meant a kind of cardboard box or simply "cardboard."

5. "Rotberg" is a German name.

6. Otto must mean "Oranienbaum," in Russia, as opposed to "Oranienburg," in Germany. "Oranienbaum" is just west of St. Petersburg. Today, the name designates the imperial estate that was founded in the area by Prince Menshikov, close advisor to Peter the Great.

7. Interestingly, though he is surely referring to ethnic Estonians (the parents of Hans' pupils), Otto refers to them as "Russians," perhaps a reflection of the level of their cultural assimilation.

8. Here, is Otto using "Eastern" to mean "Eastern Orthodox"? Eastern Orthodox Churches honor the patriarch of Constantinople and include churches in Russia, Serbia, Bulgaria, Romania, and Greece, among others.

9. As a "Greek Catholic" (or "Eastern Catholic" monk), the "Holy Ivan" was probably part of the Eastern tradition that aligned with the Roman See but retained its own, characteristic forms of liturgy, art, and organization.

10. In Otto's manuscript: "Commiserate with us!"

11. Otto's use of "Greek Orthodox," as well as "Eastern Orthodox" and "Eastern"—with no mention of the more familiar "Russian Orthodox"—is all very confusing. We can guess that he did not distinguish carefully between these

complex and differing religious traditions and communities. In English, "Eastern Orthodox" churches are sometimes referred to as "Greek Orthodox," so we may guess that Otto was thinking in English.

12. Perhaps Otto means, "the first day of the Easter holidays."

13. *Pascha* ("paska") and *kulitch* are traditional, yeasted Easter breads.

14. *Chuhna* is now more commonly spelled "chukhna." In modern usage, it is a perjorative term—an ethnic slur—for Finns and Estonians.

15. Renate:

    Otto's mention, above, of Mary's phenomenal memory and his praise of her competency reveal his view of her as an admirable woman, yet as he describes, fecundability, fertility, and the opportunity for conception played into the decisions made regarding her fate. Mary can be assumed to have been fecundable—a magnet of attraction for the widowed Jüri Lellep. Acting upon Liina's advice that he avoid marrying or even taking an interest in a woman young enough to bear him a child, Jüri seems, in Otto's eyes, to neglect Mary. Yet when Jüri marries an older woman, Otto and his siblings are spared the tension that could have readily developed upon his death, should there have been a half-sibling whose presence would call into question the expected distribution of affection and inheritance.

16. Renate:

    In the family archive, we have a long letter Hans sent to Otto. Written in Estonian, it is the only letter Otto received, or perhaps kept, from any of his siblings. Hans' letter is dated December 1939, long after the 1929 marriage of Otto and Frieda Aina Brandt. Hans died in Germany and his daughter Elsa brought his remains to Estonia for burial.

CHAPTER 8

More Studies

Mid-1890s to c. 1898

Otto age ~11–13: Near Ripsi and 1 kilometer from Wiljandi

After herding pigs during the spring, summer, and part of the fall, I entered the closest elementary school, a public school half an hour's walk from Ripsi. It had three classrooms for boys and girls from the surrounding farms. We were about eight to eleven years old. All of us slept five nights at school and two nights at home. Every Saturday afternoon I walked to Ripsi and every Monday morning I returned to school on foot. Children who lived four kilometers or so from the schoolhouse were brought back by wagon or sleigh.[1]

Food and drinks at school were simple. No hot meals were available. We drank cold water from a common water container using a ladle. I brought one week's worth of food with me on Mondays in a "bread bag," which was like today's [US] lunch box except that the food supply was simpler and it had to last a whole week.[2]

My bread bag held a five-pound loaf of coarse rye bread, and, in wooden containers, about two pounds of fat pork and one-and-a-half pounds of butter. Each of us also brought about four pounds of potatoes in separate nets marked with our names. The potatoes were boiled by the half pound daily in a large kettle in the school kitchen. Despite this monotonous, one-sided diet, in which a bottle of milk or some sauerkraut was considered a luxury, we remained healthy and cheerful. We supplemented our meals with what we ate at home during the weekends.

My clothing was as simple as my food. I wore a shirt made of flax grown in Father's fields and spun and woven into cloth by my sisters. I changed it once each week. My pants and coat were from the wool of our own sheep, converted to yarn in our textile mill and also woven by my sisters.

On my feet, I wore *pastlad*, which city people considered old-fashioned and suitable only for common, poor, uneducated farm workers. They were a homemade, inexpensive substitute for shoes on the farms. We made them at Ripsi from the tanned hides of our own cattle. Though they were not watertight, *pastlads* were convenient to wear during dry weather or on dry snow. I helped [fashion them], though it was not easy. We fastened them securely to our legs by a long string that was drawn through small holes at the edge of the leather—string I made myself, from flax fibre.

I entered public school in the highest grade and was the second to the best pupil in the group. I was an exceptional student because I had been to the famous capital city of St. Petersburg many times and had learned to speak Russian with Russian pronunciation. In addition, my brother was a prominent pastor and my father was a known public leader and businessman. One year, he was president of the Farmers' Society in Wiljandi.[3]

The teachers treated me with a little more respect than they gave the other pupils, and I was freed from menial tasks. Commonly, the boys and girls from the upper class had to keep the two large classrooms and two dormitories clean. They moved the school desks and swept all the floors. Instead, I was assigned the duty of keeping the five petroleum lamps in our school in good shape and filled with petroleum.

Each week, an assistant and I walked one kilometer down the hill to the storeroom. We carried a heavy container full of petroleum back with us. Since the holders for fuel and the cylinders covering the flames were made of glass, we had to handle each lamp carefully. The lamp wicks had to be cleaned and expertly kept in shape each day. At eleven years old, Otto was able to meet these responsibilities satisfactorily.

I liked both my teachers in the public school. The senior one was a talented instructor of singing. We learned multiplication, division, and some geography. Under pressure from the Russian government, instruction had to be in Russian, except for the class in religion. Against our will, we had to sing the hated Russian national hymn: "God Save the Czar." We also learned about thirty hymns of the Evangelical Lutheran Church.

During the break between lessons, we were allowed to run outside the building in warm clothing. When the snow was thawing, we took special joy in snowball fights. Once, the teacher himself came out to direct our battle. He divided the boys into two groups, with even numbers of fighters on each side of the narrow valley that was close to school. We prepared plenty of ammunition, and at the teacher's command, each group ran toward the other.

I was particularly eager to beat the enemy. At top speed, I jumped deep into the valley with all my strength. The sudden impact when I landed caused a painful cramp in my spine, and I became lame and then immobile. The teacher ordered two boys to carry me to my bed, where the pain soon disappeared. Another time, I had a bitter, hard snowball fight with a boy whom I did not like. We battled until we were both exhausted.

Outside of the classroom, we also joyfully sang a few patriotic songs in Estonian.[4] In April, when the weather became warmer and the snow disappeared, we boys liked to walk to a nearby hill. Our voices resounded throughout the surrounding land.

In the spring, after I completed the school year, I began my third summer as the caretaker of our pigs and worked on developing my ocarino. One day, in the pasture for cattle near the forest and the road to the Ripsi farm, an important person in fine and unusual red hunting clothes [passed by] while I was guarding my pigs. He sat upon a beautiful riding horse. Ten or twenty years before, as a member of the German nobility, he alone had owned the land of all the farmers in our district. Father [was able] to buy the Ripsi land from him because, as I have mentioned, the government in St. Petersburg had required the German landowners to sell to Estonian farmers and to allow them long-term repayment [of their debt].

The important, red-coated man was quite human. He asked whether I was the son of Lellep of Ripsi, which I confirmed. I was surprised that such an important man even talked to me, a poor swineherd. The man took a sandwich with meat from the pocket of his saddle and gave it to me. I was too shy to say much. I felt honored by him.

During my childhood, by a traditional but wrong standard, we in Estonia distinguished between three different "ranks" in our society. Rich German landowners occupied the highest rank, followed by the "burghers," the townsmen or inhabitants of the city. The poor Estonian peasants were usually at the lowest level. Later, times did change. Twenty-five years after my birth, by virtue of their native abilities, Estonians gradually became the leading group in industry, business, and government in Estonia.

In 1896, my brother, Pastor Jaan, sent Peter back to the Ripsi farm. I remember seeing Peter return from the Russian capital city wearing clothing and shoes that he had bought there. He brought back a number of interesting Russian books about economics and politics, and some modern skates that could be screwed safely to his shoes. I had only old-fashioned ones that I had to fasten onto my shoes with leather straps. He liked to skate one-and-a-half kilometers distance on the good ice of the river.

Knowing that my older brother Peter had returned from the capital city of St. Petersburg, my teacher invited Peter and me to a Sunday dinner. I was twelve years old and Peter about fifteen. During my youth, the teachers in our local public school were considered leading people in the community, so it was an honor for us boys to be the teacher's guests. Peter could talk about high school life in the capital city of Russia and about the science and politics that interested Russian youths, particularly the students in universities all over Russia.

After I graduated from the highest level in the public school, Father decided to send me to the school of the Evangelical Lutheran Church for my fourth year of education. The school was located one kilometer from Wiljandi, the nearest city to us. Mr. Kodaras served as its senior teacher. Father knew him well because Mr. Kodaras was the secretary of the Farmers' Society in Wiljandi.

The rooms in Kodaras' school were very small. Downstairs, there were two classrooms. Upstairs, the school had a single dormitory for all the boys. The dormitory room was too confined, and it had practically no ventilation. At night, the air was definitely unhealthy.

Father had made a special agreement with Kodaras, and I was entitled to get a glass of hot tea from his kitchen every evening. Most weekends I remained at school, but I needed to walk into Wiljandi every Sunday to meet Father. I took my empty bread bag and dirty laundry, and he gave me fresh food and clean laundry. I carried these back to school myself.

Again at Kodaras' school, the majority of the instruction occurred in the Russian language, which was pressed on us by the powerful Russian government. Our main subjects were the grammar and syntax of Russian; the reading of thick textbooks in Russian; writing in Russian; geometry, elementary algebra, and more complicated calculations; botany; geography; and a short history of Russia. We had brief exercises in gymnastics and often had to sing "God Save the Czar." The Russian government permitted instruction in our native Estonian only a little in writing and in religion.

Kodaras' parochial school had two classes, taught by him and a very capable assistant teacher. I liked both teachers, and learning was not difficult for me. In botany class, the assistant teacher explained that flowers have sexual organs. For an exercise in Estonian, he let us write long stories on subjects we selected. With great pleasure, I wrote a four-page paper titled "How We Obtain Bread."

HOW WE OBTAIN BREAD

In the autumn, the farmer scatters seeds of rye on a well-ploughed and aged field. In the wet soil, the seeds begin to germinate. Soon, little white roots start to develop, and green leaves [emerge] one decimeter above the ground. Then the temperature drops and the wet soil freezes. For almost five months, the green leaves of the rye remain frozen. They appear to be dead, but they are not. The lovely sunshine of the spring brings them to life from their apparent death.

The leaves of rye start to grow rapidly in May and June until they reach the height of a man. On the long stalks, ears develop, and on a warm day, tiny male and female fecundating organs appear on each ear. The dust from the male organs fertilizes the female elements and new grains begin to grow rapidly. In each ear, forty strong kernels of rye grow.[5]

The ripe, rye straw and rye ears dry on the field and nowadays are threshed by a big steam-power-driven threshing machine. The ingenious machine separates the pure kernels of rye from the straw. The sacks of grain are then transported to a miller, whose millstones grind the grains into flour, from which Mother, or nowadays a baker, bakes loaves of tasty, nourishing rye bread. Wheat grows about the same way as rye and produces wheat flour and wheat bread, which also feeds millions of people.

Estonia being a province of Russia, and Czar Alexander the Third having started the policy of the Russification of the three small nations of the Baltic Sea—Estonia, Latvia, and Lithuania—our schools were visited from time to time by Russian inspectors who came to make sure that the will of the czar was actually obeyed. One day, the Russian inspector came to our school. As I liked our teachers, I asked a few comrades among the pupils to help show the inspector that we were advanced in our knowledge of Russian. He would then remain satisfied with us and our teachers.

The inspector gave us the following two sentences in Russian:

Maltchik v sinem surtuke (The boy in the blue coat)
Dremlet sidja na skamje (is dreaming while sitting on the bench).

I was to analyze the syntax of these two sentences. I did this using the correct, difficult Russian pronunciation that I had learned in Kronstad. My comrades also attempted to satisfy the man, and in the end, we felt he was impressed by our knowledge of the Russian language. It was also understood that we would sing for him "God Save the Czar" in soprano, tenor, and bass.

In addition to my usual lessons, I studied music at Kodaras' school. While my father was in Tännasilm, he had played the organ to teach the pupils to sing hymns in church. My brother Hans liked classical music, and he considered the appreciation and knowledge of it to be an important element in education. In the Finnish-Estonian church in Kronstad, he, too, played the organ, as well as accompanying his pianist friend Rotberg on the violin.

In accordance with the wishes of Hans and my father, a small violin was bought for me, and I had to take lessons from the assistant teacher. My progress in playing the violin was poor, however. Once, during my violin lesson, I had a dispute with a schoolmate who took lessons with me. In my excitement, I beat my comrade with the little instrument, breaking it into two pieces, which were later glued together.

Altogether, my violin lessons remained unsuccessful. I had better results with my homemade ocarino. I enjoyed playing a few little melodies on it and even succeeded in selling one or two homemade ocarinos to my school comrades.

During my second year in Kodaras' school it became a little complicated to obtain my homemade food. At that time, business transactions among farm owners took place in guesthouses like Sakala, in Wiljandi.[6] Father brought my food to Sakala, where he met his numerous friends at the beer table inside. Beer loosened Father's tongue, and he enjoyed talking with his friends for hours. In Father's opinion, his friends were more important than I was as a twelve-year-old boy.

I did not like Father's lengthy talks because they hindered me from speaking with him personally. It was inconvenient and tedious for me to wait in the guest room, which smelled of beer and tobacco smoke, but after a while, I would find an opportune time to interrupt. I exchanged my empty bread bag for [one with] fresh food. I also asked Father for some pocket money and received from him a small sum. Father avoided strong alcohol, and I never saw him drunk, but the tedious waiting in the guest room influenced me, and I have avoided drinking and smoking all my life.

The railway station at Wiljandi was less than one kilometer from the church school, and it was also during my second year there, that we schoolboys [were able] to watch the construction of a new, narrow-gauge railroad connecting the county city of Wiljandi to Tallinn, the capital of Estonia, and the city of Pärnu, on the western coast.

We were much interested in this new and unusual project. I had traveled by train to St. Petersburg, but I'd never had the opportunity to observe a locomotive or see how a railroad was built. I still remember that the rail bed was cut through the hill so that the rails could be laid in a straight path. The earth that was dug was used to build the bed for the tracks in the valley. Men nailed steel rails to beams of wood laid every half-meter across the leveled surface. Then the noisy locomotive appeared, issuing smoke and steam from its chimney. It seemed immensely strong, because it pulled heavily loaded freight cars and a long train of large passenger cars, each the size of a small house.

At the end of my second school year, I finished the courses in Kodaras' school and started walking home to Ripsi, a distance of about eight kilometers.[7] I took the shortest path through the forest, but I felt tired and had to lie down to rest. Though I slowed my walking speed, I arrived home still exhausted, with a headache and fever. This is no wonder, since my diet during the entire school year had consisted of rye bread, a few boiled potatoes, bacon, and butter. I'd had no milk or fresh vegetables.

After eighty-six years of life, I know now that my food at school lacked vitamins. At home I had better nourishment. There was plenty of fresh and sour milk, as well as soup made from green cabbage. It was not customary to go to a medical doctor, and there were no Estonian doctors in Wiljandi at the time, but drinking milk and eating green cabbage at Ripsi, I felt better after a while.

That summer, for the fourth season, I started my usual work of guarding the pigs. It was 1898. I had completed my education in Kodaras' school and therefore would not return. I was not able to go to Kronstad, either, since Hans lived in his apartment with his wife, but Father intended to give me a higher education.

1. Four kilometers is only two and a half miles. Could Otto have meant "four miles?"

2. Renate: "Bogdanov-Belsky's painting 'At the School Door,' pictures a boy with a lunch bag just like the one Otto describes."

3. Otto's "Farmers' Society" might well have been one of the "Agricultural Societies" described by Raun (*Estonia and the Estonians*) as offering periodic lectures and exhibitions. Characteristically, Raun notes, these were founded first in northern Livland, which was more economically advanced. They were established in 1870 in Tartu and Pärnu, and in 1871 in Viljandi.

4. See Endnote 1, Chapter 9 regarding the role of singing in Estonia.

5. Otto wrote "corns of rye."

6. As with Carl Robert Jakobson's newspaper, *Sakala*, the name of the guesthouse harkens back to ancient Estonia and the district around Viljandi.

7. Eight kilometers is five miles.

CHAPTER 9

The Alexander School and My Steam Engine

1898–1900
Otto age 14–16: near the village of Põltsamaa

In 1898, Father took me to the Alexander School in his own horse-drawn wagon. We rode the seventy kilometers from Ripsi to the school in one day, and the following day, Father talked with the superintendent of the school about enrolling me.

Years before, the confidence of Estonians had begun to rise, in part because of weekly, and then daily, Estonian newspapers. Patriotic unity also grew through the formation of large-scale national societies for singing. In many Estonian communities, young men and women came together to learn patriotic songs with melodies by Estonian composers and words by Estonian poets. The first grand Estonian singing festival was held at the University of Tartu. It drew about 5,000 singers from hundreds of organized singing choirs and an audience of about 20,000 people from all parts of Estonia.[1]

Later festivals increased the feelings of patriotism and unity, and a plan developed for the establishment of a central school for higher education to prepare students to enter the university. Subjects were to be taught in Estonian. Money was collected from all Estonians, and a large, three-story school building was bought near the village of Põltsamaa. The building had formerly been used as a school for the sons of the rich German landowners. The Estonians named it the Alexander School, in honor of the Russian czar Alexander.[2]

After our arrival at the school, during his talk with the "inspector," or headmaster, my father must have been painfully disappointed to discover that the Russian language would be forced upon us students. The power of Czar Alexander the Third had radically thwarted the intentions and wishes of the Estonians. Hopes had been annihilated. Only Russian was permitted as the language for general teaching, and the scope of instruction was limited. Instead of gymnasium classes appropriate for preparing a student for university, the school was allowed only the programs used in small Russian "city schools."

The headmaster of the Alexander School was a non-patriotic Estonian whose wife was Russian. He was totally subservient to the Russian politicians,[3] but a small concession had been made. E. Peterson, a recognized Estonian writer,[4] was made teacher of religion and church history. He was permitted to give his lessons in Estonian. Study and discussion of the famous Estonian epic *Kalevipoeg* and writing in Estonian were also allowed.[5] Peterson conducted a choir during the free evening hours a few times per week.

In addition to Peterson, a strict and capable teacher taught mathematics, algebra, and trigonometry. An agreeable instructor who had lived in Palestine taught the natural sciences, but the man who gave the classes on the Russian language was a Russian of no outstanding talent.

The Alexander School was divided into three groups of boys ranging from thirteen to twenty years old. I wished to enter the second class, or grade, but my examination after my arrival led to bitter disappointment. The mathematics teacher tested me on the subject of religion. Because I did not know the names of certain Jewish kings, he decided I should enter the first class, which would cause me to lose one whole school year.

Fortunately, because I promised to learn a certain part of the geometry book, the strict, accurate teacher of mathematics did allow me to sit for another examination after my return from Christmas vacation. My second examination in January was successful, and I was transferred from the first grade to the second grade.

Students at the Alexander school stayed there year round, with the exception of Christmas, the Eastern holidays, and summer vacation. Almost all of them lived on food sent from their homes—bread, butter, meat, potatoes, and fruit—or they bought what they needed from the nearby village of Oberpalen.[6] It was also possible to eat ready-made food prepared at the school for a modest price. I tried this system for a short time, but it did not satisfy me, and I went back to preparing and cooking my own food, using supplies sent from home.

In the cellar of the school, there were rooms for the boys who were eating from their own food supplies—their so-called "bread bags." A huge, old-fashioned, slow-heating and difficult kitchen range was also available, but this was used only by a few pupils, since it was heated by firewood.

When I went home for my first Christmas vacation, I thought about how I might improve my nourishment at Põltsamaa. At Ripsi, I found a cooking setup called "Primus" that Jaan had used when he'd studied at Tartu. It was a small, handy, kerosene-fueled burner that consisted of a gas ring heater and a small cooking pot with a double bottom.[7] I could light it quickly and could use it for porridge without burning the cereal. My stepmother gave me a four-liter container of currant concentrate, sweet as sugar. The practical cooking equipment and the vitamin-rich concentrate were just what I needed at school.

Because of the distance between the Alexander School and Ripsi, I stayed at school during vacations, returning home only in the summertime. One Easter, hoping to avoid boredom, I cast my eyes around the surrounding area. I often played ball during vacations, a game similar to American baseball but modified by Estonians.

That Easter, since the yard wasn't sufficiently dry, I decided to risk an adventure on the Pahla River, which ran on the east side of our schoolyard. The river's west side was planted in fertile fields of rye, wheat, flax, and barley. Forestland lay a little beyond. Watching the large, broken pieces of ice being swept downstream by the running water, I grabbed a long wooden pole and jumped onto a piece of ice, hoping to make an interesting trip on the big river without paying for transportation.

My mathematics teacher happened to see me as he looked through a window facing the schoolyard, and he ran out quickly to put a stop to my journey. Had the ice broken, I would have fallen into the freezing water and drowned, so I had to obey his order to come in.

The teacher gave me my punishment in his classroom. I had to memorize a page-long piece written by the famous Russian writer Lermontov, a description of the beauty of the nightingale's singing in the southern part of Russia.[8] [Though I was punished], the teacher had saved me from drowning, so I actually felt he was my friend. He knew our family, and fifteen years later he asked my brother what had become of me.

[The Pahla River provided other amusements.] During the late winter, it formed large, snow-free, ice-covered areas over the low, surrounding meadows. These provided us with perfect opportunities for skating. One day, I joined a number of older, stronger, and more experienced schoolmates in skating about twenty kilometers to an abandoned glass-casting plant in Roika that had manufactured large and small mirrors.

A group of five boys started the long trip early in the morning. I enjoyed our trek to the plant. The stronger, older boys skated in long, curved strokes to the right and the left. I had to work hard to keep up with them. Our efforts made us hungry and we consumed all the sandwiches we had in our pockets before we reached our destination. Then, after only a short pause, we had to start the trip back in order to reach the school before dark.

Tired though I was, I decided to keep following the stronger, older boys. We were hungry, but in the wilderness surrounding the Pahla River, there were no houses where we could buy food. Despite our miserable feelings, we had to keep skating. That twenty-kilometer skating trip back and forth to the Roika glass plant in the cold of winter required the most demanding exertion of physical energy that I have experienced in my life.

On the whole, I have agreeable memories of my time at the Alexander School. Most of us pupils were the sons of Estonian patriots. I found a friendly, competent schoolmate named Parsman, who liked cleanliness and order in our cellar dining room. Parsman's uncle was a popular Estonian poet. My friend Kelder had musical talent and played the piano well. He organized a singing quartet that he conducted with strict discipline. The four boys sang so beautifully that when they appeared at our yearly school festival, to which young ladies were invited, we felt proud.

Not all of my schoolfellows were trustworthy, of course. One day, a pupil from a nearby village called my attention to tasty foods in glass containers that were sitting in an open cellar window behind iron bars. He suggested that I use a crooked stick to snag some of the containers so we could enjoy the fine food, but I did not want to steal. Another schoolmate once entertained me with pornographic stories during a long walk in the area near the school. Later, I avoided him.

The two years I spent at the Alexander School, from 1898 to 1900, left new impressions on my character and thinking. I was especially interested in the sciences that are important for technical work, such as mathematics, physics, and chemistry. The natural sciences of botany and zoology interested me, as well as the introductions to astronomy, algebra, and geometry. Calculus was necessary for my future work. My nickname among the pupils was "the chemist," although chemistry was not among the subjects taught in the school.

The Russian teacher did not know how to make his subjects interesting, but we were [once] induced to write a rather long article in Estonian by our teacher Peterson. He had himself written a few books in Estonian that were considered good literature.

A quiet place contributes to good writing. In order to concentrate on my assignment in Estonian, I went into the large garden used primarily by the teachers for raising vegetables and fruits. The theme of my article was "Our Mood During the Spring." My purpose was to express my thoughts in good literary style, which would please our teacher. I wrote a few pages, including among them some overblown sentences that I thought might beautify my writing. Peterson, however, found my inflated, flowery language unsuitable for good literature.

Sometimes, during vacations, I borrowed a modern, monthly periodical from the library and found a quiet, beautiful place on the bank of the Pahla River. There I read very interesting, and for me, new, geological descriptions of the formation of the earth's crust one hundred thousand or more years ago. The pictures in my periodicals showed the skeletons of many kinds of prehistoric animals, beginning with the simplest worms and progressing to whale-size fish and mammals the size of a rhinoceros. These existed for millions of years before us.

The new knowledge I gained contradicted the biblical story, according to which God created the earth with everything in it in seven days. Why had our teacher of religion not told us of this obvious discrepancy? Through a capable schoolfellow who boarded with Peterson's family, I learned that Peterson was an earnest, broad-minded, and deep-thinking person who tried to understand the philosophy of the Hindus and the Chinese writers. In his heart, he probably did not think that the teachings of Martin Luther were the only answer for our lives, but because of politics, he dared not teach his deeper philosophy in our classroom. Now I, as an eighty-seven-year-old man, understand that he could not talk about the discrepancy between the Bible and scientific readings or he would have lost his well-paying position.

Today, my two sons-in-law are anthropologists—scientists who have studied the origins, customs, and beliefs of mankind, as well as our physical, intellectual, cultural, and moral development. They have observed primitive and civilized nations. Most of these nations have their own religion or tradition, simple as a fairy tale or wise and deeply philosophical. The religions of the oldest civilized nations and cultures, such as the Hindus, Egyptians, Indians, Chinese, Japanese, Greeks, and Romans, preceded our Christian religion.

The teachings of the Chinese and Japanese existed before Moses received from God the Ten Commandments on stone tablets at Mount Sinai. [Though] the biblical account of creation is an incorrect, naive story, even now the Ten Commandments are valid and morally justified rules for us. Most religions have moral laws that help humans to live together more harmoniously.

At the Alexander School, I had many new experiences outside the classrooms. Each year, the teachers and pupils of the two higher classes organized school festivals, for which we prepared musical and literary performances. These lasted about three hours, from six to nine o'clock in the evening. Invitation cards with the program for the evening were mailed to each guest a few weeks ahead of time. A high platform with a piano was placed in the front of the largest room of our school. For the guests, chairs were set before the platform, as well as benches along the walls.

The power and might of the Russian empire was evident in the festival program. Because of the Russification policy of the czarist government in St. Petersburg, the talks and presentations had to be in Russian. The evening began and ended with a short speech in Russian by our chief inspector. As an Estonian, I did not like him. I considered him a traitor.

Having learned Russian in St. Petersburg and Kronstad, I spoke with better pronunciation than the other pupils, so I was placed on the program more often than they. One time, the Russian teacher had me memorize a long Russian poem, which I had to recite loudly and with correct emphasis. During my fourteenth year, I had a high-pitched voice, so I was dressed in lady's clothing and had to impersonate the wife of the mayor in a short, funny spectacle called *Gorodnitchi* ("The Mayor") written by the Russian writer, Gogol.[9]

Patriotic songs of Estonian origin were not permitted at the festivals, but we enjoyed the music of our choirs, which had trained for long months. The large one consisted of over fifty boys and was conducted by Peterson. It performed well, presenting the works of well-known musicians, including part of an opera. Kelder's quartet elicited special applause and joy, due to its capable conductor, who also sang.

My friend Parsman had [previously] given us dancing lessons. This was expedient because girls from the area were invited to the festival, and dancing always took place at the end of the festivities. Parsman attempted to teach polite manners to us uncultivated peasant boys and to show us how we should treat and talk to the young girl guests.

After the performances by two choirs, a few recitations, and the presentation of the spectacle, most of the chairs, benches, and the platform were removed to make more room for dancing, which was accompanied by piano music. [I remember being with] a young girl whom I did not know, and I am not sure how successfully I danced. I was fourteen and had no experience entertaining a young girl.

The dance was followed by a walk around the hall, each boy taking his lady by the arm. The walking couples formed a ring, and the parents of the girls sat on one side, observing our activities. Unfortunately, neither I nor the girl on my arm had any talent for interesting conversation. We were both shy and reserved, but some of the older boys and girls seemed to enjoy lively conversations.

On the whole, the school festival was a stimulating undertaking requiring use of the various capabilities and talents of the pupils in our isolated boarding school. It temporarily unified students and teachers with the surrounding population.

[Meanwhile], the progress I observed in all matters related to technology fascinated and gratified me. Technical and industrial development had been occurring in the district of Wiljandi. Dried peat, containing about 15 percent water, is a valuable fuel, and during my walks in the vicinity of our boarding school, I saw the equipment used for the large-scale production of improved quality peat.[10]

A steam locomotive first moved an inclined elevator to lift the raw mass of peat, containing about 85 percent water, from a deep pit. It was then used to grind and compress it into sausage-like lengths about twelve centimeters thick. Women loaded the material into small railroad cars and pushed them to the area where it dried during the summer. The locomotive used twenty-five horsepower. About one hundred men would have been needed to do the same amount of work by hand.[11]

The power of the locomotive particularly impressed me. Indeed, I fell in love with the locomotive and its steam engine! I decided to build a little steam engine myself. I remembered that I had seen such an engine built by a boy who demonstrated it at the farmers' exposition in Wiljandi. From time to time, the boy let his steam engine whistle. How charming! I knew that the father of the boy was a skilled machinist who had helped him build the wonderful machine, but I thought that what the boy in Wiljandi did, I could and should do too!

In my physics book at the Alexander School, I found a sketch of the simplest steam engine: a small cross section of the cylinder of this wonderful machine. Inside the cylinder, the steam pressed a piston with a rod back and forth and then escaped through a clever little arrangement. To make steam, I needed a steam boiler, which was much easier to build than the engine. Without delay and with great joy, I made a scaled design of a steam engine so small I could carry the boiler with the cylinder in my lap.

Unfortunately, since the Alexander School had no mechanical construction shop or tools, I could not build the little engine at school. With the design done, I needed the money to make it. I first wrote to my brother in St. Petersburg requesting a small sum, but he refused. I then wrote to Father, asking for the money. After some delay, he mailed me a little sum for the project.

At Pöltsamaa, I bought a cartridge of brass, fifteen millimeters in diameter, such as that used by hunters in their guns. A mechanic there was willing to build the most important parts of the steam engine cylinder for me, according to my sketches. He fitted the piston and its rod into the cylinder. The rod moved through a stuffing box and activated the crank on the main shaft, which rotated the flywheel.[12]

A Jewish handyman, who was a specialist, undertook the building of my boiler.[13] It had an outside diameter of about fifteen centimeters, a firebox at the left end, and the outlet for used fire gases at the right end. The hot gases moved through water in a six-centimeter pipe. I planned to use thin pieces of wood for fuel and calculated that a vertical stack seven centimeters in diameter and seventy centimeters high would pull the fire gases through the boiler's inner pipe.

The parts I ordered from the mechanic and the Jewish tinsmith were soon ready. I did not tell my schoolmates about my plan to build a small steam engine because they would have thought me a fantastic, impractical dreamer. Instead, I concealed the parts in a bag as though I was carrying food and hid the bag in an almost inaccessible room under the roof of our boarding house, where I kept it until I went home to Ripsi.

My friend Hendrick worked as a young apprentice in the textile department of the Ripsi mill. I convinced him that with his assistance during his free time on Sundays, we could construct the steam engine. The mill had no facilities for mechanical work but there were tools such as small drills and equipment to solder thin blank steel to the top of my steam boiler.[14]

The actual construction of the more refined parts of the engine and its connection to the steam boiler took some time for my good friend Hendrik. The steam boiler and the engine on it had a number

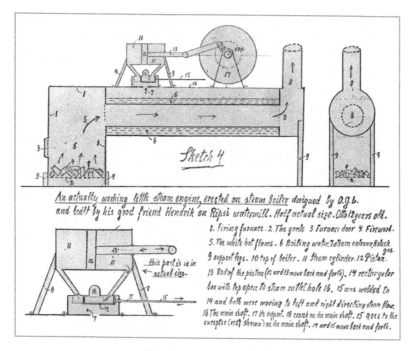

9.1   Steam engine sketch

of parts. I could only explain to him the principle of the engine and make sketches of some important mechanical details.

One Sunday, Hendrik and I conducted a test to see if my steam boiler could actually produce steam. We erected the boiler outside the smithy near the mill, filled it with water, put on the stack, and made a fire in the firebox. Soon, the water became hot and began to boil. Steam escaped with a little noise from the opening on top of the boiler. To our joy, when we held a whistle against the steam opening, the engine whistled loudly. Father passed by us on his Sunday walk, so we explained that we were testing our new steam engine and that the boiler could whistle. He was convinced, said nothing, and continued his walk. Apparently, he understood our ardent experimental work.

How happy Hendrik and I were that the steam boiler worked

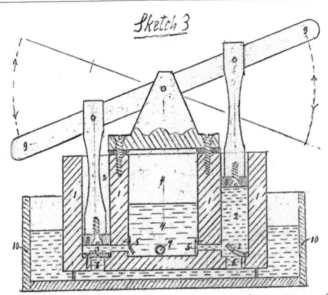

Sketch 3

Fire engine to put out fire in a burning hous with a water jet.

1. Rectangular block of birch wood. 2. Two smooth cylindrical piston holes. 3. Flexible lether covered valves in bottom of cyliders. 4. Airtigt pressure chamber for air and water. 5. Lethercovered valves in sidewall near bottom of chamber 4. 6. Water inlet holes below pistons. 7. Outlet hole for pressure water. 8. Two plungers each with tight cylindrical lether discs scrued to bottom of pistons. 9. Hand bar held by one hand on each end to swing the plungers 8 up and down sucking the water from box 10 into the cylinder 2 and pressing the water into the pressure chamber 4 and from there through hole 7 into the fire hose to put out fire.

9.2   *Fire engine sketch*

so well! We viewed our demonstration of its success with great satisfaction. At the time, steam engines provided the main source of power for machines in technical plants. The distribution of power by central electrical stations and electromotors was a later development and improvement.

Technical and industrial development had changed our area. The modernization of traffic by railroad opened up new business for Father. When Tallinn, Wiljandi, and Pärnu were linked by the narrow-gauge track, the trip from Wiljandi to Tallinn was cut to about one night, instead of requiring a two-day journey by horse-drawn wagon. Suddenly Father could ship his forest products to Tallinn, the capital city. As his business increased, he bought a large area of land in Tallinn and built a house and office for the sale of firewood.

In the district of Wiljandi, the rise of new professions and possibilities affected my father's intentions for his sons. He'd probably first apprenticed Willem to the faraway mill so that he could take over management of the one at Ripsi. As the volume of Father's sales grew, though, he took on new associates. He used Willem and Peter as his trusted agents and partners, adding his son-in-law, Anna's husband, as well. The younger generation saw more possibilities working in business than in agriculture or at Ripsi's small water-powered mill.

Thinking of my future, Father freed me from guarding pigs when I was fourteen. He'd decided that I should get further education in the real school in Tallinn, which had many students and was city-owned and city-recognized. Real school was a high school without instruction in Latin and Greek.[15] French and German were taught there, though, and I would need to study both in order to enter.[16] During the summer of 1899, to get to my private lessons in French and German with my teacher, Namsing, I had to walk back and forth from the Ripsi farm to Wiljandi, seven kilometers, three times a week. This was a hardship, but my legs grew stronger.

1. Regardless of their occupiers, Estonians have long used song as a means to affirm their language, culture, resistance, and unity. Inaugurated in 1869 to commemorate the emancipation of peasants in Livland and held later for the same purpose—or, ostensibly, to recognize tsarist anniversaries—enormous song festivals increasingly featured the work of Estonian composers. According to Raun (*Estonia and the Estonians*), the audience was estimated as high as 50,000 at the festival in 1894, and the choir featured 5,520 performers in 1896. Choral singing continued to play an important role in the period of Estonia's nationhood and in the modern era as the country fought for independence from the Soviet Union. (See the film *The Singing Revolution* for a moving history of Estonians' resistance through song.)

2. Named in honor of Tsar Alexander the First, the Alexander School movement began in the 1860s among the "rural intelligentsia" (Raun) of Viljandi County, who hoped for an institution that would use Estonian as the language of instruction and that would provide Estonians with a body of educated elementary school teachers. The movement eventually gained widespread support, though the Ministry of the Interior had not given permission for fundraising to begin until 1871. Within about fifteen years, local committees in 80 percent of the Estonian parishes had raised the needed capital (approximately 100,000 rubles). Led by Jakob Hurt and his supporters during the 1870s, the movement was later riven by power struggles between Hurt and Carl Robert Jakobson. Each side appealed to the central government to intervene, and in 1884 control of the movement passed to tsarist officials. In 1888, in a bitter blow to Estonian hopes and in accordance with the policy of Russification, the Alexander School opened as a middle school using Russian as its language of instruction. It was closed in 1906 and re-opened in 1914 as an agricultural school.

3. In Otto's text: "subdued to the Russian politicians."

4. Renate:
    > E. Peterson may have also taught technical subjects and literature in Russian. I found reference to him in 'The Role of Popular Science Literature in Shaping Estonians' World Outlook" (Mait Taits of Tallinn University, March 2013).

5. *Kalevipoeg* (Son of Kalev) is an epic poem tracing the battles and adventures of a mythical hero and leader of ancient Estonians. Written by Friedrich Reinhold Kreutzwald in a traditional form used in Estonian folk songs (*regivärss*), it was published in sections by the Estonian Learned Society between 1857 and 1861. *Kalevipoeg* played an important role in the awakening and affirmation of Estonian national consciousness.

6. Ober-Palen is east of Viljandi and west of Tartu.

7. As Renate later understood, and as mentioned, Otto remembered the value of his Primus stove many years later. In the 1950s, while traveling to Africa by ship, Renate met James Fernandez, an anthropologist who was also on board. They married in Yaounde, Cameroon in two ceremonies. The first was

officiated by the mayor of Yaounde in accordance with the Napoleanic Code, application of which persisted throughout Cameroon's late colonial days. Official statements had to be sent from the US confirming that neither was already married, and bans were published. Following the ceremony, the two were given a *cahiers de famille*, a "family book," in which they were to inscribe the names of their children. This served as an enticement for couples to procreate, given the financial reward that would follow if enough children were born. Jim and Renate were subsequently married again by local, Swiss, Protestant missionaries, who gave them a ten-gallon tin of wheat flour as a wedding present. Renate appreciated Otto's gift of the stove and tried to use it to make bread, not completely successfully. When the flour ran out, she began cooking over a fire each day.

8. I can find no reference to a poem about a nightingale written by Mikhail Lermontov (1814-1841), the beloved Russian poet and writer. Otto was perhaps forced to memorize a poem by the equally loved Aleksander Pushkin (1799-1837), "A Nightingale and a Rose."

9. In Nikolai Gogol's famous satirical play *Revizor (The Inspector General)* a "gorodnichi" ("mayor") named Anton Antonovich and his wife Anna appear as two of the characters.

10. It is unclear where the following description of the processing of peat belongs. Otto offers similar descriptions of peat production at two different times in his story. At one point, he says he saw it near the Alexander School; at another, he remembers observing it in Moscow (Chapter 14). Using my best guess, I put the description in this chapter.

11. Renate notes that Otto's language is interesting here. He again writes of work done by women, but he measures the work itself in terms of that which can be done by men. As mentioned before, nouns and pronouns are not assigned grammatical genders in Estonian. While the effects of that language—Otto's first—are perhaps evident in this awkward use of "women" and "men," his attitudes toward "men's work" and "women's work" are also at play.

12. In Otto's text, "flying wheel."

13. Here and later in his book, Otto's mention of several of his helpers as "Jewish" (not "Russian") contrasts with his reference in this passage to the Estonian parents of students in his Kronstad school as "Russian"—not "Estonian." Throughout her childhood and adulthood, Renate never recalls hearing him speak of anyone as "Jewish." In his few words (he spoke little), he referred to people as "American" or "Estonian", or, more often, "capable" or "not capable." It would seem his use of the marker "Jewish" in the memoir reflects the significance of that identity in tsarist Russia.

14. Blank steel is an unfinished piece of metal stamped out of a larger piece and used for forming a part or container.

15. "Real school" is "Realschule" in German.

16. In mid-eighteenth century Germany, real schools (Realschulen) evolved as alternatives to Gymnasium, which prepared students for university entrance. Real schools were distinguished by their practical curriculum. Otto's school in Tallinn was perhaps an Oberrealschule—a secondary school of later development that emphasized modern languages and the natural sciences rather than Latin or Greek, thus preparing its students for advanced technical (not university) study.

CHAPTER 10

German, French, and Technical Wonders: the Juckum and Real Schools

c. 1900–1902
Otto age 16–18: Tallinn

During the spring of 1899, when I was fourteen-and-a-half years old,[1] Father transferred me to the house in Tallinn that had been built by the Lellep and Company firewood business. He planned to give me a higher education, but he also needed me to keep an eye on the sale of a large amount of firewood. Jaan, [not my brother but] the son of Father's lifelong partner Lorup, was a year younger than I and also intended to enroll in the real school. He moved into our new house, and we lived there with a taxi driver and his unmarried, elderly sister, who cooked and cleaned for us.

I planned to enter the third-year class at the real school, but I first had to submit to strict examinations in French and German. The French teacher, a native of southern France, dictated a short, simple story in French. To me, the teacher's correct French sounded entirely different from the French spoken by my Estonian teacher in Wiljandi. I was able to understand only a few words, and though I wrote them on my dictation sheet, in my excitement,

10.1   Father at sixty

I missed the subject of the little story. Consequently, the teacher rated my understanding of French utterly unsatisfactory. The

German teacher, a native German from Wiljandi, also found my knowledge insufficient. These results established that I could not enter the third class in the real school.

Fortunately, there were in Tallinn a few classes in a private juckum real school,[2] where the boys of rich German estate owners and the sons of the prosperous Germans and higher Russian officials were trained. Of necessity, remuneration for schooling in the private institution was considerably higher than that for the city-supported, official real school. After I inquired of Father, I learned that he was able to afford the tuition, so I was able to begin in the private school. Since Father's firewood business was on the periphery of Tallinn, I walked three kilometers back and forth daily to study there.

Before my arrival in Tallinn, I had already attended four different kinds of schools, all intended for the common people. I'd spent two years at my brother Hans' school in Kronstad, one year in the elementary school in our own village near Ripsi, two years in the parochial school near Wiljandi, and two years in the Alexander School.[3] In contrast, the pupils of the expensive juckum school came from the German aristocracy and the prosperous German families who governed the city at that time. The first day of school, when I packed my textbooks into a large handkerchief, the much younger pupils found it ridiculous. They were carrying their books in knapsacks on their backs.

I was the only pupil in the third level from the Estonian peasant class, a rank not generally esteemed by the average pupil at the school. I did not take my situation as any kind of tragedy because I was one of the best pupils in the third-level class, with the exception of [my performance in] German and French, which hadn't been taught in my previous four schools.

In the juckum school, the instructors of German, French, and Russian were from Germany, France, and Russia. Classes were taught in Russian, except religion, which was in German. During the first religion lesson, the German pastor called on me, the supposedly underprivileged peasant boy, and told me haughtily in the despised Estonian language that I should learn the Ten Commandments in German. Inside myself, I found his arrogant, lordly command revolting.

I spent one year at the juckum school. I quite easily fulfilled its requirements because I had already learned many of the subjects at the Alexander School. Transferring to the real school was not difficult either. Many teachers at the juckum school were also teaching at the city school, and the entrance examination was easy for me.

It became clear to me that I should improve my German and learn the ways and manners of educated city people. After discussing this with Father, I moved from my crude living quarters at our firewood depot to a good German boardinghouse for German-speaking boys and girls. Three boys from the real school and two girls from the gymnasium lived there.[4] Among the boarders was a young German from Riga who was in the highest class at the real school. He had a wide knowledge of world affairs and great intellectual capacity. Everyone liked him, particularly the girls. The other boarders were prosperous Germans.

In the boardinghouse, I met three sisters. Management of the house and all its rooms lay in the hands of the first sister. The second sister was an educated, widely traveled, and intellectually capable woman who earned her living by giving lessons in German, French, and English. The third sister worked as a cashier in the beautiful German theater in Tallinn.

I took English lessons from the second sister, studying both reading and speaking because I thought I might some day travel to the United States, the leading country of the world. I also made gradual progress in learning German and French, since I had to speak German every day in the boarding house.

At school one day, every pupil had to give a talk or speak before the entire class in the presence of the German teacher. For my presentation, I memorized in its entirety, Schiller's long, famous poem about a bell.[5] The teacher thought I pronounced only certain words incorrectly.

I enjoyed reading a few German books without difficulty, and in the French class, I read a small book assigned by the teacher—the love story of a thirty-five-year-old man who attempted to win the heart of an eighteen-year-old girl. We had to understand and memorize the text. In addition, I bought from the bookstore *L'éducation de la volonté*.[6] Using a French dictionary, I read and enjoyed this book. I also learned a little French conversation.

Around this time, I had an idea for my first invention and had the courage to ask my physics teacher for his critique of it. I conceived of a motor somewhat similar to the famous diesel engine, but rather than using oil, I proposed injecting a small amount of gunpowder after each second stroke [of the pistons]. My teacher was unenthusiastic, besides which gunpowder could not compete with oil, a cheaper fuel.

[I found many ways to learn.] The school had a voluminous library, from which I borrowed numerous books on technical subjects. In one of them, I found a description of the powerful, large locomotives that were able to pull long rows of heavily loaded wagons at high speeds. This seemed to me like a miracle! The description of tall metallurgical blast furnaces for the production of liquid cast iron and pictures of large vessels, so called Bessemer converters, which were able to transform one hundred tons of brittle cast iron into valuable, strong steel in fifteen minutes, appeared to me to be another miracle.

Among the students, I made a friend with whom I practiced my German as we walked home from school. His sister was married to a mechanical engineer, Lender, who was employed in the great industrial plant, Dvigatel,[7] which specialized in building large, beautiful, and convenient passenger cars for the Russian railroads. Mr. Lender was willing to show us this famous plant personally.

When I saw the huge, clean power station full of shining and powerful machinery that was able to generate many thousands of horsepowers of energy, I was very enthusiastic. In another large hall called the smithy, I saw a mighty forging hammer, which was so powerful it could, with a few strokes, shape the white-hot steel into a regular railroad wagon wheel! This visit to the Dvigatel plant convinced me finally that I should become an engineer to build and manage such mighty machines.

In the real school at Tallinn, I became friendly with another pupil, whose father was a senior machinist in an electrically driven flour mill. Together with this new friend, I was allowed to inspect and see the operation of the mill. In one of the rooms, we saw an electric dynamo machine about 35 centimeters in diameter.[8] I was surprised when I was told of its capacity. You could say I fell in love with the machine, which could produce the power of ten horses though it was merely the size of a dog! I asked my new friend to loan me a drawing of the motor, and I copied the outside dimensions of it very carefully.

In my physics textbook, I found a sketch of another technical wonder: the Bell telephone. Its design was surprisingly simple, yet this apparatus was capable of transmitting the human voice from Tallinn to St. Petersburg and back, instantaneously! Falling in love with the Bell telephone, I decided to build one with the help of my Estonian school friend and his father, who had a lathe for the turning of pieces of wood and other mechanical equipment.

The Bell telephone consists of only four essential parts. The first is the handle—two pieces of wood screwed together. The wooden handle holds the second essential component: the round electromagnet, which is 90 millimeters long and 8 millimeters in diameter. It consists of hard steel that is permanently and strongly magnetized. The handle also holds the third component, a thin diaphragm of common sheet steel, close to the end of the

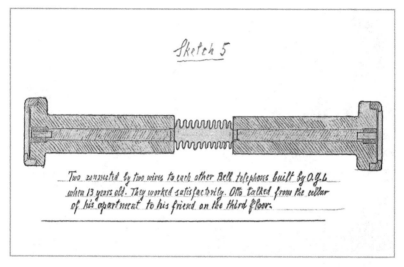

Sketch 5

Two connected by two wires to each other Bell telephones built by O.G.L. when 13 years old. They worked satisfactorily. Otto talked from the cellar of his apartment to his friend on the third floor.

10.2   *The Bell telephone*

electromagnet but not touching it. The soft piece of sheet steel is only 18 millimeters long and about 4 ½ millimeters in diameter. Around it is the fourth component: a small spool filled with about one hundred windings of thin, insulated copper wire. The copper wire's two ends are connected to an identical Bell telephone, via two thicker insulated wires of one hundred meters or even one hundred fifty kilometers length.

I built a satisfactory Bell telephone when I was thirteen years old. From the cellar of my apartment, I spoke with a friend who was on the third floor. I was proud of my homemade equipment, and I talked about it to two friends at the real school.

[In addition to studying and learning, I spent time with friends and family in Tallinn.] I was happy to discover two older Estonian schoolmates who had graduated from the Alexander School and were employed in the Russian governmental control department. They and I went for long walks on Sundays into a beautiful area

10.3 I am seated on the lower right, age sixteen, posed with my two Estonian friends, who studied in the same high school as I.

outside of the city, to the coast of the Baltic Sea. Father also let me buy a bicycle, which enabled me to ride long distances more easily. During holidays, I rode to the resorts of Nömme and Kopli.

I was quite happy that my brother Willem lived in Tallinn. At first, he was a soldier in the Russian army. Then, because of his expertise in handling tools and machines, he had the privilege of serving in a military workshop. He'd visited us quite often at the house of Lellep and Company, but after his military service and his marriage to a girl he had admired at her father's watermill,[9] he took over the management of the Lellep and Company firewood business. Willem improved the house belonging to the company to suit him, his wife, and their growing young family.

My sister Juuli was also in Tallinn when I was a pupil in high school. During the warm summer months, her daughter, her co-workers, and I once arranged for a boat ride, rowing to the famous ruins of a monastery in the beautiful surroundings of Pirita, near Tallinn.

Photography interested me when I was in Tallinn, and I bought the smallest and cheapest photo camera available. It cost only one Russian ruble, which nowadays corresponds to about five dollars. The camera took pictures 5 x 10 centimeters in size. (The photo of my father when he was sixty years old was taken with this simple camera.) Later, I bought a fairly good lens with a controllable diaphragm and built for it an adjustable camera made of a thick carton. Its photos had a dimension of 9 x 14 centimeters.

By selling my photos, I was able to earn a little money, with which I bought a regular camera with an adjustable bellows and a tripod for support. Willem was a precision mechanic, and he gave me three caskets, or plate holders. I had to develop my negatives at home, so I made a portable darkroom of black, dense fabric. I bought chemicals for the developing and printing of photos with the money I earned.

Photography became my hobby. With my portable camera, I climbed to the top of the church tower of St. Olaf, the highest tower

10.4   *This photo and the one at right bring back dear memories of my student years. Top row, left to right: My exceedingly capable but unsystematic brother* Peter, *my dear niece* Leeni *(daughter of sister Juuli), my practical niece* Maria *(sister Liina's daughter). Bottom row, left to right:* Julie *(brother Hans' wife); my brother* Hans; Else *(Hans' daughter, above and to his right); the young lady who was a practical and dependable helper in sister Juuli's store (next to Hans);* Miss Luha *(the lady with the most charming smile—also a helper in the store) and my wise and businesslike sister* Juuli, *the owner of the ladies' apparel store.*

in all the Baltic states. The light was favorable and the snapshots I took were beautiful. I sold two hundred copies, and the local Estonian daily paper wrote an article about my photos.[10]

During summer vacation, I rode by train to Wiljandi and Ripsi, carrying a large number of negative glass plates, copying paper, and my portable dark room with the necessary chemicals. I photographed the main building at Ripsi and the mill from many sides.[11] I also took my equipment to Tännasilm and made snapshots of my sisters' children.

10.5 *One Sunday in Tallinn, we organized a trip and rowed on the river Pirita from Tallinn's harbor to the old ruins of a Catholic monastery (the Pirita Monastery). From left to right:* Miss Luha, Leeni *(sister Juuli's daughter),* me, Lulla *(sister Liina's daughter),* Alice *(the little girl in the lace hat, daughter of my brother Jüri),* Alice's mother Elizabeth *(Jüri's wife),* and Maria *(Liina's other daughter).*

The village of Walma, where my father was born and where my friends and relatives were living, was not far from my sisters' farms. My cousin Jaan Lellep and his beautiful sister Mari were living at Father's birthplace, on the farm, and naturally I gave them photos I had taken. I also photographed my granduncle, who was almost ninety. The photograph of my granduncle, titled "Uncle on the Lake," showed him dressed characteristically in old-fashioned, totally homemade clothing, including his *pastlad*—the leather, moccasin-like footwear.

My granduncle was the "medical man" of our community. He was a wise, kind, and popular healer when there were no medical

10.6 My granduncle

doctors available to country people. He used two methods of treatment: (1) holding his patients' hands, he murmured words to ease their minds, and (2) he gave them medicine he made himself from dried herbs, blossoms, roots, and minerals.[12]

I later learned that my granduncle asked my father to see him before his death. At that time, he disclosed the secret of his ability to heal others. His words in the presence of his patients had simply been the famous New Testament Lord's Prayer.

1. If he had been born in 1884 and graduated from the Alexander School in 1898, Otto would have been fourteen when he moved to Tallinn. At one point, he dates his move there to the spring of 1899, though he also says that he spent the summer of 1899 living at Ripsi and studying French and German with his teacher Namsing (Chapter 9).

2. I can find no definition or description of "juckum school," which Otto contrasts with the real school.

3. I have used this passage to date Otto's movements from school to school, taking 1893 as the year he left for Kronstad with Hans and adding the subsequent periods he ascribes to his study at each school. When conflicting dates or references appear in his text, I have left them as he wrote them.

4. Gymnasiums prepare students for university educations.

5. Otto made an audacious and ambitious choice in selecting Schiller's well-known poem "Das Lied von der Glocke," or "The Song of the Bell," as it is over four hundred lines long. The poem describes the creation of the bell—the boiling of copper and tin, the addition of alkali, the casting, and the destruction of the bell casing—a process that was surely of interest to Otto. It may also be seen as a complex fugue. In Marianna Wertz's reading ("Friedrich Schiller's 'The Song of the Bell,'" *Fidelio* Volume 14, Number 1-2, Spring-Summer 2005, pp. 36-45): "The first voice is the technological process of forging a great bell. The second voice, for which the bell is also a metaphor, deals with the development and life of the individual. The third voice concerns questions of statecraft and the French Revolution . . . . The fourth voice, which enters for the first time in the person of the poet, introduces Schiller's method to ensure the success of republican revolutions."

6. In English: *The Education of The Will: The Theory And Practice Of Self-Culture* by Jules Payot (New York and London: Funk & Wagnalls Co., 1914). From the preface to the first edition in English: "We have had to investigate the

causes of the weakness of the will. . . . 'The means of forming and strengthening methods of self-enfranchisement, of annihilating or suppressing impressions antagonistic to self-mastery,' might have been the subtitle of the book. . . . Instead of treating the education of the will '*in abstracto*,' we have taken as the essential subject 'the education of the will such as is demanded by prolonged and persevering intellectual work.' We are convinced that students and intellectual workers generally will find here much very useful information."

7. From the website for Ulemiste City, accessed June 7, 2018 (http://ulemistec-ity.ee/en/innovators/area-history/): "On 25 October 1897 Nicholas II, the last Emperor of Russia, being in his residency in Tsarskoye Selo, approved the articles of association of a new company—public limited company Dvigatel. The plant started operation on 9 May 1899, its main activity being maintenance of planned railways, primarily production of cars as well as maintenance and repairs of locomotives. The plant employed 4,000 people, including 70 engineers." In later years, more than one attempt to save the company from bankruptcy failed, and today the Dvigatel grounds have been made into the site for a business technology park in Tallinn.

8. An electric dynamo produces direct (not alternating) electric current using electromagnetism. A "generator" produces alternating current.

9. Willem probably met his wife at the mill where his father sent him to work.

10. Renate:

    Otto's account here differs somewhat from what he told me at home, years later, when I was a teenager in Wauwatosa. This was during the period following World War II, as the Cold War was about to begin, when Mutti was helping to settle refugees displaced from war-torn Europe. She and Otto received Estonian refugees in our home—professional men and women unable to resume their careers in the United States because of their age, language, and lack of certification. Otto spoke repeatedly and with pity of the refugee engineer who could only make a living in the US by repeatedly refilling chewing gum machines.

    My father must have considered the refugees' difficult situation as a teaching moment for his daughter. Thinking of the value of a fallback position in handcraft, he talked often about how he had made a peephole camera from scratch, climbed *Der Grosze Hermann* (a legendary, historical tower in Tallinn)—not St. Olaf's—and earned pocket money for food from the sales of the photos he took.

11. We can guess that the photographs of Ripsi appearing in Chapter 3 may well have been the ones Otto refers to here. If so, he somehow managed to hold onto them throughout his moves from country to country and the passage of almost six full decades.

12. Renate remembers hearing that this relative, "a shaman," as she thought of him, had a trained bear. Her father repeatedly spoke of his granduncle, dressed in leather (as she remembers it, but probably actually wearing rustically woven garb and *pastlad*), leading his bear by a chain. According to Otto, the healer massaged his patients by having the animal walk on their backs.

CHAPTER 11

A Loosening of Power and the Revolution Begins

c. 1902–1905
Otto age 18–21: Tallinn and Riga

At eighteen years old, I made a trip by railroad to Petrograd (formerly called St. Petersburg).[1] There I looked for my childhood friend, Jon Watto, whom I had known when I was in school in Kronstad. Jon was a few years older than I and was already studying electronics in an institute in Petrograd.

I met Jon in the dining hall of the electrotechnical institute. Russian students were often the children of poor parents and were supported by the state. As a Russian student, he wore a beautiful uniform. For our meal, large plates filled with slices of brown, coarse rye bread had been set on all the tables. We could eat as much bread as we wanted without paying for it, and a large cup of soup containing some meat cost us only ten kopecs (five US cents). At the time, Russian peasants mainly ate brown rye bread and meatless cabbage soup.

My friend Jon showed me the splendid palace built in Petrograd by Czar Nicholas the Second.[2] The czar created it for the amusement of the people of the city, but his generosity did not raise the living standard of the poor. The incompetent Russian bureaucracy had been unable to improve life in the villages. Though the higher

Russian institutes and universities had excellent teaching programs, a large majority of the people lived in poverty, most of them without even an elementary education. And though Russia was by area the largest country in the world, [in 1905], the country was defeated in Manchuria by little Japan.

The unsuccessful war with Japan and the large masses of uneducated, impoverished Russians angered the Russian students. In Petrograd, students met and criticized the monarchical government of the czar. Jon showed me the busy, famous Nevsky main street during the day, and at night, we saw semi-secret activities there.

While I was in the city, I also visited my brother Jüri, who was for all his life a botanist in the Imperial Botanical Garden of Peter the Great. I saw an especially rare blossom of the Victoria Regia growing in a greenhouse there. One leaf of this beautiful, huge water lily was almost one meter in diameter. Its edges turned up, and it was said that it could support the weight of a nine-year-old child. Its blossom was pink as it was opening, but it became pure white and fragrant when fully developed. In another building, high, tropical palm trees grew below a ceiling of glass.

After I returned to Tallinn by train, my life and learning in the real school proceeded as usual. I earned some pocket money by giving private lessons in mathematics, algebra, and geometry to a prosperous Russian boy. He liked to draw, mostly pictures of Russian cathedrals with gold covered towers in the shape of onions.

I also gave Estonian lessons to a German engineer at Luther's, an internationally known plant for the production of plywood. Luther's made unassembled boxes for the shipping of tea from China to England. Its plywood was so waterproof we even used it for pails. The engineer, a gentleman of noble character, was quite unhappy when the Japanese ruthlessly destroyed the Russian fleet of warships that traveled to Manchuria to help the Russian army.

Some Estonians formed a group for dancing during the evenings, and I joined them. Girls were included. In addition to the polka and mazurka, we learned a French dance, the quadrille, which was not practical or interesting to me in terms of the normal dancing that was done at the time. I was eighteen years old and no hero in dancing!

I and a few patriotic Estonian pupils in the three highest classes of the real school also organized a secret Estonian group called Lindanisa.[3] [When we met], I gave lessons in the Estonian language to my schoolmates. The Russians still prohibited the teaching of Estonian in Tallinn, but I had learned it from our teacher, the writer Peterson, at the Alexander School.

In the United States, everyone has equal social standing and equal rights, but as I have mentioned, during my youth in Estonia, the situation was quite different. Estonia was a Russian province, governed by the czar in St. Petersburg. His highest local official, the Russian governor of Estonia, lived in a palace on the most elevated site in Tallinn. The large Russian cathedral with its gold-covered towers stood near his residence.

In Russian-governed Estonia, we had equal rights on paper, but in Tallinn, as elsewhere, tradition dictated three ranks in the population: the rich German land barons; the old city inhabitants, who were mostly Germans; and the large majority of Estonians, who formerly lived on the farms. All educated people in the capital city of Tallinn could speak Estonian, Russian, and German. Street names were printed in three languages.

At the time, Tallinn was known by the German name *Reval*. Germans comprised perhaps 15 percent of the total population. Actions [proposed] by the city government had to be confirmed by the local Russian governor, but Tallinn was in the hands of the Germans, industrially and politically. When I arrived in Tallinn, they governed it, as they did other Estonian cities.

Estonian influence began to grow gradually. About 85 percent of the Tallinn population consisted of Estonians. Under the management of the energetic lawyer Päts, a daily paper, the *Päevaleht*, was published in Estonian.[4] Tönisson edited the periodical *Postimees* in

Tartu and other parts of Estonia.[5] An Estonian Credit Society began to support Estonian merchants and businessmen, and Tallinn had an Estonian society and theatre, where plays of world-famous authors were presented from time to time. The entire Estonian nation particularly liked one excellent actor, Pinna, for his outstanding talent.[6] He presented the plays of the famous Norwegian writer Ibsen, which deeply touched and affected me.

For centuries, Tallinn had been ruled by the Germans, but gradually it became clear to the Estonians in Tallinn that the city government should be in the hands of the majority: in other words, the Estonians. Editorials in *Päevaleht* supported this position and the interests of Estonians in the city.

During my youth, Estonians began to take over city governments from the former German burghers, or townsmen. In 1902, a general vote by the entire population of Tallinn was held to determine who should govern the city and serve as its mayor.[7] The resulting decision was that the Estonian majority should govern the city, and for the first time in centuries, an Estonian mayor was elected. General improvements in the city were begun. Plans were made to enlarge the electrical power station and improve the pavement of many streets. The size and number of city schools was increased.

During my last year in the real school, from 1904 to 1905, Doctor Köhler, a medical doctor, invited me to live in his house for free. In return, I was to give his ten-year-old son extra lessons. The doctor's famous nephew, Professor Köhler, had done a large painting of the Caucasian mountains that hung in the house.[8] Professor Köhler was an outstanding painter who had lived in Petrograd and was influential in the circle of men close to the court of the czar. The lawyer, Otto Strandman, who later became president of Estonia, ate with us at Dr. Köhler's.[9] Often, we were served roast hare because Dr. Köhler's patients who came from the country paid for his services with hares instead of money.

During my walks in the century-old park of Katerinenthal, I also happened to meet and become acquainted with the lawyer Päts, the owner and chief of *Päevaleht*.[10] He became the last president of the free Estonian Republic and was [still] in office in 1941 when the Russian Bolsheviks illegally invaded Estonia, and the country's leading persons died in Bolshevik prisons and prison-camps in Siberia.[11]

In the spring of 1905, after our final examination in the real school, we were entitled to enter universities and higher technical institutes. That summer vacation, I stayed in my small, rented room in Dr. Köhler's house and began to prepare for the difficult entrance examinations to higher technical institutes. The summer heat did not contribute to my progress.

I also learned from my friend Watto that only a very small percentage of the candidates trying to enter the good technical schools in Petrograd would be accepted, so I understood that my chances for further study in Petrograd were poor. As a citizen of the Baltic provinces, however, I would have no difficulty entering the higher polytechnical institute in our governmental capital city of Riga.

During my younger years, Father could not know how my learning capacity would develop or how his business income would change with time. His forest products company grew considerably, with members that included his lifelong partner, Lorup; a son-in-law; and my brothers Willem and Peter. He decided to give me the highest technical education only when he had sufficient resources and I had made good progress in the real school in Tallinn.

I had to pass through six schools to obtain the right to seek the highest technical education. Boys born in big cities needed to pass through only two schools for the same right. I lost two or three years of my life attending too many schools, but this loss is almost negligible for a man who is yet healthy at eighty-seven years of age.

In the autumn of 1905, I began to study at the polytechnical institute in Riga, specializing in building engineering (for houses and other structures). For the first two months, my learning progressed normally, but the general political situation in Russia was tense. The progressive people of Russia did not like the monarchist government of the czar, who consequently agreed to the establishment of the Duma, a kind of weak parliament in Petrograd. The progressives, and particularly the students in all higher educational institutes, wanted more rights for the people. Acceding to their wishes, the weak czar nominated Witte, a liberal-thinking prime minister.

Witte recommended that the czar give the people all the rights they wished for, and the czar accepted his radical suggestion, agreeing to bestow unlimited rights of publication and free speech in meetings. All persons with liberal ideas, particularly the students in the highest educational institutes, celebrated the news jubilantly. They were happy, exulting in their freedom and the ability to tell millions of simple working people how they could and should improve their everyday living conditions.

There was no free area sufficiently big enough to hold a meeting of twenty thousand people in the center of Riga, but outside the city, the students found open fields, where they built over a dozen elevated stands for student speakers. A large portion of the population went daily to the meetings held outside Riga.

I had been a student at the polytechnical institute only a few months and consequently could only help the experienced, older Estonian students print the revolutionary proclamations they distributed to the working men at the meetings the next day.[12] We used a duplicating machine.

Our eager and zealous work lasted for about ten days, and then the czar fired the liberal prime minister Witte. The czar's reactionary advisers believed that if extreme liberal reforms continued, the revolutionary leaders would eventually overthrow him, removing him from his throne. The czar's new orders gave power to reactionary generals. With subordinate soldiers, they were sent to all parts of Russia to suppress any revolutionary movements and shoot their leaders. Thousands of revolutionary leaders were put to the wall and shot!

I left Riga and traveled to Ripsi, where I talked with Father. As young students, we had all become ardent, convinced readers of Karl Marx. The mild Marxists were social democrats, not communists, a movement that spread later. We pored over the revolutionary, red-covered booklets about the great teachings of Marx, who wished to free the world, human society, and industry from capitalism, reorganizing life on socialistic principles. Though I kept my revolutionary opinions secret from outsiders, I disclosed them to my father, attempting to convert him to Marxism, with no success. Once, when no one saw me, I risked tearing down the czar's picture, which was posted on the corner of a street in Wiljandi.

The reactionary movement did not immediately reach our district. The poorest people in the community, the peasants, wanted their own land to cultivate for profit. Elsewhere, some mansions belonging to rich landowners were burned down, but in our district of Wiljandi and in its surroundings, the revolution caused no extreme actions.

My brother Peter, who was a well-known socialist leader in our community, organized a large meeting of many people at our school. He was the main speaker. I [spoke] very little.

When the armed soldiers and officers came [to our area], our family remained undisturbed. Peter disappeared. He lived secretly in a nearby forest, and the [local] police officer, [who was] a family friend, did not report him.

At home, I waited and thought about how I could continue my engineering studies. All the universities and higher institutes for engineering studies in Russia were closed for long periods. It was impossible to study in Riga. Instead, Father was broadminded and prepared to let me study abroad.

---

1. In 1914, at the beginning of World War I, St. Petersburg was renamed "Petrograd," a name deemed less German. Here, describing it as the site of student unrest, Otto refers to it as "Petrograd," but later, writing of it as the home of the tsar's garden, where his brother Jüri worked, Otto reverts to "St. Petersburg."

2. The first version of the Winter Palace in Petrograd (St. Petersburg) was actually a small building constructed for Tsar Peter I in 1704. Vastly expanded, redesigned several times, and later reconstructed after a fire destroyed the interior in 1837, the palace served as the official residence of the Russian tsars, but Nicholas II and his family had left St. Petersburg and were living in Tsarskoye Selo, in the Alexander Palace, at the time of the revolution.

3. Lindanisa was an ancient Estonian fortification in what is now the city of Tallinn. It was destroyed by the Danes in 1219.

4. According to Raun and Miljan, Konstantin Päts (1874-1956) published the nationalist newspaper *Teataja* (*The Herald*). I find no record that Päts himself ever published or managed *Päevaleht*.

5. According to Raun (*Estonian and the Estonians*), Postimees (*The Courier*) was the first Estonian daily paper, birthed in Tartu in 1891. Miljan (*Historical Dictionary of Estonia*) describes Jaan Tõnisson as having joined the editorial board of *Postimees* in 1882, after he graduated from the University of Tartu with a law degree. He worked for two years in Russia (1894-1896) as an apprentice judge and court investigator, before he helped to buy the paper and assume its editorship. "Tõnisson's liberal democratic ideology, to which he remained true to the end of his life, led him to oppose not only the ongoing Russification of the late 19th century and the Baltic German reactionaries but also Estonian radical democrats and socialist revolutionaries. Thus, he came into early conflict with Konstantin Päts, and remained in lifelong opposition as the quintessential liberal democrat to the pragmatic social-democratic authoritarian Päts." (Miljan, p. 478)

6. "Estonia," a song and drama society, was founded in 1870. This became the basis for a professional theater established in 1906 by Paul Pinna and Theodor Alterman, though more serious dramas had already been presented from the start of the twentieth century. "Estonia" became today's Estonian National Opera. (Estonian National Opera website—http://www.opera.ee/en/rahvusooper/—accessed March 2, 2017)

7. According to Miljan (p.13), the elections in Tallinn in 1904 resulted in an Estonian-Russian takeover of Tallinn's city council. Under the leadership of Konstantin Päts, the Baltic Germans were removed from council power. Raun notes that between 1901 and 1914, Estonians were able to gain control of municipal governments in six of the ten major cities of Estland and northern Livland. I find no mention of an election in Tallinn in 1902.

8. This is probably the painter, Köler, of Otto's first chapter.

9. Born in 1875, Otto Strandman studied law at the University of Tartu. During 1905, when he pursued autonomy for Estonia in the Russian empire, he attracted younger members of the Tallinn intelligentsia and Social Democrats who found Jaan Tõnisson and Konstantin Päts too moderate. Strandman assumed many positions of leadership in the provisional and later independent

Estonian governments. Rather than facing Russian deportation and imprisonment in 1941, he committed suicide. (Miljan, pp. 446-447)

10. Konstantin Päts worked for the political autonomy of Estonia throughout his life. Following the abortive revolution of 1905, he fled to Switzerland, returning to Estonia a few years later. In the first decade of Estonia's independence, he served as head of state (Riigivanem) five times. He ruled with an authoritarian hand from 1934–1937 and was elected Estonia's first president in 1938. In 1940, the Soviet occupation forces arrested and deported Päts and his family. He died in 1956 while forcibly confined in a psychiatric hospital, because, according to the Russians, he continued to assert that he was the president of Estonia.

Päts' daughter-in-law wrote a long account of the families' arrest and the death of Päts:

> Toward the end of 1954, K. Päts was taken to the Jämejala Hospital in Estonia. Later, Dr. Nõges told me in Viljandi that he had been summoned to examine K. Päts. I had not returned home yet. K. Päts, totally wasted from malnutrition, did not have diabetes anymore. In the mornings he was conscious, but in the evenings he appeared to fade. My sister-in-law, Erna Lattik, with whom my son Matti stayed after my second arrest, went to Viljandi to have Matti visit his grandfather. The chief of staff [a female physician], Dr. Lellep, did not allow Matti to see his grandfather.

> I will explain the unusual return of K. Päts to Estonia in the following way. Some time after Stalin's death, I received orders as the head of the dispensary in Kazakhstan to send all the disabled internal exiles back to their homes. No doubt such orders went out throughout Russia. At that time, they were also sending released prisoners back to their homes. And then, in the summer of 1955, when I had returned to Estonia for the second time, I was summoned to Pagari Street. And why? Again some chief asked me if I had heard that K. Päts had been in Viljandi, at Jämejala. I said nothing. Then he continued, "There was a deranged man who imagined he was the president!" That was the extent of our conversation. But great fear had gone through me again when I got the call from Pagari Street.

> I hope that these lines in this notebook will serve to remind us that it is from home and our homeland that we derive our strength to travel through today's storms and the darkness of suffering.

("Personal Memories of the Fate of the Family of 1939 Estonian President Päts," by Helgi-Alice Päts, accessed March 25, 2019:

https://truecostmovie.com/img/TSR/pages/section_01/1940-55_Memoirs_Fate_of_President_Pats_Family.pdf)

11. The war years brought tragedy. Soviet forces occupied Estonia in June of 1940. In July, the country was proclaimed the "Estonian Soviet Socialist Republic." The Soviets arrested 10,157 people and deported them to Russia on June 14,

1941. Less than one month later, German forces drove the Soviets out of the Estonian mainland and conquered Tallinn. The Red Army returned in August of 1944, and the Soviets re-occupied the country, resulting in more arrests, the nationalization of industry, and a massive influx of Russians and other Soviet peoples in a renewed effort to "Russify" the country. Thousands of Estonian men disappeared into the forests, many of them resisting through guerilla warfare.

12. More than once, Otto told Renate that he tried to address some of the crowds in Riga as he stood upon what he called a "soap box," also admitting to her, however, that he realized he was unsuited for delivering "stirring orations."

CHAPTER 12

The Practice of Mining: From Russia to Claustal, Germany[1]

1905

Otto age 21: Liège, Belgium; and Lautental, Germany

In order to investigate which higher level technical institute I could enter, I wrote to one in Liège, Belgium and one in Glasgow, Scotland. I received positive answers from both, but before I could consider going to either, I had to secure a statement from the Russian district office in Wiljandi that I was a true citizen of Russia.[2] No one had reported my tearing down the czar's picture, so this was possible. With Father's money in my pocket, I rode to Riga, the capital of Livland,[3] where I received the necessary passport for my trip abroad.

In February 1905, I traveled by rail [from Russia] through Berlin and Cologne to Liège (Lüttich, in German) in Belgium. Crossing the frontier into Germany, I noticed the greater prosperity of the Germans. The buildings, as well as the fields and forests, were in better and more orderly shape than in Russia. I changed trains in Berlin without visiting the city because I had to save money, but I observed that the common people wore nicer clothes in Germany. In the Ruhr district, a group of masons dressed in white clothing entered the train. Their cleanliness surprised me.

Waiting for the train to Belgium in Cologne, I had time to admire the colossal cathedral. I noticed the first green grass near the south wall of the mighty building, reminding me that I was in a warmer climate than in Estonia, which at that time was covered in deep snow.

In the late afternoon, I arrived in Liège, Belgium. After spending two days riding on the hard seats of the third-class coach, I was quite tired, and I spent the first night in a hotel. The next day, I bought a map of the city and a daily paper. Under the listing of available rooms, I found a few close to the university and selected a modest place where the landlady would also serve three meals [a day].

My next task was to learn French. I was able to comprehend the meaning of the texts in French books, but that did not mean that I, as a foreigner, could understand a scientific lecture given by a professor. It is much more difficult to quickly take notes on a lecture than it is to read. Clearly, I had to learn a lot in a very short time if I wanted to be able to follow the university lectures.

Regular lessons in another language were expensive. To save money, I thought I would try to pay for French lessons by giving German lessons in exchange. I put an advertisement in a Liège daily paper, and after receiving a few responses, I went to see one of the teachers. She was a young lady of twenty-two, about my age, who lived with her family. Her father was employed by the Belgian customs service. We agreed to work two hours daily, five times per week.

Our French and German lessons took place in the living room of the young lady's home. These were interesting discussions between two serious persons. The young lady's parents did not disturb us in any way. Poor as my French was, I told her about my life and education in Estonia, especially mentioning my short period of study in Riga and the stormy, interesting meetings of hopeful people outside of the city. I worked intensively, reading out loud from a French book or newspaper and asking her to correct my pronunciation. In my rented room, I tried to write down my conversation with her in French. I also asked her to read from a German book and corrected her speech, but I felt that I learned more French from her than she learned German from me. We were really just cooperating. Neither of us attempted to force the other or to calculate the relative size of the effort we were each making.

I also became acquainted with a young Jewish student from Russia who had already studied one year in Liège, and I visited a meeting of Russian students belonging to different political parties. There were usually strong arguments between the students of socialistic and communistic opinions at such meetings. The arguments did not please me at all, and I did not go to listen to the bitter fights about socialism and communism.

[On my long walks, I learned about nature, people, and industry in the area.] I saw large iron and steel plants on the Mozel River,[4] with tall blast furnaces for the production of cast iron. An old fortress stood on a hill outside the city. Soldiers marched through Liège and sang delightful songs, and on the street corners, small traders sold hot *pommes frites* by the handful. These were little fried sticks of potatoes that we could eat while walking. At the time, they cost five centimes (or one cent).

I inquired more closely about the educational programs of the university and discovered that in accordance with French methods, students learned only theory during the first two years of their study of technical subjects. This seemed tedious and impractical to me, so I inquired about the School for Mining and Metallurgy in the Royal Prussian Academy at Claustal,[5] in the Harz Mountains of Germany. There, students were required to have a half-year of practical experience in their chosen specialties before entering the academy, a much more appealing system.

When I wrote to the school at Claustal to see if I could enroll, I received a positive and friendly response. Although I decided to go there, my two and a half months studying French in Liège were useful. I could easily make myself understood in simple, practical conversations, and I'd read two thick books by Émile Zola, as well as enjoying the interesting biography of the famous French scientist Curie, written by his daughter.[6]

It was a little painful to disclose my decision to leave for Germany to my nice French teacher. She wrote to me for at least a year. I answered her letters very briefly from time to time. Apparently, she had expected marriage, but I had decided to marry only after I completed my student years.

I was very pleased with Claustal once I arrived. The School for Mining and Metallurgy was located in mountains eight hundred meters tall, in the midst of surrounding forests. Because of its high elevation, the little city's climate was almost like that of Estonia: cold winters, lots of snow, and moderate summer months filled with the aroma of fir trees.

My half year of practical work began in the very small town of Lautental, at a plant for melting lead and silver. This plant for the production of both metals had been supported by the Prussian kings for many hundreds of years because its precious silver could be pressed into *thaler*[7]—valuable currency.

I found a room in Claustal and rode daily by railroad to the plant. During my half year, a German student worked there, too. We wrote our notes on a table in a small room lit only by a little electrical lamp hanging from the ceiling. The light seemed too dim, and I wanted to screw the bulb out of its socket to see how many watts of electrical power it carried. My strict, disciplined, and accurate Prussian comrade found my investigation inappropriate and told me so. I found his extremely limited Prussian orderliness and discipline unjustified, but I kept my opinion to myself.

My practice in the metallurgical plant interested me. Lead is a heavy metal used for hunters' bullets, and I had the opportunity to observe how it was produced. I also learned that silver is present in a very small percentage in metals containing silver sulfide and lead sulfide. Both were found in sulfide ore, which was mined from approximately eight hundred meters below the land in the Claustal area. This depth is equivalent to about ten church towers, stacked one on top of the other.

Miners painfully hacked out the black sulfide of lead with sharp, heavy, steel picks. The crude rock, which mainly consisted of useless minerals, was taken to a separation plant, where it was crushed by complicated machinery. Ingenious equipment was then used to divide the valuable components from the worthless ones, and the concentrated ore was sent to the Lautental plant. There, the powdery lead and silver sulfide was placed in a thin layer at the bottom of long, red hot furnaces and moved along by a man using a shovel. [Eventually], the sulfur burned out and formed sulfuric acid, a product that could be sold. The ore was converted into lead oxide containing a little precious silver.

The next phase of separating the precious silver from the large weight of lead occurred in a "shaft furnace."[8] At about 1000°C, the lead oxide was reduced to liquid lead. The product was then cast into heavy bars, each containing a trifle of silver.

I was especially interested in the final refinement of silver from lead. In my day, this was done in a round, flat furnace 2 ½ meters in diameter, at red-hot temperatures. The surface of the molten metal was heated with a flame made from coal mixed with air. This oxidized the lead bath into liquid lead oxide, which ran out of the furnace in a small stream. The silver, which was not subject to oxidation, concentrated itself in the bottom. From time to time, raw bars of the lead, each with its trifles of silver, were added. Through a chemical analysis of the metal, the silver content of the bath was tracked as it increased, and the laboratory was able to predict the approximate day and hour when all the lead would be oxidized.

We new students were anxious to observe the most interesting moment: that point when the last dirty lead oxide slag would run off from the surface, leaving pure silver. It was said that the silver would shine like a mirror. We talked often about the long-awaited appearance of the "silver mirror."

One day, the manager of the Lautental plant informed us that he expected the silver mirror to appear during the coming night. I and a new German student, who also practiced at Lautental, decided to stay at the plant until that moment. From time to time as the night passed, we looked inside the furnace through a dark glass, but for long hours the dirty lead oxide slag covered the surface of the bath.

In the morning, the lead oxide slag began to thin. Our waiting time was much longer than we had expected, and we were dead tired, but finally the layer of lead oxide on the silver metal bath decreased to the thinness of paper. We thought, *Now! Now! The silver mirror will appear!* And it actually did. Before our own eyes, the thin layer of lead oxide ran off to the side. Shining before us was the clean, mirror-like surface of the precious silver.

It had been a long process. A few hundred tons of lead had been gradually charged into the refining furnace and transformed into lead oxide slag until about nine hundred kilograms of pure silver accumulated on the furnace's flat bottom.

At that point, the outlet groove in the side lining of the furnace was deepened. Clean forms of cast iron were laid below the groove and pure molten silver bars were cast, weighed, and carried by trusted men into the treasury room of the plant. Our long, tiresome nightshift without sleep was finished. Exhausted, we rode back to Claustal.

1. Now "Clausthal-Zellerfeld" but always "Claustal" in Otto's text.
2. Here, in naming himself a "citizen of Russia," Otto acknowledges his status in terms of the realities of political power. Reading this and later, similar references to his identity, Renate was stunned. She had only recognized her father—as seen through her eyes and through what he told her—as Estonian.
3. German crusaders established the late medieval state of "Livland" in present-day Latvia and Estonia. After 1560 when Sweden conquered Estonia, and following the Polish-Swedish war of 1690-1629, the province of Livonia was created from the southern half of Estonia and today's Latvian province of

Vidzeme. The remainder of present-day Estonia was known as "Estland." Sweden ceded Livonia and Estland to Russia as a result of the Great Northern War (1700-1720).

4. Now known as the Meuse River.

5. Today, called the Clausthal University of Technology.

6. I've found no record of a biography of Pierre Curie written by his daughter. The MacMillan Company published Marie Curie's biography of her husband, Pierre, in 1923 (in English). According to R.F. Mould (*Current Oncology*, 2007 April; 74–82; accessed 7/28/2018: https://www.ncbi.nlm.nih.gov/pmc/articles/PMC1891197/), this is the only biography that has been written. Though we do not know what materials were available in French in the early 1900s, Otto's probable confusion may strike the reader as curious, as it did Renate. To her, this passage underscores Otto's inability to regard women as capable of doing science or of having them participate in the same workspace as men. Though he admired the "competence" of some women, Otto did not or perhaps could not easily ascribe genius and fame to a woman rather than a man.

7. *Thaler* are silver coins issued by various German states from the fifteenth to the nineteenth centuries.

8. A shaft furnace is loaded at the top and tapped at the bottom. Inside, an ascending stream of hot gas is forced through a descending column of solids.

CHAPTER 13

The *Bergakademie* at Claustal[1]

c. 1906–1910
Otto age 22-26: Claustal, Berlin, and the Ural Mountains

When I finished my practical work at the lead and silver plant, I gave a report of my observations to the academy as requested and began my studies. I was enrolled in one of the first higher technical schools in the world. In Germany, there were three higher institutions for training in mining and metallurgy: one in Berlin; one at Freiberg in Saxonia; and the third, the *Bergakademie* at Claustal. The two oldest were located in Claustal and Freiberg. Mining and metallurgy techniques used there were described in Latin, in the first technical textbook published, *Metallurgia* ["Metallurgy"].[2]

The Prussian government owned the lands, forests, mining and metallurgical plants in the Oberharz area near Claustal, and the Royal Prussian Mining Academy at Claustal was supported by the Prussian state. The school stood in the center of the city, a large, new, stone building with modern rooms for lectures and laboratories. The numbers of students increased later to many thousands, but in my time, there were only about two hundred. The small ratio of students to the large, well-equipped laboratories gave us the opportunity to choose research projects according to our own wishes. The professors knew each of us personally.

My social life during my first year at Claustal was enjoyable and interesting. I felt quite comfortable in the city, surrounded by beautiful forests. I became friendly with an interesting German who belonged to a prosperous and educated family, and I took long walks with him into the beautiful surroundings of Claustal. We had serious talks about scientific, and even philosophical, subjects.

As the mining school was one of the first in the world, a large percentage of its students came from other countries. The Germans wore colored caps and were mostly members of social clubs called "corporations." The non-Germans were almost all members of a club for foreigners.

As a Russian subject, I joined the club for foreign students, introduced by an older, friendly Russian who was one of its leading members. Among the fifteen members, I met people from Holland and its colony, Java; the United States; South America; Peru; Russia; and Greece.

During my first semester at the academy, I lived in a small, student room on the main street of the city. A Dutch student from Java, whose features revealed an admixture of Javanese blood, lived there, too. He liked to sketch pictures of Javanese faces. The landlady served me hot coffee or tea for breakfast and suppers, and I bought food for the morning and evening in nearby stores. I ate substantial mid-day meals with other members of the foreign students' club at the best restaurants in Claustal or in nearby Zellerfeld.

The foreign students' club had permanently rented a large room in a building in Claustal, where it held its social meetings once or twice a week. We members usually gathered after we'd eaten supper separately in our own rooms or a city restaurant, sitting down on both sides of a long table lit by a large, alcohol-burning lamp. In accordance with the habit of German students, a small barrel of beer was bought, and we drank it from large glasses. To elevate the mood of the group, we sang cheerful student songs, reinforced by drinks of beer. Sometimes, someone made a funny speech.

My membership in the club lasted only one or two semesters. The food was good but too expensive for me, and the conversation during the meals was, for my taste, superficial and uninteresting. Beer drinking at the meetings in the club also did not interest me, so I found a large room in a private house where the landlady had two young daughters. They fed me quite well.

Most of the local inhabitants in Claustal had little income. They looked upon the students, who were usually from prosperous families, as gentlemen. The ladies who had daughters were interested in the students because the young men occasionally married their daughters. I had no intention of marrying early, however. I bought a used bicycle for summer and new skis for winter. These gave me bodily exercise and helped to keep me in good health.

As my specialty at the academy, I chose the metallurgy of the noble metals silver and gold, although on occasion I attended lectures concerning iron and steel production. [I had several professors.] The mining teacher often organized interesting trips to mining plants near Claustal. Because of our small numbers, we students were able to talk to him during those visits. He was elderly and world-renowned, and he served as the general director of the academy, as well. The professor for mineralogy and geology was also very capable, but the physics professor was quite old, and I didn't like him. He did not distinguish the important subjects from the unimportant, so I avoided as many of his lectures as possible. A young, energetic, and capable professor taught inorganic chemistry, a subject that was very important to me. With interest and pleasure, I concentrated mainly on inorganic chemistry lectures and practical laboratory work during the eight semesters of my studies.

Through good fortune, I became acquainted with a young assistant professor, Mostovitch, who was Jewish. He was a friend of the professor of metallurgy and specialized in nonferrous metals, though he was only working temporarily at Claustal. "If you are studying metallurgy, then base your knowledge on that of the Americans," he said. He particularly recommended an American textbook, *Metallurgical Calculations*, by Professor Richards, an outstanding teacher at Lehigh University, Bethlehem, Pennsylvania. I especially appreciated Richards' excellent books. Through his three volumes, I learned the theory and methods of calculating the efficiency of industrial and metallurgical processes and furnaces. Later, I visited him many times in Pennsylvania.[3]

Mostovitch and I took long walks, during which we spoke in Russian, since we were both citizens of Russia. As a result of our friendship, he found me a paid position in a small nickel production plant in Oberschlesien, Germany (also called "Silesia"),[4] where I was employed as a common workman for six months. The manual labor was often tiresome, but as I moved through every section of the plant, I thoroughly learned the successive stages of producing nickel and had ample opportunity to study the design of all the machinery—including the automatic presses for creating briquettes of nickel ore before it was melted in the vertical, water-cooled shaft furnace. I sketched all the equipment and noted exact measurements. My notes were very useful to me later, in Russia, when I planned to build a production plant for this important metal, which was then used as a component in armor and canons.

[In 1908],[5] after two years of study without seeing my father and brothers, I wanted to visit Estonia and Father during my summer vacation. When I went back, I found my father sick at Ripsi. He had been ill for a few weeks, and my sisters were living far away. I felt it my duty to help my father. He had always sent me funds for my living expenses abroad, and I esteemed him as an Estonian patriot and a man of outstandingly high character.

I first went to Wiljandi and asked an Estonian medical doctor to ride to Ripsi and examine my father carefully. X-rays had recently been invented, but they were not available in our city, and the doctor's examination did not reveal the cause of Father's sickness.

In order to feed my father better food, I bought a portable, petroleum cooking stove and prepared easily digestible meals for him myself. I slept in his room in order to help him during the night. As his suffering did not lessen, I brought the medical doctor to Ripsi a second time. Again, he was unable to discern the reason for Father's illness or to prescribe a definite medicine for him.

To get steady, better care and nursing, I brought a lady from Wiljandi whom our family had long known as a friend and helper. We found a little blood in Father's feces, indicating that something was wrong with his bowels, but we were unable to cure him. After about four weeks of sickness, he died.

13.1 *["I give my peace to you" ("Oma rahu annan mina teile"): the gravesite of Jüri Lellep (October 11, 1841–September 2, 1908), Liisu Lellep (May 3, 1839–August 4, 1893), and Mari Lellep. We know from a note on the back of the photo that Mari was Jüri's second wife, though she is never named in Otto's manuscript. (See Chapter 7.)]*

13.2   Father's funeral. Top row, left to right: Otto (23 years old and studying metallurgy in Berlin), brother Willem (manufacturer of doors and window frames for houses and owner of the first steam-engine-driven plant in Tallinn, brother-in-law Jüri Toss (member of Lellep Forest Products Company), brother Hans (teacher and pastor's assistant in a parochial school in Gatschina, near St. Petersburg). Bottom row, left to right: Brother Peter (member of Lellep Forest Products Company), sister Juuli (owner of a store for ladies' apparel and accessories in Tallinn), sister Liina (married to a famer in Tänanasilm), Julie (wife of brother Hans), brother Jüri (botanist in the Imperial Garden of Peter the Great).

All the members of our family and a large number of Father's good friends were invited to his funeral. The row of horse-drawn wagons was unusually long. My brothers living in Tallinn, St. Petersburg, and Gatchina in Russia came with their wives.

Unfortunately, Father had made no will before his death, and consequently, some disagreeable discord arose from my oldest brother concerning the distribution of Father's property. The largest portion went to Willem at Tallinn, as he managed the greatest part of Father's business.[6]

Willem started to pay the expenses for my education in Germany. In addition to the Prussian Mining Academy at Claustal, I knew of the Prussian Mining Academy in Berlin, where I also wished to study. Spending the winter semester of 1908-1909 in Berlin, I was able to perform a few quantitative chemical analyses of minerals. I also particularly enjoyed the lectures of the professor of mechanics and machinery. He had a special talent for using diagrams and pictures to explain the design and construction of various machines. He taught so clearly and so interestingly, it was a pleasure to listen to him. In addition, after each lecture, he gave us a number of calculations that helped clear up and elaborate on the subject of his talk.

In 1909, because of Professor Mostovitch's kind introduction, I received a paid position in a Russian copper plant in the far Ural Mountains near Siberia. [This was a remote area.] To give a sense of the geographical distances in Russia, I should say that a trip from Petrograd to the Ural Mountains required three days of railroad travel.

My work in the copper plant consisted of my copying large technical drawings by hand. Machine copying was a far cheaper process, but it was not yet used in the remote Ural Mountains. I was also assigned the task of suggesting means to improve the roasting or oxidation of the lumpy copper ore. The simple and efficient American cintering machine was not used in Russia either,[7] but a talented and friendly Russian engineer, Pomeranzev, explained a new, regenerative "open-hearth" furnace for the refining of copper.[8] I studied and collected data about the plant's open-hearth furnace. It utilized dried wood for fuel, which was cheaper than coal or oil in the Urals.

Back at Claustal, I specialized in the study, development, and efficient operation of fuel-fired, high-temperature furnaces for metallurgy. The professor of metallurgy kindly gave me a free hand to experiment in his laboratory, where I improvised and tested a small Dwight-Lloyd grate for desulfurizing ore.[9] I also set for myself the difficult task of constructing a small laboratory furnace to produce exceedingly high temperatures with gas fuel. Though I succeeded in building the furnace, in which the air for combustion was preheated in seven porcelain tubes to about 1400°C, the process worked for only a few minutes. When the temperatures rose to about 1700°C to 1800°C, my air preheating tubing melted.

My experiments in my professor's beautiful, clean, metallurgical laboratory did not please him, but he was a kind and likable person. One day I told him that I intended to become an inventor. I had decided this during a walk I had taken with a good friend at Claustal. We were discussing the kinds of positions or occupations we would like to have as engineers, and I told him I wanted to become the director and manager of a plant. My friend looked at me doubtfully.[10] His expression told me that he did not think me suitable for directing the activities of others. I myself also felt that I was more suited to do research or perhaps to be an inventor, and I decided to develop the latter capability. I remembered well that when I herded pigs on Father's farm, I made many objects with my own hands. Some of them were toys, but others were useful, such as the straw hats.

[Finally, in 1910], I received my diploma as a metallurgical engineer.[11] I used the data I had gathered at the copper plant in Russia to work out the complete heat balance of the wood-fired, regenerative furnace used there.[12] I presented my calculations and sketches in a study of the efficiency of heat utilization in large-scale industrial furnaces: "Heat Utilization in Fuel-Fired High Temperature Furnaces for Metallurgy."

After I received my diploma, I had to decide in which country I would apply my theoretical knowledge. I could speak and write fluently in Estonian, Russian, and German. In addition, I could explain myself in French and English. My capabilities in five languages opened almost all the world for my future work.

Both the United States of America and Canada had immense natural resources, and great possibilities were available there, but my brother Willem, who had given me funds for my studies after Father's death, wanted me back in Estonia. He had taken over

Father's business, and there were possibilities of employment in that family business. I would not be able to utilize my four years of study in metallurgy, but love of our native country and of my brothers was calling me back there. Estonia was part of Russia, so I also had to fulfill my two-year duty of military service in the Russian army.

1. A *Bergakademie* is a school of mines or mining. Today, the school is known as the Clausthal University of Technology.

2. We think that Otto's *Metallurgia* is actually a reference to *De Re Metallica*, a book published in 1556 discussing the state of the mining, refining, and smelting of metals.

3. Otto first met Professor Joseph W. Richards in person after the Russian Revolution of 1917, when he traveled to the US to investigate the possibilities for nickel production in Russia (Chapter 18).

4. The region known as Silesia is now in southwestern Poland. Otto doesn't give dates for his work at the nickel plant, but he seems to have done it sometime before he graduated from Clausthal. The text is unclear regarding the exact chronology of his studies and his work at the nickel and copper plants.

5. Jüri Lellep's tombstone lists his death date—and hence, Otto's summer visit home—as 1908.

6. Renate:

    Otto's mention of "discord" may suggest to many a reader that Hans, the eldest of Jüri Lellep's nine offspring, opposed the passing of the largest part of the Lellep inheritance to one son, Willem. Hans may, of course, have created discord concerning this matter, but not necessarily solely so. Tension might have resulted from other issues, as well. Perhaps some wished for a readjustment of wealth, given dowries that may have been deliberately passed on prior to Jüri's death—for example, to the precipitously widowed daughter Juuli for start-up business funds, or to Jaan's twin sister Liina upon her marriage to a farmer selected for a husband (not a Ripsi associate) by Jüri himself. One or another of this couple's three offspring, Jüri's grandchildren, may have been seen by some of Jüri's sons as deserving educational support that the children's parents could not provide. (After all, Hans had refused Otto's request for funds for one of his early experiments—support that Jüri did provide.) The interests of Jüri's succeeding generations and their variably perceived promise could well have produced discussion readily regarded as distasteful discord to Otto.

    As well, I notice that Otto mentions the offspring of Juuli, Liina, Jüri, and Willem more than once: of Hans only once—in a photo. So scarce a mention leads me to consider the possibility that inheritance discord may have turned on an implicit assumption that the inheritance should pass only to those perpetuating Jüri Lellep's bloodline over descending generations (especially those perpetuating the family business, such as Willem). A simple sentence in Otto's memoir may hide or suggest parts of a four-generation family saga. We can only try to read between the lines of the text.

7. "Cintering," or "sintering," as it is now more commonly spelled, is the process by which a powdered material forms a solid or porous mass through heating, and usually compression, without liquefication.

8. The open-hearth process, or the Siemens-Martin process, was developed to increase the temperature in a metallurgical furnace. The furnace's fumes (otherwise wasted heat) were first directed through a checkerwork of loosely stacked bricks, heating them to a high temperature. Air was then introduced through the same pathway, entering the furnace preheated and thus increasing the temperature of the flame. The open-hearth process has been replaced by the basic oxygen process and the electric arc furnace in most industrialized countries, but for the majority of the twentieth century, it dominated steel production throughout the world.

9. Like a conveyor belt, the Dwight-Lloyd grate moves continuously, carrying materials that are sintered through controlled combustion on the grate.

10. Otto told this story to his daughter Renate many times, always mentioning that the friend who looked at him doubtfully was Gustav Klaas. (See Chapters 14, 17, and 18.)

11. My dating of the year of Otto's graduation is based on a resume he wrote many years later.

12. The heat balance of a given system is the distribution of heat energy—both useful output and losses.

CHAPTER 14

"Do Not Think!"

c. 1910–1914

Otto age 26–30: Moscow, Borodino, and Estonia

While gaining my higher education in Germany, I forgot to declare and formally assure my right to serve only one year in the Russian army. I attempted to correct my mistake in Petrograd, where I had the means to make an indirect approach to the prime minister, but he refused to help me. Consequently, I was obliged to start my two-year military service as a twenty-eight-year-old[1] in the pioneer battalion in Moscow.[2] This was a bitter and unavoidable necessity.

Although I had my diploma as a graduate metallurgical engineer, the military authorities had to handle me exactly as they did the uneducated, young boys from Russian villages, some of whom were even unable to read a book. Standing among a group of village boys for our first inspection by a pompous, young Russian officer, I began four months of rough, painful, disgusting military training. We were in the poorly ventilated soldiers' rooms, and I was dressed in simple but clean clothing. Observing my dress, the officer yelled: "*Captenarmus!*[3] Why has this man better clothing than the others?" He pointed at me. "Give him the worst things you have!" They handed me filthy clothes. The insides of the pants were covered with the miniscule, shiny eggs of lice! I had to obey and put them on.

This was followed by the first hour of training for young soldiers. "Lellep, man, what are you thinking there?! Do *not* think! Hold your head higher and stretch your chest forward! Listen and do exactly what I am telling you!" For sixteen years I had studied at several different schools to learn to think *better*. And now I had to learn not to think at all.

Military training in all countries, for examples Germany and the United States of America, requires unquestioning obedience to authorities. At the age of twenty-eight, having lived all my life among free-thinking persons, I found it difficult to change my habits and fall in with strict and rigid military discipline. At times, I almost despaired.

Luckily, this painful, almost hopeless situation lasted only the first four months, during which I completed the basic training for new soldiers. One night, before the end, I was on duty with an educated, young officer who was the son of a general. I felt that he would understand my emotions, so I risked entering his quiet, little office. Talking frankly, I explained I felt almost able to kill the young, pompous training officer and then to shoot myself. He tried to soothe and quiet me and promised to see what he could do to improve my situation.

After the four-month training period, conditions changed. I was given interesting work calculating how much food had to be prepared in the soldiers' kitchen for the varying numbers of soldiers. I also received the privilege of visiting places of historic interest in Moscow. I saw the Kremlin, many centuries old, with its high and thick walls; a dozen or more French cannons that Napoleon had left in Moscow; and a few Orthodox Greek cathedrals, some with golden, onion-shaped towers—sights really worthy of attention.

One time, on a Moscow Street, I met a schoolmate who told me of a firm named "Lellep," somewhere in the city. I found the firm in the central part of Moscow, the first business in the city selling sewing machines to poorer people on long-term credit. The owner invited me to visit him in his big, modern house. He was a rich businessman with a wife and two young, school-aged daughters. He thought that as Estonians, we were at least remotely related, and he often asked me to visit. I was glad to do so. This Lellep from Moscow later moved to the Estonian university city of Tartu, thus saving his property when the Bolsheviks took over the Russian government.

In Moscow, I also met my dear old friend Klaas,[4] a highly capable engineer who was employed at a steel plant in Tula, not far from Moscow. I had become acquainted with Klaas when I was in Claustal and he was studying electrical engineering in Hannover, Germany. We'd had an unforgettable vacation in the forest-covered Harz Mountains. For a whole week, as we took our long treks in the beautiful countryside, we talked with each other in our dear Estonian language. We were satisfied with the least expensive foods, mainly eating black bread, butter, and salt herring. We drank refreshing spring water and slept in simple huts provided by the Prussian government, the proprietors of the land.

[All in all], my life as a soldier in Moscow became tolerable. I was assigned to a special class in our pioneer battalion. An educated and trained officer taught our group of Russian soldiers from primitive villages how to use dynamite to destroy buildings, bridges, or other enemy structures during war. He knew that I was a trained engineer, so I was able to sit in the back of the class without participating. Instead, I busied myself trying to figure out how to simplify the metallurgy of nickel production. I studied modern periodicals that I ordered from the United States and planned a few experiments that I could perform, even while I was a soldier. [Fortunately,] I was able to use the battalion's bathroom for my work. It was occupied on Saturdays but was unoccupied the other six days of the week.[5]

Each of my tests required a few hours of [labor]. I first had to carry my equipment from a secret corner in our bathroom and assemble it. To melt the nickel, I used the newly discovered method of surface combustion, building a little furnace and an experimental crucible that I made of burned magnesite.[6] I asked Willem to send me a simple pair of bellows in order to obtain high-pressure air. With compressed liquid gas as fuel and an air blast from the bellows, it was easily possible for me to fire the furnace to a temperature above the melting point of nickel, though it was almost impossible to regulate it without an expensive pyrometer. Still, I kept thinking about inventions that could bring me a fortune in the future.

In 1912, towards the end of my military service, Russians celebrated the one-hundred-year "jubileum" of the time they drove Napoleon from Moscow.[7] Our pioneer battalion was assigned the task of reconstructing the military trenches of the Russians and French at Borodino, sixty kilometers from Moscow. I was the only man in the battalion who could read and understand the French drawings of the trenches.

[While we worked], I lived in a primitive house belonging to a Russian peasant and slept on a bench without a mattress. The grandfather and grandmother of the house spent each night lying on a very large oven with thick walls. This kind of oven was typically used for heating and baking. I ordered fresh milk as a special food, and they cooked it in a particular kind of pot in the oven.

My military service in the Russian army ended in the summer. As was usual for that time of year, our battalion was temporarily housed in a beautiful military camp near the Oka River. Luckily, about twelve of us soldiers with a high school or university education had passed our examination and been promoted to officers (*prapor-shchik zapasa*).[8] We, the educated soldiers, recognized the end of our military service by ordering some alcoholic drinks. Our celebration lasted all through the night. Normally, I avoided alcohol, but in this particular case, [the end of our military service], I did make a slight exception.

[At this point], Estonia lured me, and I decided to return and manage the family sawmill. My brother Willem had bought two fairly primitive sawing machines and one circle-shaped saw. During the first months, the engineering work of erecting a power plant with a thirty horsepower locomobile and mounting the saws kept me busy and interested.[9] Later, the supervision and direction of the fifteen, mostly Russian workmen and the selling of the sawn boards did not hold my attention.

I stayed in primitive living quarters while I managed the mill. I was mostly interested in converting the logs of relatively thin fir trees into boards. Sales of the boards of thick firs had been profitable, but a Jewish-owned sawmill had used up [the thick firs] and then discontinued operations.[10] It was not easy to get rid of the thin boards.

As a large stock of our lumber accumulated, I saw a partial solution. Estonia had two fair-sized cement plants needing short, thin boards for the barrels they used to transport and ship Portland cement. I made a special trip to Russia where such boards were produced, and we bought two inexpensive cylindrical saws. At my suggestion, we hired two men from Russia for our mill near Narva. They were experts at using the saws, but our stock started to grow again. Sales of our lumber required a talent that I did not possess. We needed a skilled salesman to handle every kind of board we were accumulating.

After about twenty-one months at the sawmill, I felt that I could not use my training as an engineer there. I was inclined toward research, especially toward inventing. I also thought that Willem's idea of founding the mill was not justified financially. [Fortunately], this was when it was Russia's policy to diminish German influence in favor of the Estonians, and an Estonian engineer I'd met when I was a student in Riga had become mayor of Tallinn. When he offered me a position as an engineer in the city, I gladly accepted.

One of my tasks as an engineer in Tallinn was to find ways and means to supply the city with economical fuel. There were large areas of land covered with deep layers of peat outside the city,[11] reminding me of the peat production I'd seen during my military service in Moscow. After I'd heard that one of the largest installations in the world for dried peat was located outside of that city, I'd gone to inspect the place before I left. There, I had found thirty working units for peat production. Each unit used a locomobile heated with dried peat as a source of power.[12]

I wrote two long technical articles about the economical peat industry in Moscow and published them in the daily Estonian paper, *Päevaleht*.[13] In them, I concluded that the same procedure could be applied profitably in Tallinn to produce cheap electrical power. [But in the end], my service to the city of Tallinn lasted only a few months.

1.   I have the left the text as written, but if Otto graduated from Claustal in 1910 (as he later noted on his resume), he must have been twenty-six at the time that he entered military service.

2.   Pioneer battalions prepared roads and terrain for the passage of the main body of troops.

3.   *Captenarmes*, "Capitaine d'armes," or "captain of arms," is perhaps best translated as "quartermaster": the supplier of quarters, clothing, rations, etc.

4.   This is the first mention by name of Gustav Klaas, the important friend who appears throughout Otto's accounts of his time in Germany, Russia, and the United States. Renate notes that Gustav's father worked in Russia but identified himself as Estonian. Gustav himself was raised in Crimea and was never able to spend more than a day in Estonia. Nonetheless, as Otto mentioned repeatedly and admiringly to his family, father and son spoke to one another solely in Estonian.

5.   Renate heard Otto tell this story many times. He spoke often of the lice, the unwashed soldiers who could not read a book, and the unused bathroom (but for once a week when the men were permitted to wash).

6.   To generate heat using surface combustion, Otto forced air or combustible gas through a material resistant to melting, or he had the gas impinge on the material's surface. Magnesite becomes magnesium oxide when burned and is a refractory (material resistant to melting) commonly used to line furnaces.

7.   Renate:
     The force of the word "jubileum" resonates through generations and from Otto down to me. On May 8, 1994, I was in St. Petersburg—or Leningrad, as it was called. I'd left a cruise ship I'd taken from Stockholm. On shore and somehow separated from my tour group, I was caught up in what I was given to understand was a jubileum celebration marking the end of the siege of Leningrad and VE Day. The siege had actually been lifted on 27 January 1944. More than a year later, on May 9, 1945, VE had been

officially declared. The jubilant celebration I experienced may have rested upon the collapse of both dates into a series of what had been officially pronounced an uncertain number of "vacation" days in May.

A taxi driver accompanied me to the cemetery. The city's mayor was to speak there as the crowd broke bagels into bits and, in remembrance, threw them onto geometrically laid out lines of mass graves. Night was falling. On tall poles, shallow bowls of Olympic-like fire lit up the night, the fog, and the huge crowd below.

My taxi driver and I spotted a group of women who were at least half a century old, carrying long poles. They lifted up the poles at the end of the mayor's speech, each woman boldly unfurling her flag: a sickle on a field of red. "Yes," the women told me. "When we were young, we carried them high and believed in what we were doing. But now, we are grandmothers. Some of us have grandchildren who live in Germany, and we visit them there. We are enemies no longer, but when we were young, we participated with all our hearts. We don't want that to be forgotten."

So intense was this occasion of jubilation and remembrance that I lost my sense of time and missed the ferry returning our group to Stockholm. I was stranded in St. Petersburg, unable to rejoin the ship for two days... But that is another story.

8. *Praporschick* are junior level officers in the military reserves (*zapasa*).

9. A locomobile is a steam-powered vehicle.

10. In the original text, the referent for "used up" isn't clear, but it seems that Otto probably meant the trees, not the boards.

11. Otto notes, as well, "The city of Tallinn also had large quarries, where limestone [was present] in layers about 9 meters thick. The geologists named the various layers, which they knew had been formed over millions of years from the remains of microscopic animals that lived in the water when the land was covered by the ocean. Their bodies contained some lime, which was deposited on the ocean's bottom after their deaths."

12. Otto either saw this once near the Alexander School (Chapter 9) and once in Moscow, or he places a single memory in both places.

13. Otto's awareness of possible uses of peat moss did not abate in the United States. Renate recalls receiving a gift from Otto when their second child, Luke, was born. She and her husband were then living in Northampton, Massachusetts. From abroad, Otto instructed Renate's Mutti to commission a metal-worker to make a metal bed frame sized to fit the newborn grandson.

Renate:
> Mutti brought us the bed, keeping her doubts to herself about how well the system would work, given our circumstances.

> Following Otto's instructions, we put a fairly thick layer of peat moss

within the frame and stretched a cotton sheet over it. When the sheet got wet, Otto suggested, it could be easily changed and a handful of the wet peat thrown onto the compost for fertilizer or used for fuel.

We purchased a bale of peat moss at a local garden center in Northampton, but Otto had not considered the question of whether or not a compost pile would exist in the urban, academic setting in which we lived. Soon, it became clear that we could not find a place to put the soiled peat moss. In good humor, we had to give up the gift-bed from Luke's inventive grandfather.

CHAPTER 15

The Battle of Lodz

1914

Otto age 30: Tallinn, Finland, Lodz, Warsaw, Petrograd

In 1914, the First World War began. As a reserve officer in the Russian army, I was called to military service.[1] Given my status as a graduate engineer, I attempted to obtain some kind of technical assignment, but this was a time when the well-organized Germans were successfully defeating the Russians in Poland, and people in the nearby military office told me, "Everyone will be useful in the fighting trenches."

For about ten days, until I was moved, I was put to work helping to build barracks for the Russian soldiers near Tallinn. Our battalion was then taken by railroad from Tallinn through Petrograd to Finland. Because the Finns and other Scandinavian people were friendly to the Germans, the Russian government apparently felt that Germany might eventually invade Finland and from there attack the Russian capital city.

Our battalion remained in Finland for about seven weeks. Life was easy for me there. It was simple to buy milk products and other food. For cleanliness, I went to the famous saunas of the Finns, where the bodies of men were rubbed by women.

[In Finland, however, we did have to practice military maneuvers.] Our division of 16,000 was first divided into two sections for a mock war.[2] Each side was distinguished by signs on its uniforms marked "Friend" or "Enemy."

As an officer, I had command of one hundred or more Russians. I found it somewhat difficult to drive the peasant soldiers to run faster on the poor roads and in the fields and forests in order to surprise our "enemies" and defeat them. They were younger than I, but they were old enough to have beards. "Sir, be merciful," they complained. "We're tired and can't run anymore."

In September of 1914, 16,000 men and [our] auxiliary equipment were loaded onto railroad wagons and directed toward the real German army. We were transported into Poland to fortify the Russian side in the so-called "Lodz" operation.[3] I had bought a collapsible field bed that I carried in a large suitcase.

Late one afternoon, we reached a Polish village that had earlier been in the midst of the fighting. It was almost impossible to find food and a house where we could spend the night. With effort, we officers discovered some bacon and coarse rye bread that had been left by the Russian soldiers. We ate them because we were hungry and drank tea afterwards. I had my field bed, but I threw it away because I did not want to be different from the other officers. We all slept on straw on top of the ground.

The next morning, even the simplest food tasted fine to us. After a rapid formation, our 16,000-man division was ready for the battlefield. A quick-step march was prescribed on the poor roads. My bearded soldiers, younger than I, soon complained about being tired, but we had to maintain our pace.

At noon, we reached the field chosen by the authorities for the start of the battle. An open meadow stretched between the German enemy and us. Our men were distributed along a front three-quarters of a kilometer wide. Allegedly, the Germans were concealed behind a stone wall about one-and-a-half kilometers away. They could see us, but we could not see them.

We had to advance against the Germans though we had no

artillery and they did. Soon they began to attack us with grenades. This was my first, painful and terrible experience of the war. The shells exploded with a hellish, thundering noise among our soldiers and officers. With my own eyes, I saw some soldiers hit by the splinters of the grenades.

As we approached our enemies, they began shooting us with machine guns. Our commanders had ordered us to lie flat on the ground to rest, then to get up and run rapidly forward before we rested again for a while. We officers were behind the row of soldiers and were obliged to order them to run forward. I was under the fear of death and do not remember whether I gave the order or not, but we moved forward during the afternoon. Toward evening, the battlefield became somewhat hilly. For my resting periods, I always selected the lowest possible point on the ground, but I was fully exposed to the bullets of the Germans whenever I ran forward.

When evening came and darkened the battlefield, I was hit by a bullet in the muscle of my left arm. Blood ran from the sleeve of my overcoat. I knew that if I didn't get medical help soon, I might die from loss of blood. I was lying behind a hill and was protected from the bullets of the machine guns.

Gradually, it became darker as night fell, and the Russian front moved forward. I was over one kilometer away from the point where the wounded were being aided by doctors, but with my last ounce of strength, I began to crawl backward to find medical help. Near a poor Polish village, I came to an area that looked like a slaughterhouse. The blood-covered parts of soldiers' bodies lay in disorder on the ground. Doctors worked near well-lit tables. The wound in the muscle of my upper arm was nicely cleaned and bound up there [but] the village was totally dark, and I did not know where to go. Someone said, "Look! The wire of a field telephone is lying here. Follow it and keep walking. You will reach a house where the wounded officers are lying."

Staying close to the wire, I walked into the darkness and came upon a poor house, empty of inhabitants. I was very thirsty since I hadn't had anything to drink or eat all day, and I found in the kitchen a large cooking pot full of water. Whether or not the pot was clean, I drank from it.

Walking further into the darkness, near the wire, I finally reached the house for wounded officers. The beds were filled with the wounded. I saw blood and heard the complaints of suffering people, some lying on the floor. With difficulty, I discovered a bed where two wounded men were already lying. There, I found a narrow space for myself. It was the most miserable night of my life.

The next morning, we had good luck that changed our hell to heaven. Outside our night quarters, we saw the magnificent train of the Red Cross waiting for us. Red Cross nurses appeared, as neat and dear as angels. They helped us into the upholstered seats of the clean, second-class railroad cars. Lovingly treated and fed, we arrived at Warshava, the capital of Poland, where the great polytechnical institute had been converted into a lazarette, or hospital, because of the war. We were treated as heroes with love and grace by the beautiful, volunteer Red Cross nurses. Their care of us exceeded our expectations.

After a few weeks in the hospital, I was sufficiently strong to take walks into the city, [where] the young Polish girls were willing to become friendly with us Russian officers. It was easy to make friends with them and to win relationships of mutual respect.

[Having gained strength, I considered my position.] In the Lodz operation, the Germans were defeating the Russians with great success. From our division of 16,000 men, only 2,500 remained able to fight after the first battle. I was no Russian patriot—I had studied in Germany to become a metallurgical engineer. It was clear to me that if I remained on the front, I would likely be killed during the next battle.

[Fortunately], as an honored, wounded [Russian] officer, I had the opportunity to find and accept a technical position far from the fighting on the front. Seeing a number of officers and soldiers riding in cars or on motorcycles in Warshava, I thought, *Surely that kind of life would be safer and more agreeable than returning to battle,* [so] I took a risk. Without asking permission from my superiors, I rode far away to the Russian capital, Petrograd, and found the repair shop of the military automobile school.[4] There, I saw a small electric furnace that stood idle.

"I am a metallurgical engineer recently wounded in the Lodz operation. As a specialist, I could put this furnace into operation," I said to the chief of the repair shop.

"Very fine," he replied. "Go back to Warshava, and we will ask your superiors to send you here."

Back in Warshava I had to report to the local commandant. "You left this city without my permission," he said. "Do you realize that I can have you shot to death as a deserter?" I was not shot, however, and in a few days an order came from Petrograd: "Send *Praporshchik* Otto Lellep to the automobile school in Petrograd."

I was saved.

1. According to Miljan, nearly 10 percent of the ethnic Estonian population— approximately 100,000 men—were conscripted into the imperial Russian forces. (*Estonia and the Estonians*, p. 95)

2. Otto's original text uses "battalion" here but he must have meant "division," since he uses the term in the later paragraph ("After a rapid formation, our 16,000-man division was ready for the battlefield.") A "battalion" is a smaller military unit varying by country and branch of service, but it might contain three hundred to eight hundred men.

3. Though it is now part of Poland, Lodz was within the Russian empire at the beginning of World War I. The engagement at Lodz was the last in a series of ferocious battles between the Russians and the Germans during the early months of the war. The two sides fought for twenty-five days in freezing winter weather, ending in complete Russian defeat.

4. Otto does not explain how he made the long trip from Warsaw to Petrograd (St. Petersburg): 1,030 kilometers, or approximately 640 miles. He probably had no money. Were trains running? Did he somehow get possession of a motorcycle?

CHAPTER 16

The First Nickel Produced in Russia

1914–1916[1]

Otto age 30-32: Petrograd, Novgorod, Peterhof, the Urals

I spent [only] a short time in the repair shop for motorcyles. There were over a hundred foreign-made cycles of about twenty different makes in need of repair, but no new parts were available for them. Apparently, officers with higher education in engineering were rare in the Russian army, so I was transferred from the shop to the officers' classes. There I was to serve as a lector or teacher, training the men to use and ride motorcycles. This was an excellent and relatively suitable occupation for me.

My class of twenty-five officers ranged from those in the lowest rank, such as myself, up to the level of *polkovniks.*[2] Before long, I was allowed to work out my own program of teaching and to select helpers from among the soldiers. From 1914 until 1917, persons of Jewish descent *could not* become Russian officers, but I was able to select educated Jewish engineers for my school to help me prepare working models, as well as pictures, plans, and diagrams of the design and functioning of the motorcycles. My lectures were easily understood but were also rich in content, so they were popular.

The military soon transferred the school for automobiles and motorcycles from Petrograd to Novgorod, and a few months later to the beautiful resort city of Peterhof, not far from Petrograd. Peterhof had served as a summer resort for Russian czars. It included a palace in a beautiful park with splendid fountains and a large number of stables for the czar's horses. During the war, the stables were used for the storage of military cars and motorcycles, and special buildings were found for use as repair shops, the school of auto riding, a schoolroom for motorcycling, and a fine house for my personal living quarters.

As I have mentioned, my earlier experiences at Claustal in Germany had made clear to me that I was not suited for leading other people. I liked research, experimentation, and the process of invention. Fortunately, my lectures lasted only two to three hours daily, so I could devote the rest of the time to my metallurgical experiments, [which I began and then continued as our schools moved from place to place].

[In my work, I built on the experiments I'd begun when I was first a soldier in Moscow and had used the newly discovered process of surface combustion to construct the small, high temperature furnace in our battalion's bathroom.] I tested the use of surface combustion again in Novgorod, where I built a fairly large furnace, but our move to Peterhof opened up especially favorable conditions [for my research]. In the private house I had for my own use, I had electric lights and could organize a small laboratory for high temperature experiments in metallurgy.

Nickel interested me. In Germany, France, the United States of America, Canada, and the rest of the world at that time, nickel sulfide was refined in two steps. It was first converted into nickel oxide and then reduced with carbon into metallic nickel, a complicated process. I decided I would simplify the process and reduce its expense. I wanted to obtain in a single step, pure nickel from nickel sulfide or Monel metal sulfide (a natural alloy of nickel containing 30 percent copper).

This would be a significant invention in itself, but [I was additionally motivated by circumstances.] Nickel was necessary for

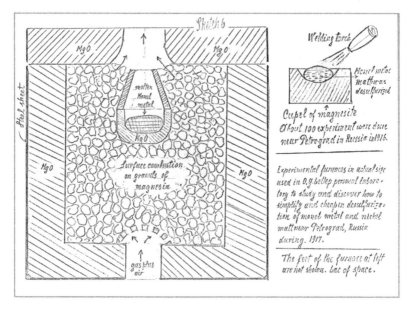

16.1   Sketch 6: Furnace for nickel experiments in Peterhof

Russia's war efforts since it encased rifle bullets and was used in armor, but all of it had to be imported from the United States. [What if I could simplify the production process and make it possible for Russia to produce its own nickel?] My superiors in Peterhof would not have anything against my experiments. Perhaps they would even have supported me.

I made a modestly sized, fairly useful furnace in my house in Peterhof. It utilized surface combustion and had an inside volume of only about two liters. I filled the interior with small pieces of magnesite and placed in it a small crucible for melting and holding about 30 grams of nickel metal. I could observe the surface of the melting nickel from the top of the furnace through an opening [that let me see into] the white hot cone of magnesite covered by grains of magnesite.[3]

I did a few experiments in my Peterhof furnace using an optical pyrometer to measure the level of heat inside the crucible. [Unfortunately], these tests required considerable time. My Jewish assistant, a graduate engineer who served as a common soldier, suggested that for heat I instead try the kind of oxy-acetylene flame that's employed in welding. [Agreeing, I turned to] the repair shop at the automobile school, where I ordered containers with compressed oxygen, acetylene, and a welding torch with rubber tubing. I had already gotten magnesite powder from England, and the repair shop also made the forms for pressing the small crucibles that would contain up to 50 grams of nickel.[4]

The production of nickel requires temperatures of over 1450°C, close to the melting point of steel, but using the welding torch, I found it easy to heat the crucible inside the furnace to nickel's melting point, and I was able to complete a precise experiment that included the regulation of the temperature in less than an hour. The furnace was a success, and I was pleased with my equipment.

I did about one hundred simple, quick tests in Peterhof, directing the flame of a welding torch on about 30 grams of nickel sulfide (N_2S) or Monel metal sulfide (its natural alloy), within the cavity (the "cupel") of a small piece of magnesite brick.[5] I melted the mixture and obtained matte, [a mixture of molten sulfides]. I then regulated the flame of the welding torch to the point of oxidizing, and it burned out most of the sulfur in about 30 seconds. When I reduced the flame until it slightly oxidized and then made it almost neutral, all the sulfur burned away, leaving either pure nickel or pure Monel metal. I was proud of obtaining such useful results from the simplest of equipment.

[A further explanation might be helpful to readers unfamiliar with the metallurgy of nickel. Dr. Roger Soderberg, a chemist, offers the following summary.]

> In Europe, Canada, and the United States, the common method of obtaining nickel from sulfide ores was a complex, multi-stage process. First, the sulfide ore, usually containing

a lot of iron and small amounts of copper and nickel, was "roasted"—heated in air to a high enough temperature to cause most of the sulfur to be oxidized to sulfur dioxide. Next, the resulting "matte," a mixed sulfide of uncertain composition, might be heated to its melting temperature and blown with air to remove the remaining sulfur. Silica (sand) and limestone might be added to remove most of the iron in a molten slag.

The resulting complex, mixed oxide of iron, copper, and nickel, might then be reduced carefully with carbon monoxide (produced by burning coke in an oxygen-poor atmosphere) in the presence of sodium hydrogen sulfate to give crude nickel metal—usually alloyed with some copper.

Otto's technique, proposed by his Jewish assistant, was to heat the matte with an oxygen-acetylene flame—at first adjusted to be oxygen-rich to remove the sulfur as sulfur dioxide and then adjusted to be neutral or slightly reducing (oxygen-poor) to produce molten metallic nickel or a nickel-copper alloy (Monel) if the sulfide ore contained appreciable copper. It is not clear how well this would work if the sulfide contained significant amounts of iron.

In Peterhof, I also made a small, electric melting furnace, which I kept in my apartment. [For the body, I used] a food can lined with magnesite powder. I equipped it with two horizontal electrodes. The electric current came from the wiring for electric lamps, which I regulated through a saltwater resistor in an insulated wooden barrel.

My little furnace consumed about one kilowatt of power, but I could use it to melt up to 50 grams of nickel sulfide at 1400°C to 1500°C. When I added nickel oxide, I caused a stormy reaction: $Ni_2S + 2NiO = 4Ni + SO_2$.[6] The result was so violent that some of the white-hot material overflowed and damaged the costly parquet floor of my room. A corresponding reaction between the sulfide and oxide of copper is widely familiar but no one knew of one for nickel. My discovery of this new, industrially profitable chemical reaction for nickel metallurgy [and the purification of nickel] made me very happy.

[One day,] I traveled by streetcar to the largest polytechnical institute in Russia, which was located in Lesnoi, near Petrograd. There, I visited a young professor of metallurgy. I became friendly with him, and he allowed me to try a few high temperature nickel reactions in his laboratory. We did quantitative analyses on the sulfur content of my samples of nickel, and I sent him other, Monel metal samples from my private laboratory in Peterhof.

[Meanwhile,] I also inquired at the Mining (Gornoi) Institute in Petrograd to see if there were any known nickel ore deposits in Russia. The answer was positive. It was generally known that some nickel ore had been found in the Urals, in the Serginski Ufaleiski District (SUD).[7] The general office of the SUD was also located in Petrograd, so I was able to talk with people there about my work in the German nickel plant and the faster, cheaper process of making nickel that I had discovered in my private laboratory. With their permission, and at my own expense, I made the long trip to the mining district to see about its nickel ore. This was during my summer vacation in 1915, and it took me four days to get there.

When I spoke with local management in the mining district, I not only confirmed the existence of nickel ore, but I received a few pounds of impure, unconcentrated samples. Returning to Peterhof, I prepared some pure cubes, about 1 centimeter in size: the first pure nickel ever made in Russia.

After I took my samples to the people of SUD's main office, they became interested in organizing a nickel production plant. A young professor from the Gornoi Institute in Petrograd was sent to the SUD to search for nickel ore and report on its location, kind, and quantity. In 1916, it became clear that there was sufficient ore of suitable quality to warrant the building of a nickel smelting plant as large as the one in which I had worked in Germany. Consequently, the main office of the SUD organized a meeting in Petrograd between the manager of SUD, a professor of metallurgy from the Gornoi Institute, and me. The purpose of our meeting was to discuss whether or not the founding of the first Russian nickel production plant was feasible, and if so, how it could be done.

I explained my six months of work in Germany and showed my drawings. I had complete, practical data, including the dimensions of the equipment, detailed sketches, and descriptions of the methods of operation. I also talked about the numerous small-scale, high-temperature tests I'd done in my private laboratory and mentioned my discovery of the means to shorten, simplify, and cheapen nickel metallurgy. I said I had applied to patent this improvement in Russia and the United States of America, and I concluded that there was full justification for building a nickel smelting plant in the Russian Ural Mountains.

The consulting professor from the Gornoi Institute in Petrograd viewed my suggestion as practical, but the manager of SUD saw many difficulties. First, there were as yet no detailed drawings of the equipment for two water-jacketed smelting furnaces and the furnace for desulfurizing the nickel sulfide. Neither was there a detailed drawing of the briquette press needed for compacting the nickel ore with gypsum. He mentioned that it would take about six months to work out such drawings. Then it would be necessary to find plants to build these machines. Because of the war, the machinery plants were overloaded with orders for the army.

I saw that the manager's objections were valid. For the time being, regrettably, it would be impossible to fulfill my hopes for the immediate construction of a nickel plant. However, I mentioned, the largest nickel-producing company in the world had its main office in New York City and the United States of America had in many ways supported Russia in the war against the German Kaiser and the monarch of Austria. [I knew that] one small New York skyscraper was full of Russian agents buying American supplies for [use in] fighting the Germans. Gustav Klaas, the Russian subject of Estonian nationality who became my best, lifelong friend, had been sent by the Russian government to the United States just to buy machines for the first large Russian automobile plant, which was located near Moscow. He did this supported by American, Russian, and English capitalists. Chrabrof, a Russian general, supervised the agents in New York.

I expressed my willingness to travel to New York at my own expense to explore the possibility of buying machinery for an SUD nickel production plant in the Ural Mountains. [In return,] I expected the main office of SUD in Petrograd to help free me from Russian military service, a very difficult task during the period when Russia was desperately fighting the German Kaiser.

SUD was willing to send a request to the central Russian military management, but it took many months for this to be routed through a number of offices. The final decision had to be made by a bureau under the direction of Czar Nicholas the Second, who was somewhere near the western front fighting the Germans, but finally, I was freed from the service.

[Meanwhile], my widowed sister Juuli had earned considerable money selling ladies' accessories in Tallinn and had moved to Petrograd to enjoy life in the capital city. She could speak Russian and German well, and she was also learning English. Her daughter Helene had finished her course in painting at the Institute of Arts. I decided to move from Peterhof to Petrograd, where I could live with my sister Juuli.

1. Otto dates these events from 1914–1917 elsewhere in his manuscript, but in the following chapter, he places his first attempt to travel to America in the year 1916.

2. A *polkovnik* is a colonel.

3. This is a confusing passage in Otto's text. Apparently, he used the pieces of magnesite inside the furnace for surface combustion, hoping he could attain temperatures high enough to melt the nickel in the crucible. He makes no prior mention of a "cone." He may have made a cone to hold a crucible, the cone itself may have served as the crucible, or he may have intended to write "cupel" (a container used for refining precious metals by melting them with hot air, thus oxidizing lead and other base metals).

4. I assume Otto had the crucibles made from the magnesite powder.

5. Otto must have intended to write "NiS" as the chemical formula for nickel sulfide.}

6. Dr. Soderberg finds no indication that sulfur exists as Ni_{2S}. The most common nickel sulfide is NiS. He believes the actual reaction may have been: $NiS + 2NiO = 3Ni + SO_2$. Theoretically, this could have been one way to purify nickel, but he is uncertain of its ultimate practicality.

7. The "Serginsko-Ufaleisky" mining district is in Siberia, in what is now called Nizheserginsk, not far from the city of Ekaterinburg, east of the Ural Mountains.

CHAPTER 17

Eyes on the United States[1]

1916–1917

Otto age 32-33: Petrograd, Torneo, Oslo, Trondheim, Germany,
Southern Norway, New York

While I was living in Petrograd, I practiced speaking English with some British officers living in the city. I also became friendly with a young lady of Finnish descent. After having spent many years in the United States, she was working as the secretary of an American businessman. We fell in love, and she was willing to marry me. *What should I do,* I wondered. In the midst of war and with my future unsettled, I had no financial means to start a family. I had to follow through on my plan to travel to the United States. It was painful for me and probably also for this good girl when I decided to leave.

Late in the fall of 1916, I made my arrangements to travel from Russia through Sweden to Oslo and then by steamship to New York City, [but this first attempt to travel to the US was affected by the war and Russia's increasing troubles]. The Germans and Austrians were defeating the Russians on all fronts. Under the leadership of the liberal prime minister Kerensky and the weak Russian czar, Nicholas the Second, the Russian government was unable to change the situation.

Because the Germans occupied the long Botnik Bay,[2] I couldn't travel directly from Petrograd through Stockholm to Oslo. Instead,

167

I had to make the long trip through Finland to Torneo,[3] on the northern end of the bay, and from there to Stockholm and Norway. Finally arriving in Oslo, I was told the direct journey to New York had been cancelled because the Germans had threatened to torpedo any Norwegian ships attempting it. I was very disappointed and had to make the long trip by railroad back to Petrograd.

Meanwhile, three years of war had used up Russia's resources. Germany and Austria were industrial nations with educated populations, but Russia was an enormous country of peasants, lacking the industries to supply cannons and rifles. The central government of the czar was unable to get its soldiers ammunition, or even food. In one extreme case, allegedly, Russian soldiers had to fight with wooden sticks against Germans bearing machine guns and cannons. Necessary discipline was lost. Angry soldiers revolted against their officers, tearing the epaulets off the officers' uniforms and chasing the officers away. Battles were lost to the Germans on the long fighting fronts.

During the winter of 1917, a revolution against the czar's government began in Petrograd. While I waited patiently for the Norwegians to obtain German permission for their ships to sail to the United States, I had the opportunity to see the development of the struggle between the Russian revolutionaries and the friends of the czar in Petrograd.

I observed open revolution. Soldiers rode on the main streets sitting in large trucks, their uniforms criss-crossed with the bands of cartridges they wore over their overcoats. I saw that the government of Prime Minister Kerensky had lost its authority. No one revealed what had happened to the czar.

In the large halls of Petrograd, the leaders of the revolution organized huge meetings of the common people. Young, capable, socialist-minded speakers gave fiery talks. They extolled the advantages of a socialist regime [to be achieved] in accordance with the teachings of Karl Marx. The rotten and unjust government of the czar would be replaced. The people would gain happiness through socialism.

For generations, most of the uneducated Russian peasants had been members of the Greek Orthodox Church, whose leader was the Russian czar. He had governed them for many centuries, and while I was in Petrograd, even during the revolution, a large number of them still believed in his authority.

One day, guided by an Orthodox priest of the church, thousands of the common people marched to the czar's palace. They were all believers, and they wanted to present the czar with a petition explaining how he, as head and leader of the common people, could save holy orthodox Russia from socialism. They asked the czar, with all his might, to save Russia from communism.

The huge mass of people moved gradually and slowly to the palace. Suddenly, quite unexpectedly, the soldiers guarding the palace opened fire on the trusting mass of the czar's followers. Many hundreds of men fell on the blood-stained ground. The large majority of people in Petrograd were becoming believers in socialism. The minority, believers in the czar, were killed in the bloody shootings.

I'd bought a number of booklets explaining the advantages of socialism while I was a student in Riga, but [at Clausthal] in Germany I'd stopped studying socialism and concentrated my efforts on technical subjects. I felt I could benefit humanity by creating useful inventions. I did not bother myself with Russian politics and did not know much about the tendency towards communism that was growing in Russia.

[In contrast], the thoroughgoing Germans had systematically followed the opinions and theories of the Russian revolutionaries. The kaiser's political advisers had studied the ideas of the Russian revolutionaries who lived in Switzerland, and they knew there was a radical leftist group led by Lenin. They also knew this group was an enemy of the czar. Germany had defeated Russia on the fighting front, but the country was still a monarchy. To defeat Russia politically, the Germans put Lenin and his friends in a closed passenger car and transported them [to Russia].

During the winter and spring of 1917, when I was still in

Petrograd, I and most Russians did not know where Lenin and his followers were. Lenin did not dare show himself because the friends of the czar would have killed him.

One day, on the street where we lived, a gunfight broke out between the revolutionary soldiers and the conservative czarist cadets who studied at a school for young officers faithful to the czar. During the battle, my relatives and I lay on the floor of the apartment to protect ourselves from the bullets. It became difficult for us to buy food, so, as a precaution, we bought a whole box of canned fish.

As a professional inventor, I kept a neutral attitude concerning the revolution.[4] Still trying to get to the United States, I wrote to a friendly soldier I'd known in the Russian automobile school. He was the son of Chrabrof, the general in New York who was managing the buying of war supplies for Russia. The son did not sympathize with the rebellious Russian soldiers, and he was willing to write me a letter of introduction.

Finally, in August 1917, I received a letter from the Norwegian shipping company saying that my planned trip to New York was possible. The Germans were willing to forego torpedoing the ship during its trip to the United States, so I packed my belongings and repeated the long railroad trip to Oslo. Arriving in the Norwegian capital city, I was informed that the start of the trip was somewhat delayed. We could not depart from Oslo but would have to leave from Trondheim, further north.

[Before our departure, I wanted to see] a [Norwegian] metallurgical plant producing nickel in Germany. It sold its metal to the Germans for [their] war [effort]. I had made arrangements to visit the plant officially. In addition, I also wanted to go for an unofficial visit to a nickel plant in the southern part of Norway.[5] Unfortunately, this was a poor decision. I hadn't made prior arrangements, and the Norwegians accused me of being a Russian spy. With some difficulty, I explained my special situation to the Russian consul in southern Norway. He himself was a Norwegian, and he helped me leave the country.

I had only a small amount of cash to use while I waited for a week to leave for the United States. During the war, I had saved some money, which I'd transferred to a New York bank. I had paid for a first-class ticket to cross the Atlantic, but before I could finally sit in the luxurious, first-class area of the ship headed for New York, I had to live in a cheap hotel and eat only bread and canned fish. Once we left, the sole other passenger in my small room was an agreeable young Norwegian student who intended to study anthropology in the United States.[6]

When I arrived in New York [at the end of August], my cash had fallen so low that I had to borrow ten dollars from the Norwegian student. My English was sufficient for me to telephone my dear Estonian friend, G. Klaas, but unfortunately he was away from his office. This gave me some time to visit a few streets in the most modern city in the world.

During my first walk in the splendid downtown district of New York, a well-clad young man joined me. "My uncle is the auto manufacturer Ford," he said. "I have some interest in the people arriving from Europe, and I congratulate you on your arrival in New York." I doubted that a young man with a millionaire uncle would be interested in me, so I excused myself and entered a nearby hotel, where I mentioned the peculiar person claiming to be Mr. Ford's relative. When I returned to the street, the alleged nephew of Mr. Ford had disappeared. I was happy to be rid of the swindler.

After that incident, I looked at a map of downtown New York and went to the office of my lifelong, best Estonian friend, G.F. Klaas. He was a manager and had four employees who helped him select and send machines to Russia for its auto plant. I saw for myself the skyscraper on Madison Avenue where he, Chrabrof, and the other Russians worked.

1. Renate:
    Having grown into adulthood during the Cold War years, I was at first confused by this chapter. I had long thought of Russians as opponents and had seen my father as Estonian—never as Russian. Yet here, my father is,

by circumstances, undeniably Russian. Further, he is describing and experiencing battles in which Russia is the vanquished, though in the largest political context, by virtue of its allies (England, the US), the country was among the victors.

2. Otto's "Botnik Bay" must be the "Bothnian Bay" that is bounded by Finland on the east and Sweden on the west.

3. "Torneo" is today's "Tornio."

4. Otto's conscious decision to think of himself as an inventor, not a patriot of any particular country, is evident in his complete silence regarding Estonia's successful attainment of independence from Russia in 1919. (See Chapter 18.)

5. In his original text, Otto writes: "There was a metallurgical plant producing nickel for Germany. I had made arrangements to visit this plant officially. The nickel produced there was sold to the Germans for war purpose[s]. Besides visiting one Norwegian nickel plant officially, I found there was another nickel plant in the southern part of Norway that I also wanted to visit, but unofficially." I think Otto meant the reader to understand that the first plant was Norwegian.

6. Renate observed: "This was an interesting foreshadowing of the future, when Otto had two sons-in-law who were anthropologists." And, it might be added, a daughter, since Renate herself has done fieldwork throughout her adult life. She obtained a doctorate in anthropology from Rutgers University and is the author of *A Simple Matter of Salt: An Enthnography of Nutritional Deficiency in Spain* (University of California Press 1990).

CHAPTER 18

In New York and Pennsylvania

1917–1923

Otto age 33-39: Bronx; Maine; Bethlehem and Egypt, Pennsylvania

Gus Klaas, my Estonian friend, was the son of a skilled blacksmith who lived in the Russian capital city and later in Sevastopol,[1] on the Black Sea.[2] Klaas' parents were capable and energetic. His mother's business selling milk had enabled his parents to give their three girls and Gus university educations.

I had come to know Klaas when he was studying electrotechniques in Germany and I was learning metallurgy at Clausthal. I visited him when he had his first paid position as an electrical engineer in Duisburg, Germany, and, during the time of my military service, also saw him in Moscow, where he worked in a steel mill not far from the city. Later, I visited him in Petrograd, when he was manufacturing shrapnel bombs during World War I. It was a great pleasure to meet him again in the United States. Huge orders for machines and materials worth millions of dollars, all intended for the Russian automobile plant in Moscow, were passing through Gus and his fellow Russian agents in New York.[3]

Klaas was acquainted with a leading group of intellectual Russians. Among his friends were a world-famous Russian pianist,

Madame Dontchakova; a professor of biology at Columbia University; and [Igor] Sikorski, a renowned inventor of airplanes.

I visited Sikorski on Long Island. In Russia, he'd built a twelve-passenger airplane, the largest in the world at the time. Escaping from Russia, he'd come to New York without a cent. With small means, he and a group of poor Russians organized themselves in a shop on an abandoned Long Island farm and started to build the prototype of an airplane he designed. Their first plane crashed [and smashed] to pieces. Undiscouraged, he improved the design and built a second, successful version. After that he [worked with] American capitalists in Connecticut, where he developed a helicopter that found worldwide use. Perhaps he is now a millionaire.

I had come to New York to inquire about the nickel industry in the United States and Canada, [so after my arrival, I set to work]. As a Russian citizen, I wanted to be useful first to Russia. I had the letter the young soldier Chrabrof [had written on my behalf, which I got into the hands of] his father, General Chrabrof. I also traveled to Bethlehem, Pennsylvania to visit Professor Richards, whose textbook I had studied in Claustal. He kindly listened to me talk about the simplified method of nickel making I'd discovered. Talks between me, General Chrabrof's office, and Professor Richards lasted some time. [In the end], the general informed the International Nickel Company (Inco) of my invention, and Professor Richards wrote me a letter of introduction to them.

One day, I went to the Inco office on Wall Street, taking Professor Richards' letter with me. Though I told the personnel there of my discovery, they were suspicious of me because I had studied in Germany and showed them some German literature. Given that Germany was at war with Russia, and Russia was supported by the United States, the Inco people may have thought that I was or might become a German spy.

[Soon, my circumstances changed.] In October [1917], the US papers carried news of surprising and sad developments related to

18.1   A photo taken by my best friend Klaas, in his office in New York, shortly after my arrival in the United States in 1917. I was thirty-three and look quite self-confident, despite the fact that all my big plans in Russia were ruined. [Renate: "The curl above Otto's forehead is striking and puzzling. Why the curl? Was it fashionable? And yet Otto never cared about fashion."]

the Russian revolution. The monarchy in Russia had prevailed about eight hundred years, but it had become weak and incompetent, and it was replaced by the extreme socialism of the communist regime of Lenin. The communists made the family of the Russian czar their prisoners and sent them under strictest guard to the Ural Mountains, about four day's train ride to the east of Petrograd.

The radical shift from the monarchy to the regime of the extreme communists did not please the democratic government of the United States. All connections with Russia were interrupted, whether by telegraph or post. I was convinced my invention was sound and that its demonstration and realization on an industrial scale could bring me a decent sum of money, but the plan to build a nickel plant in Russia had clearly become impossible. As an immigrant to the United States what could I do? I was happy I had earlier transferred a few thousand dollars to a bank in New York.

[After some thought], I decided to try to sell Inco my nickel invention by building a very small electric furnace at my own expense and demonstrating my idea to them. When I enquired of a professor of metallurgy at Columbia [University], I received a friendly response. He permitted me to use the metallurgical laboratory at the university, provided I built the furnace and its components myself.

The professor's laboratory was almost free of students and offered sufficient room for my experiment. [I intended to duplicate the results of my work in Peterhof, where I'd combined nickel sulfide and nickel oxide to create pure nickel.][4] Taking a round, flat can used for fish conserves,[5] 11 centimeters in diameter and 7½ centimeters high, I cut the tin sheet, steel casing in half and lined it with magnesite powder moistened with linseed oil.

I used two carbon electrodes 0.8 centimeters in diameter and regulated the 110-volt laboratory electric current in a salt water resistor. At about 1500°C, it was easy to bring up to 40-gram charges of nickel sulfide and nickel oxide to a violent reaction that could be confirmed by the production of ill-smelling SO_2 gas. The design

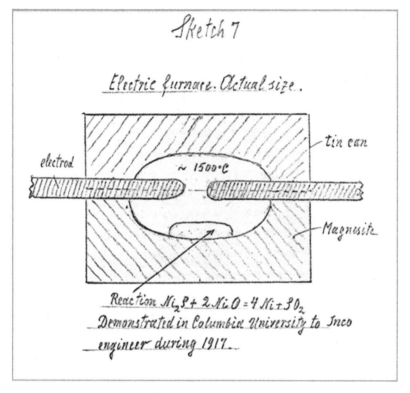

18.2 Sketch 7: Electric furnace for nickel experiments at Columbia University

of the furnace and the equipment to control its temperature were extremely simple, but doing everything with my own hands—inventing the devices and finding the best way to operate them—required about a month of arduous work.

I informed the engineers at Inco that I had built an electric furnace at Columbia and had repeated my experiments proving that the reaction between nickel oxide and nickel sulfide would produce metallic nickel. I asked them to come see me demonstrate my discovery. I was sure this reaction would reduce the cost of nickel production, but [as of April 1917], the United States had entered the war. With the French and the English, the Americans wanted to defeat the German kaiser.

The engineers from Inco finally came to Columbia. I heated my little electric furnace to a white-hot temperature and pushed in the prepared pellets of nickel oxide and nickel sulfide. The reaction could be seen through an observation hole in the side. As soon as the temperature reached 1500°C degrees, a violent reaction occurred, metallic nickel was formed, and foul-smelling sulfur dioxide gas escaped from the furnace. I added more nickel oxide pellets until the reaction stopped. After cooling the furnace, we found around 40 grams of nickel metal on the bottom.

I presented samples of the nickel, nickel oxide, and nickel sulfide to the Inco representatives as controls and asked them what they thought of my invention. "Your demonstration is quite interesting," they replied. "But what can we do with it now? The United States has entered the war against Germany. We have to produce nickel for the war effort, and we have no time for the development of your invention."

I was bitterly disappointed. My first few months in the United States had definitely been unsuccessful. First, the communist revolution in Russia had destroyed my hopes of organizing the first nickel production plant in Russia. Second, my demonstration of the new nickel production process had not interested Inco. Third, my savings in the bank were gone.

My position appeared almost desperate, but thinking things over, I realized I had a few advantages that most immigrants did not: I had my training as a metallurgical engineer, I could speak and write English, I had made my first invention, and I was in good health. Then came a positive idea: advertise in a metallurgical trade publication for employment!

For many years in Russia, I had been an interested reader of the *Journal of Mining and Metallurgy*. I therefore advertised in the magazine as follows: "Metallurgical engineer who has built with his own hands a number of experimental high-temperature furnaces is looking for a suitable position." After a few days, I received an offer from the Surface Combustion Company, which was located in the

Bronx, an uptown section of New York. After a short talk with me, representatives of the firm offered me a job testing and experimenting with industrial furnaces. I was very happy!

The Surface Combustion Company was a young and relatively modest business that built small industrial furnaces. Most were for the hardening of steel tools, which were heated to an exact temperature and then suddenly cooled in water. Heat hardening furnaces, and others, were designed, built, and tested in the plant for acceptable performance before they were shipped out.

The company's business was based on the principle of surface combustion, which had been discovered by Professor Lucky of Columbia University. When an almost theoretical mixture of gas and combustion air contacts a porous refractory material, complete combustion occurs almost instantaneously, and very high temperatures on the surface are obtained.[6] A well-known example of this takes place on the porous, finger-shaped net of thorium oxide that can be observed in street lamps, where the temperatures of the net can be 1600°C or higher.

I was pleased by how effectively the functions of the company were coordinated. [Working to meet] each customer's instructions, engineers calculated how large the furnace had to be, its highest and lowest gas consumption, and what kind of gas burners were needed. After draftsmen created drawings based on the engineers' specifications, the construction shop used the drawings to build the furnace. Testing engineers put it into actual operation to determine whether or not it satisfied all the requirements of the buyer.

[I was employed by the Surface Combustion Company from 1918 to 1923.][7] In my first job there, I worked with an experienced engineer, testing gas burners. I was then transferred to the engineers' room, where I sat at a table and calculated the size and number of gas burners needed in various furnaces. After one or two months, I was sent out to customers to install the furnaces in their plants and get them running. This took me to various New England cities and pleased me very much. I enjoyed the opportunity to observe life in different areas.

During my first year of employment, I received two raises in salary, an indication that the company was satisfied with my work. [I was fortunate, but] the Russians who had been paid by the czar's government fell into a miserable situation once the czar's regime ended and the sale of American goods to Russia was halted. Happily, my friend Klaas had worked with an English firm helping to build the auto plant in Moscow. He had saved a substantial amount of money and, with the permission of the firm, was able to travel to England to clear his account. [When he came back], he started a business in New York, [though] that did not please him.

For a while, when I was at the Surface Combustion Company and Klaas was unemployed, we lived in separate rooms in the same house on the west side of New York. He had a small sailboat that we could use as a rowboat on windless days. We could prepare our own food on board, and we sometimes spent a few hours on the ocean.

One hot summer, in about 1919, Klaas and I had the happiest vacation of our lives. We were uncomfortable living in New York, so we decided to arrange for a two-week holiday in the cooler climate of Mount Desert Island, off the coast of Maine. When we arrived on the island, we hired a driver with a horse and carriage, and we loaded on our belongings and a rented boat. The driver was a local man, so he knew that the beautiful, hilly spot we found on the coast was free for camping. Various berries grew there, and it was entirely empty of other people.

Klaas put up his tent, and we carried our boat close to the water. Our fishing lines had three hooks, and the fishing was so good that we caught three fish at a time. I am not exaggerating, as you can see by the photo of me posed with over a dozen fish by my side. Gus was a diligent cook. He worked in front of the tent, which we hardly needed since it did not rain. We picked berries, and no one disturbed us.

Klaas was also a fine sailor, improvising a sail out of a bed blanket. One day, we rowed about a mile out into the ocean. Suddenly, a storm arose. Our little boat was in real danger of sinking in the

18.3   On Mount Desert Island, we hired a man with a horse and carriage to carry our belongings and the rented boat.

18.4   Proof that the fishing was excellent

18.5   Klaas cooking in front of his tent

18.6   A sail made from a blanket

18.7 Klaas and I on the water. [Renate: "I wonder why Otto is wearing a tie!"]

waves. We were lucky to return alive, but in spite of [the danger], this vacation was the most satisfying of all our long lives.

After World War I, because of a serious economic depression throughout the world, the Surface Combustion Company lacked sufficient orders, [and I lost my job]. [I found a new position through] a Mr. Lesley, who was one of the stockholders of Surface Combustion. [Robert W.] Lesley was called "the father of the United States cement industry" and was apparently a millionaire who owned a splendid mansion and a park in the fashionable outskirts of Philadelphia.

I'd met him once at the Bureau of Mines in Pittsburg when I was demonstrating a very small gas-heated furnace I'd built. The furnace could produce exceptionally high temperatures and was even capable of melting platinum.

Mr. Lesley hired me as an efficiency engineer for his Giant Portland Cement Company in Egypt, Pennsylvania.[8] There, I learned that heat utilization in rotary cement kilns was extraordinarily low: about one half of the total heat input escaped unused into the stack. Mr. Lesley asked me to give speeches at two meetings of the Portland Cement Association, one in New York and a second one in St. Louis. He wanted me to call attention to the poor heat utilization in cement burning. I told the listeners that something should be done to decrease the waste.

With Mr. Lesley's support I built an experimental shaft kiln for efficient heat utilization in his cement plant, but my experiment was interrupted due to insufficient funds. I had lived modestly and had saved money, so during the summer of 1924, I rented a stable at my own expense. I put in a few windows, and Klaas came from New York to install electric lights and power for two little electrical fans that I used to create compressed air for my two test furnaces. I hired an Estonian student from Harvard, Woerman, the son of a pastor in Estonia, as an assistant for my research and workshop.[9]

While I was employed at the cement plant, I continued with tests in my private laboratory. I used one furnace that was six square decimeters in cross-section to study the flame of powdered coal. In another, I burned small cubes of an unburned cement mixture into good cement with low fuel consumption. I blew powdered coal into the furnace with compressed air and moved the cement through the horizontal section by using a steel stick poked through a small hole in the furnace wall. I cooled the white-hot cement clinker with incoming cold air in the cooling section of the kiln.[10]

I had a hard time regulating the furnace but I did produce some well-burned clinker. I learned one important fact from these

18.8   *My personal laboratory when I was a research engineer at the Giant Cement Company in Egypt, Pennsylvania. The electromotor driving the air blower is on the left. The cone containing powdered coal, which was burned as fuel in the small experimental cement-burning furnace, is on the right. The experiment was only partially successful, showing that the exit gases heated by a flame of 1000°C in a rotary kiln could be used to preheat a layer of pelletized raw cement 15 centimeters thick. The exit gas was transmitted with 92 percent efficiency.*

inexpensive experiments: the heat in the kiln's exit gas was well utilized by my preheating a layer of small cement cubes 15 centimeters thick. (This later helped me develop the fundamental concept of the Lepol kiln, which in one plant in Paris later produced 2,000 tons of high-grade cement daily, with almost one half the usual fuel consumption.)

[I also continued to think about nickel.] My first demonstration of the simplified production process I'd discovered was not sufficiently convincing, since I had produced only about 50 grams of nickel metal per charge.[11] I wanted to demonstrate success with a one-hundred-times-larger charge, using a cheap gas for fuel rather than [employing] electrical energy as a heating agent in order to create about 5 kilograms of metal.

Working for the Surface Combustion Company, I had acquired practical knowledge and experience in building and operating industrial furnaces. For my renewed effort with nickel, I built a round, flat-bottom furnace with an outside diameter of 35 centimeters and a height of 18 centimeters. The furnace was lined with magnesite and heat insulated with a porous refractory. Its top was detachable and had a round hole in the middle for the exit gas.

From Inco, I ordered sufficient nickel copper matte, a sulfide of Monel metal containing about 65 percent nickel and 35 percent copper. [See glossary.] I used two tangential gas burners to direct a flame upon the liquid surface of the metal. As before, I melted the matte, raised the temperature to about 1450°C, burned out the sulfur with an oxidizing flame, and converted the Monel metal matte into ductile Monel metal in a single process.

I had a very difficult time getting a competent person from Inco to come see my simple and more convincing experiment, but I felt justified in calling Dr. Merica, the director of research there. "I am a metallurgical research engineer who has worked many years to simplify and cheapen the production of Monel metal," I told him. "After a number of unsuccessful tests, I am now able to convert Inco's Monel metal matte into pure ductile Monel metal. I can do this in your presence at Columbia University."

1.   Sevastopol (now "Sebastopol") is on the Crimean peninsula.

2.   A brief biography of Klaas appears in "Estonians in Southern California."

> Gustave P. Klaas was born in 1882 in St. Petersburg (later Leningrad). His parents, both Estonians by birth, had migrated to Tsarist Russia, and had eventually settled on the Crimean peninsula. Gustave Klaas had acquired his higher education in Germany. He became an electrical engineer and worked in several places in Southern Russia. The living conditions during World War I in Russia were such that he preferred to go to America. While he was on his way to America he had to travel via Estonia where he stayed for two days. These were the only days he spent in his ancestral land. From 1916 to 1923 he worked in New York. In 1924 he arranged for his widower father the passage from Sebastopol, Russia to Alhambra, California. His father died in 1952 at the age of 98. In 1937 Klaas constructed

in Alhambra what was in that time the largest stress-relieving oven in the oil industry. He also made several discoveries in oil cracking technology, which were of military importance. He became an ardent supporter of the Estonian House of Los Angeles (INCD-AS).

By Walter E. Niilus (LA LEP 2017; http://lalep2017.com/wp-content/uploads/2017/01/EstonianHistory-SC.pdf), accessed on August 2, 2018.

3. Gustav Klaas is mentioned in "Men of the Iron Trade," an article published in *Iron Trade Review* (Vol. LIV, No.13) March 26, 1914: "Gustav Klaas, a noted mechanical engineer of Riga, Russia spent the week of March 16 in Cincinnati, inspecting the different machine tool plants in that city. Mr. Klaas will attempt to introduce American made machinery into Russia extensively upon his return to that country." (https://books.google.com/books?id=3SBKAQA AMAAJ&pg=PA582&dq=gustav+klaas&hl=en&sa=X&ved=0ahUKEwiHjt OJ3MLcAhVMs1kKHXVDCXEQ6AEIODAD#v=onepage&q=gustav%20 klaas&f=false), accessed on July 28, 2018.

   Klaas is also mentioned in the *The Iron Age*, Vol. 97, June 22, 1916, p. 1532: "Some extensive buying is being done by the Russo Baltic Carworks Company, 1 Madison Avenue, Room 242. . . . John Karmazin, 650 Madison Avenue, New York, with whom is associated Gustav Klaas, has been purchasing for the Moscow Automobile Works, Moscow." (https://books.google.com/books?id=Ot2Juxbi0WcC&pg=PA1532&dq=gustav+klaas&hl=en&sa=X&ved =0ahUKEwjEkLL92MLcAhXKtlkKHTQjCE8Q6AEILzAB#v=onepage&q=gu stav%20klaas&f=false), accessed on July 28, 2018.

4. See Otto's description of the original experiment in Chapter 16.

5. From Otto's description and sketch, this could well have been a large tuna fish can!

6. In an email to K. Noda (November 21, 2017), B. J. Bernard, president of the Surface Combustion Company explained:

   A theoretical mixture of gas and combustible air is the mixture required to fully combust the gas (e.g. convert the gas and air to nitrogen, carbon dioxide, water vapor, and heat) based on stoichiometry. For example, for methane (the principal component of natural gas), the theoretical mixture is approximately 1 part methane to 10 parts air. The theoretical mixture is different for different types of gas. [Stoichiometry: "The relationship between the relative quantities of substances taking part in a reaction or forming a compound, typically a ratio of whole integers." (Oxford English Dictionaries)]

   In 1915, natural gas was not readily available. Manufactured gases, such as "producer gas," "water gas," and others, were the primary gaseous fuel sources in cities. These gases had much lower heat content than natural gas and were difficult to fully combust. With the advent of surface combustion, these fuels were able to be fully combusted more easily.

For your reference—the inventor of surface combustion was Charles Edward Lucke [Otto's "Professor Lucky"]. He was the head of the Department of Mechanical Engineering at Columbia University. In the UK, William A. Bone, a professor at the University of Leeds, independently discovered surface combustion. I do not know who the inventor in Germany was.

Lucke and Bone came together to form the Surface Combustion Co. in New York City in 1915.

7. Dates from Otto's resume. (See Chapter 28.)

8. In 1883, Robert W. Lesley formed the American Improved Cement Company (AICC) in Egypt, about seven miles from Allentown, Pennsylvania. The AICC and the Copley Cement Company combined their assets in 1914, resulting in the Giant Portland Cement Company. The company established a major production plant in South Carolina in 1947 and closed its plant in Egypt in 1969. (Giant Cement: About Us," from http://www.giantcement.com/corporate-information), accessed August 2, 2018.

9. In his text, Otto dates his experiments with the Harvard student as occurring in 1924, but he also describes the work that followed this, at Inco, as beginning in 1923—a date confirmed by his resume.

10. Otto put a raw mix of ground materials, probably including limestone and clay, into his high-temperature, experimental furnace, where the heat and agitation caused them to sinter (coalesce) into clinker—incombustible matter that is fused together in lumps or nodules, such as the residue of burned coal.

11. To "charge" a furnace is to load it, so one "charge" is one furnace load.

CHAPTER 19

Cuba, Inco, and Readiness for a Wife

1923–1926

Otto age 39-42: Cuba; Huntington, West Virginia; Copper Cliff, Ontario; Tallinn, Estonia

Dr. Merica promised to come for my demonstration at Columbia, and I invited my friend Klaas to serve as my co-worker during the test. We charged into the furnace the pieces of broken Monel matte (a sulfide of the metal) that we'd received from Inco. Dr. Merica took samples of the charge. After the metal became molten at about 1450°C, I made the flame an oxidizing one. Immediately, it became difficult to breathe because of the ill-smelling sulfur dioxide exit gas. As before, I made the flame less oxidizing after about twenty minutes and later made it neutral. About half an hour later, the samplings became quite ductile. They could be bent to 180 degrees without breaking.

Dr. Merica witnessed the simplified process and took some samples of the Monel metal. The next day, I gave him a pound more of the results of the experiment. "I can't tell you today what the company thinks of your process," he said. "Come back in a month and we'll be able to give you our opinion." This satisfied me.

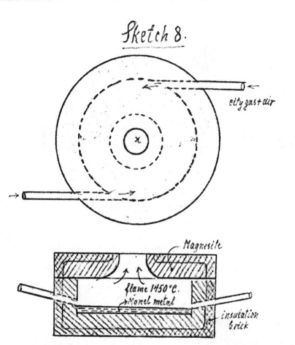

Sketch 8.

city gas + air

Magnesite

flame 1450°C.
Monel metal

insulation brick

In my private laboratory in Peterhof near the russian capitol city Peterburg, after about 100 experiments I had discovered that Monel metal matte (⅔ nickel, ⅓ copper) could be freed from sulfur in much simpler way than used in nickel industry. After patenting my invention I intended to demonstrate the useful idea to the director of research, Doctor Merica of International Nickel Co. I built in Columbia University a small demonstration furnace for 5 kg of Monel matte. The above sketch is 3½ times smaller than my furnace. After repeated invitation Dr. Merica came to see my new simplified and less expensive method.

19.1   Sketch 8: Demonstration furnace built at
Columbia University to refine nickel

*19.2   My best, dear friend Gustav Klaas
during our trip to the Isle of Pines*

With the expectation that Inco might be interested in the further development of my simplified production method, I made a lengthy trip from New York to Havana with Klaas. We took a steamship, which was pleasant for both of us, but especially for sailboat-owning Klaas.

Klaas and I lived in a small hotel in Havana. We took numerous walks to see the city and the old fortress near it, which had extremely thick walls to protect it from cannon balls. We also enjoyed the city

19.3   *Me, in a quiet cove on the Isle of Pines. The swimming was not quite safe because of sharks.*

parks. Outside Havana, we swam in the ocean, though there was some danger from sharks.

When Klaas and I took longer trips into Havana's tropical surroundings, we saw large areas planted in sugar cane. Cutting off pieces of the cane, we chewed the sweet substance inside. At a large, modern mill, trainloads of sugar cane were cut and pressed until the sweet juice ran out. Large boilers concentrated the liquid, and raw sugar crystals were formed. American capitalists owned the sugar cane fields and the huge sugar mill.

Life in the large city of Havana in the midst of the tropical heat did not particularly interest us. We wanted to know how people lived in the country, so we moved over to the Isle of Pines, a small island close to Cuba.[1] There we lived in a little guesthouse, where we also had our meals. At the weekly market, we saw huge toads, many kinds of tropical fruits and vegetables of all colors—red, blue, and white—and colorful tropical fish. Everything was sold at very reasonable prices. We'd never before seen such sights.

When we walked or drove into the country, Klaas and I passed fruit and vegetable farms. I saw how clusters of bananas were grown, and how the tropical climate allowed for the production of lettuce, tomatoes, and cucumbers, which could be exported to nearby America for a good price. We tried our luck with fishing rods we bought, and we actually caught some small, red fish, which we fried over a fire we made by the shore of the ocean. Because of the warm weather, we bathed in the water, too, but when we talked about it at the guesthouse, people told us we were lucky. "The big fish and crocodiles could have eaten you up," they said.

Klaas and I were told about an enterprising American man, "Jungle John," who lived about ten kilometers away from the village on a piece of fertile land he had bought and developed into a very interesting farm and business. I hired a cab and rode out to visit Jungle John and his establishment.

Jungle John grew many kinds of topical fruits, plants, and trees. A small creek ran through his property, where he'd built a simple house. He showed me his home, which contained all he needed for his simple life. I saw many books about tropical plants and trees and a desk with an organized file for letters. He corresponded with a number of people and institutes in the United States in order to exchange or sell tropical plants and trees.

[Before I left], Jungle John showed me a particularly interesting tree. It produced yellow balls of about 15 centimeters in diameter, inside of which were hundreds of small cacao beans. After fermentation, the beans were separated from the useless substance around them, dried on tables in the hot sun, and sold for a good price.

Our vacation in Cuba lasted about one month. Klaas had grown up on the coast and preferred a direct return to New York on an ocean steamer. I wanted to go through the various states south of New York, which I had never seen before. I took the short trip by steamer from Havana to Tampa and then travelled by train through Georgia, Virginia, Maryland, and New Jersey.

Looking out the train window, I saw a landscape that in many cases indicated poor living conditions. The houses were old and primitive. I was surprised that some people seemed to live in poverty.[2] My trips as an engineer of the Surface Combustion Company had exposed me mainly to the New England states, Pennsylvania, and New York, where the people generally lived in more prosperous surroundings.

Upon my return, I learned that my demonstration of the desulfurization of Monel metal matte had convinced Inco that my process could eventually be useful to them, and they hired me as a consulting engineer at a high salary. I accepted the contract as they formulated it. If a test on a larger scale confirmed the good results demonstrated in the 5-kilogram capacity furnace at Columbia, Inco could buy my patent rights for $20,000. The buying power of $20,000 at that time was approximately equivalent to that of $60,000 today.

Inco decided I should conduct further tests at their plant in Huntington, West Virginia, on the Ohio River, and I began my work there in 1923. The Huntington plant received its raw product from Copper Cliff in Ontario, Canada: a brittle sulfide of Monel metal

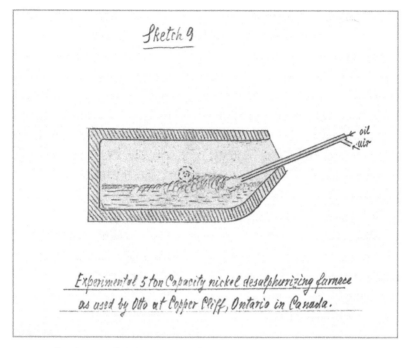

19.4   Sketch 9: Nickel de-sulfuring furnace created at Copper Cliff, Ontario

consisting of about two-thirds nickel and one-third copper sulfide. The metallurgical task was to convert the sulfur-containing matte into a sulfur-free, strong, and ductile Monel metal.

Over the course of a year, the capacity of my testing furnaces gradually increased from 5 kilograms to 110 kilograms, and later to 1,000 kilograms. The Monel metal I made in my top-blown 100-kilogram capacity furnace was so ductile that a 6-millimeter wire could be drawn from it. [I] made a knot from this wire and mailed it to Inco in New York. Someone hung it on a wooden board on the office wall of the chief engineer, a Mr. Thompson, as a sign of the successful tests at Huntington.

Inco suggested that I continue my experiments on a larger scale at the main Inco smelter at Copper Cliff.[3] The manager of that plant was a practical executive who'd had no engineering education. Without consulting me, he had bought an old, used, side-blown, 5-ton converter for my large-scale tests. At that time, the large-size steelmaking Bessemer converters were all bottom blown.[4] I saw that converters of 100-ton capacity or larger were used for practical, large-scale work at Copper Cliff, and in my mind, a side-blown converter was unsuitable for my new process. The question of whether the converter should be bottom- or side-blown did result in a disagreeable discussion with the manager at Copper Cliff, [but] I simply proceeded with my idea of a bottom-blown converter.

My experiments at Copper Cliff required two years of work. During that time, we found that it was impossible to eliminate the sulfur to zero percent in the Monel metal that was our final product. We had achieved such a result at Huntington using sulfur-free natural gas, but only fuel oil was available in Copper Cliff, and it contained a small percentage of sulfur.

Because of the presence of sulfur, the end product of our tests at Copper Cliff was unsalable. Additionally, we could not compete with the Swedes and Norwegians. They had developed an electrolytic process for separating copper and nickel from Monel metal. This left a bottom sediment containing precious metals of the platinum group and brought an extra profit we could not offer.

[Given the circumstances], I discontinued my experiments at Copper Cliff. Since Inco could not use my simplified process—in 1926, they actually bought one of the competing companies owned by the Swedes and Norwegians—they did not pay me the full sum we had originally agreed upon. Instead of $20,000, I received only $10,000. Fortunately, I had also saved that much from my high monthly pay during the three years of my work, so I had total savings of about $20,000, the equivalent in buying power of $60,000 today, [in 1971].

Traveling from Canada to New York City, I allowed myself a two-week vacation in the beautiful Adirondack Mountains near

Lake Champlain in New York. There, I thought about my fortune. I felt I had saved enough money to marry and establish a family, and I decided that after nine years of work as an engineer in the United States, I would visit my dear native country Estonia and find my future wife.

I left from New York by steamer bound for France, then traveled [by train] through Paris and Berlin to Lübeck. From there, I took a steamer to Tallinn. Arriving at the harbor in Tallinn, I met a woman who told me she had recognized me on the steamer, though she hadn't approached me. About twenty years earlier, when I lived on my father's farm in Estonia, she was the daughter of a neighbor, a girl famous as a talented student. She'd studied in Switzerland, and as the capable writer [known as] Helene Taar,[5] published interesting stories in Estonian newspapers about her eventful, happy student life abroad. Helene had married an Italian professor, and they had come back to vacation on her father's farm, Nuia, near my birthplace, Ripsi.

1. The Isle of Pines (now Isla de la Juventud—the Isle of Youth) is about sixty miles off the south coast of Cuba.

2. After growing up, traveling, studying, and working among white people, Otto may have seen black people in New York City—or not. Although he must have been exposed to large numbers of them in Cuba or in the southern United States, he never mentions race in his descriptions of people or travel. This contrasts with the many times he notes the Jewish identities of colleagues, professors, friends, and fellow soldiers.

3. Inco's "Copper Cliff" operations were located in Sudbury, Ontario.

4. In the Bessemer conversion process (see Introduction), the impurities in iron are oxidized by air that is blown through the molten metal, either through the bottom or the side of the converter.

5. Helene Taar obtained her doctorate from the University of Bern in 1912, writing a dissertation titled *Die beiden Schlözer (The Two Schlözers)*, probably an examination of August Ludwig von Schlözer, a German historian with an interest in political science and statistics.

CHAPTER 20

In Tallinn:
A Tumbling Invention

1926–1927
Otto age 42-43: Tallinn, Berlin

I was glad to be back in my native country, particularly in Tallinn, its capital city. My brother Willem had become a prosperous businessman and had built himself a large house, where he lived with his wife and three sons.[1] His wife arranged everything to please me, and I spent many happy days there.

After my arrival, I made a trip to Pärnu, the summer resort city on the Baltic Sea where my capable and successful widowed sister Juuli lived with her daughter, Leeni. They had rented a house close to the beach. It was very pleasant to see my beloved relatives. [While I was there], someone introduced me to a pretty girl on the beach.

After a few happy days in Pärnu, I returned to Tallinn. Given my nine years of a very busy life in the United States, I now decided to take a few restful weeks and do nothing. To my surprise, the planned "do nothing," lazy weeks had a negative effect on my health. I felt almost half sick! As a result, I decided to find an interesting task that would keep me busy—something in the line of new inventions.

I knew there were reasons for improving large, industrial furnaces. As I've mentioned, while I worked in the cement plant in

Egypt, Pennsylvania, I learned that 30 to 50 percent of the heat in the existing rotary cement kilns was wasted in the high temperature of their exit gases. I had twice presented reports at meetings of the Portland Cement Association, emphasizing that changes could and should be made. I'd started to work on solving the problem during the summer [of 1923 or 1924], when I'd hired the Estonian student from Harvard [to help me], and I decided to take it up again.

I needed space for experiments, and I had to invent, design, and build the necessary equipment. My sister-in-law left a room in the cellar of the house free for my use. It had electric wiring. Willem borrowed a special quicksilver thermometer from a friend so I could measure the temperature of exit gases during cement burning.[2] It read up to 400°C. I had previously bought a small, high-pressure fan able to produce pressure up to 400 millimeters water gage,[3] but such fans were not available in Tallinn. I had to make a drawing of one and have it built in a local machine shop. I myself knew how to build simple orifice meters for measuring flowing gas and gasoline. [In preparation, I also] ordered a full barrel of dry, raw cement mixture from Asserin, a dry process cement plant in Estonia.[4]

After the tests I'd run in my laboratory in Egypt, I knew that for efficient heat utilization, the exit gases of a kiln had to pass through a thin layer of small pellets made of the powdered raw mixture of cement. My brother Peter had many talents, and during the winter of 1926 when he came from Narva to visit us in Tallinn, I asked him how he would produce small pellets of powdered, raw cement in mass quantity. "Otto," he said, "I have seen how a candy manufacturer transformed a fine powder of sugar into nice, small, round pellets. He used a rotating drum, charged the sugar into it, and moistened the powder with a spray of water. The pellets were formed through the tumbling of the powder."

Peter's suggestion was excellent. Soon afterward, I had a rotating drum built. Willem's son Endel turned it with a crank, and when we sprayed the raw mixture of cement with water, we easily converted it into small pellets. They were the size of large peas and could be made even bigger. I called them "granules."

From 1926–1927, I continued my experiments in Willem's house to find ways and means of utilizing the exit gases from rotary cement kilns. The test furnace and the instruments I'd obtained made it possible for me to measure the heat of the fuel input, the temperature of the exit gases, and the weight of the cement granules before and after the test. After I'd analyzed the data of a number of experiments, a very happy idea came to me in bed early one morning after a good night's sleep. I could combine a shortened rotary kiln (with exit gas temperatures of around 1000°C) and a traveling grate carrying a layer of raw mixture cement pellets. Before the pellets entered the kiln, I could use a fan to pull the hot exit gases through them. This would radically improve heat utilization in the rotary kiln.

My first attempt to burn a 20-centimeter layer of raw cement pellets into cement was a total failure, but [I did not give up]. As a forty-two-year-old, practical man, I tried to think realistically about the development of my exceedingly promising idea. The little hand-rotated drum for pelletizing the moistened cement raw-mix powder was not yet a readily available, practical machine, but in my mind, I saw that a power-rotated, lengthy cylinder with a slight inclination toward the outlet end would be quite possible. An automatic stationary scraper inside the drum could remove the moist adhesive raw mix layer [from the sides].

I had an experimental version of the rotating drum built in a shop and mounted on four wheels outside on Willem's property. It included a spraying pipe with drilled holes for water drops and a stationary scraper to remove the raw mix adhering inside. Willem's son Endel provided temporary power. Using one hand, he rotated the pelletizing drum with a crank. Using the other, he shoveled a regulated amount of raw cement mix into the drum.

My engineering calculations and experiments showed that fuel costs could be cut considerably through the combination of the rotary kiln and the traveling grate. The large cement mills near Egypt had red-hot exit gases of 800°C in the stacks at various times [during production]. By effectively utilizing exit gas heat, I reduced the final temperature of the exit gas to 100°C in the pot furnaces filled with pellets in Willem's basement. Visualizing an application for this economical method of cement burning in many countries of Western Europe and the United States, I applied for patents in both Germany and the United States.

Meanwhile, in Tallinn, I became friendly with the young, pretty lady I had met at Pärnu on the beach when I first arrived. She had grown up in an educated, prosperous Estonian family. We had many talks while we drank tea in her apartment, and she visited me in Willem's house. Our friendship was never too intimate. Even kissing was strictly forbidden.

The young lady probably had some hope of marrying me, but various considerations caused me to painfully break off our relationship. I knew from the three years of work on my first invention that a fundamentally original idea, such as a new process for the production of nickel or cement, would require large capital and years of arduous work on the part of the inventor. In addition, there was a fifteen-year difference in our ages.

Thirty years later, [in the 1950s after the end of the war], I met a relative of the young lady. [I learned that] she had escaped to Germany when the Russians invaded Estonia in 1941 and lived in the city of Dresden.[5] During the Second World War against Hitler, the United States and England destroyed Dresden by bombing. This good girl was one of the thousands who were killed during the bombardment.

Given my discoveries at my brother's house in Tallinn, I decided to write to Mr. Lesley, who was known as "the father of the cement industry in the United States" and who was part owner of the cement plant in Egypt, Pennsylvania. My process promised to radically reduce fuel consumption in cement burning, but fuel—coal, as well as oil—was about twice as cheap in the United States as in Western Europe. When I asked Mr. Lesley if he or his friends were interested in developing my new idea he answered me negatively.

[While I was still in the United States, in 1923], I had become a US citizen.[6] Now I decided to leave Estonia [again] and try my luck at developing my invention in Germany. Traveling through Berlin, I looked up a world-famous German professor who had written a huge textbook about Portland cement and who was teaching in the largest university near that city.[7] I talked to him about my invention and gave him a short report about my promising results in Tallinn. "I had similar ideas about cutting the fuel consumption in cement burning," he said, "but, to be frank, I do not think much of your idea." Still, he was kind enough to add, "Try your luck with the German companies that are building machinery for cement mills." He gave me the names and addresses of five such firms, the Polysius Company in Dessau among them.

I went to see the agent and representative of the Polysius Company in Berlin and told him about my invention. His answer: "This idea and invention is old and worth nothing. But I am not an engineer. Send the description of your idea and the test results to the company in Dessau. Expert engineers there can understand and evaluate them properly."

1. Otto never mentions that Willem was living in an independent Estonia.

2 Quick silver is mercury.

3. Water gage (w.g.) is a measurement commonly used for small pressures (eg. 400 mm w.g.).

4. Asserin was founded in 1899 in northeastern Estonia. It was primarily owned by banks in Russia, and its Portland cement was exported from there. After Estonia's independence, exportation ended, but the domestic market was too small for Asserin and its rival, the Kunda mill, and Asserin gradually ceased production in the late 1920s. ("Estonia 1929: Portland Cement Works Asserin Ltd," Scripophily, accessed August 3, 2018 at https://www.scropolhily.fi/product/30147/)

Renate:

>"Asserin is in or near Narva, perilously located on the border, under threat by the Russians, Soviets, and now the Russians again. Narva figures importantly in our family history. From the Lellep Family Archives, we know that Alice (Veinbergs), daughter of Otto's brother Jüri (the botanist), grew up and studied as a schoolgirl for at least a number of years in Narva during the Estonian's first independence."

5. The Soviets occupied Estonia, Latvia, and Lithuania in 1940—and again in 1944 and 1945 when they re-took the region from the Germans, holding it through 1990.

6. Otto makes only glancing reference to his decision to become a US citizen. In 1923, Estonia was an independent nation. Renate notes that his decision in the United States perhaps indicates his sense that his commitment to a future as an inventor would necessarily take him away from his homeland. In addition, he probably also understood that further restrictions limiting immigration to the United States were soon to be enacted. In 1917, the country had imposed a literacy test and tax on new immigrants, as well as barring entry to those from the "Asiatic Barred Zone." Passage of what became the Immigration Act of 1924 was in the offing. That act further limited the number of immigrants permitted entry and completely excluded people from Asia.

7. From Otto's letter of October 9, 1945 (Lellep Family Archives), we can guess that this was probably Professor Kühl of Technische Hochshule Charlottenburg (now the Technical University of Berlin).

CHAPTER 21

Success and the Edge of Bankruptcy: The Lepol Kiln

1927–1930
Otto age 43-46: Dessau and Rudersdorf, Germany

The day after I sent my letter, a telegram summoned me to the Polysius Company. There, I talked to a competent engineer who understood the importance and significance of my invention. He informed the two Polysius brothers of my arrival.

The next day, I found a rotating drum and made a pailful of raw mix cement pellets in the experimental workshop at Polysius. The *granalien*, [granules], as I called them, were from 6 to 10 millimeters in diameter.

Pail in hand, I entered the best reception room of the firm. Both owners of the firm and their top engineers sat in soft armchairs around a large conference table covered with a red cloth. I introduced the name *granalien*, which was new. Karl Polysius, the younger owner, took a piece of the moist raw granule between his fingers and said: "But these will crack to pieces in the heat of hot gases!"

I had a piece of very thin steel wire in my pocket. I bent it into a loop to support the granule and heated it in the flame of a match. It did not crack! This was a simple, convincing demonstration. The Polysius firm and I [then] worked out an agreement for decent remuneration. I would help develop the idea of the rotary kiln combined with the traveling grate for preheating the pellets. If the idea proved successful on [a small], then industrial scale, the Polysius firm would have the right to produce the grate kiln system by paying me $50,000. (The buying power of $50,000 in 1927 was about as much as the buying power of $125,000 today [1969].)

Forty-three years ago, [in the late 1920s], a normal cement kiln in Germany produced about 300 tons of cement every twenty-four hours (9,000 bags per period). No firm would be willing immediately to build a new invention on such a large scale. It was decidedly safer to start with less expensive, smaller units, so I became very busy testing equipment at Polysius to see if my concept was actually feasible.

We first constructed a small, inexpensive rotary kiln, 3.5 meters long and 0.7 meters in diameter, with a traveling grate 0.6 meters wide and 1.6 meters long. Tests at Dessau using the kiln and grate were successful. Combined, the two burned 360 bags of cement a day.

This convinced us that the concept of the Lepol kiln was sound,[1] but the output was too small to interest cement manufacturers. To persuade them, we had to demonstrate success in an actual cement plant with an industrial scale Lepol kiln that could produce one hundred tons (2,000 bags) of high-grade cement per twenty-four hours while consuming half the typical amount of powdered coal, which was the usual fuel.

The Polysius Company had connections with a cement company in Rudersdorf, near Berlin. The two companies agreed that Polysius could construct a plant at Rudersdorf at their own cost.[2] With the usual German meticulousness, a committee from the German cement industry organized the operation and the later measurement of fuel consumption in the kiln we built. Ten members of the industry from Western Europe were invited to observe

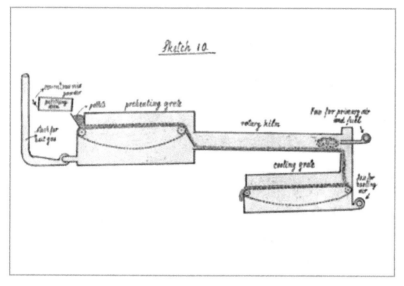

21.1   *Sketch 10: A sketch of an early Lepol kiln*

its testing. The results were fully successful, which gratified me and the Polysius Company.

After my successful demonstrations of the Lepol kiln at Rudersdorf, I freed myself from regular work at Polysius. In my modest living quarters in Dessau, I decided to work out a longer analysis and written description of how the idea of the Lepol cement kiln had grown in my mind. [I used this as my] doctoral dissertation from the Institute of Technology at Brunswig [the Technische Universität Braunschweig].[3]

I began my dissertation by remembering my work as a student at Claustal, when I was actively interested in the efficiency of industrial furnaces. In the report I had done before receiving my engineering diploma [in Germany], I had described the design of the wood-fired regenerator furnace in the copper plant in the Ural Mountains and how the total heat generated by the burning of fuel, the so-called "heat balance," was utilized in different functions and parts of the furnace. My last task at Claustal had been to develop a little furnace with recuperative air preheating, but it reached

Wärmetechnische Untersuchungen
über den Wärmeaufwand beim Zementbrennen
Verbund-Rost-Drehofen

Von

Dipl.-Ing. Otto Lellep
aus Alt-Woidoma (Estland)

von der Technischen Hochschule Carolo-
Wilhelmina zu Braunschweig zur Erlangung
der Würde eines Doktor-Ingenieurs genehmigte

Dissertation

Eingereicht am 11. April 1930.

Berichter: Professor Dr.-Ing. Ernst Terres.
Mitberichter: Professor Dipl.-Ing. Richard Düll.

1930

21.2   *[Otto's dissertation has disappeared from the Lellep Family Archive,
but a photo of the cover remains.]*

temperatures so high that the preheating porcelain tubes melted together. My idea was impractical.

In my work as an efficiency engineer in Mr. Lesley's cement plant in Pennsylvania, I saw how approximately half the total heat in rotary cement kilns was wasted in hot stack gases as high as 800°C. I was very happy the morning at Willem's when the idea came to use the wasted heat and the rotary kiln stack gas for preheating a layer of pelletized cement raw mixture. Through tests and development work in my little laboratory, I demonstrated clearly that the large amount of heat in the exit gases of numerous rotary cement kilns could be utilized with 90 percent efficiency by passing them through a thin, 15-centimeter layer of small granules or pellets on a traveling grate connected to the upper end of a rotary cement kiln.

[Meanwhile, at some point], the Polysius Company sent a letter that made me happy. Based on the successful tests of the small, industrial-size Lepol kilns near Berlin, the company had sold six normal-size kilns in Germany, Switzerland, and Spain. Each kiln had the capacity to burn from three hundred tons to five hundred tons of cement per twenty-four hours. Customers were attracted. They could cut their fuel costs by half and pay for the kilns from their savings in about two years.

Although the first experimental Lepol kiln at Rudersdorf had worked without difficulty for five weeks, the six Lepol kilns sold in Western Europe exhibited serious problems—an unexpected handicap for me, as well as for Polysius. The pellets, or granules, cracked in the 1000°C flame over the grate in all the Lepol kilns we'd sold, and the crumbled pieces and powder filled the spaces between the pellets, preventing the passage of the exit gases and hindering the operation of the furnace. The temperature of 1000°C in the gases appeared to be too high.

The cement plant operators of the new Lepol kilns complained bitterly to the Polysius Company about the impossibility of operating their new kilns. The company did not know how to alleviate the trouble, endangering the good reputations of the firm and myself, as the inventor. The complaints were so serious that a younger member of the firm almost wept, [moaning] "We are bankrupt!"

[In response], Polysius hired a capable young engineer named Bernard Helming,[4] the son of a family of medical doctors, and took me back, as well. Helming and I had to work full speed to find a solution. We ordered samples of the ground raw cement mixture from all the plants where the pellets on the grate had disintegrated. First working together during the day, we later split up. With me working alone in the day and he alone at night, we found that the raw mixture from the plants differed. The pellets made from the Rudersdorf raw mix hardly cracked, in contrast to those from the plants in Switzerland, France, and Spain.

Helming and I found a solution. The cracking of the moist pellets could be prevented if they were not submitted [subjected] to the 1000°C gases suddenly but were pre-dried for about one minute in gases of low temperature—about 300–400°C. This necessitated a change in the design of the furnace surrounding the traveling grate. Instead of using a single, large chamber, we divided the kiln, creating a small, pre-drying chamber with the lower temperature and a longer chamber with the higher one. Our solution was a bitter pill for the company to swallow because of the unforeseen expenses, but no other answer was feasible, so it introduced the expensive improvement. After that the kilns worked satisfactorily.

The Lepol kiln reduced fuel consumption radically, [putting] the Polysius Company in a position to profitably sell about one hundred of them before World War II. The firm's financial standing improved considerably, and they paid for my invention in accordance with our agreement. This also improved my financial standing.

[Throughout the time I worked on developing the Lepol kiln, I remained single], in part because I thought my savings were insufficient to support a wife and children. But as the strength of my finances began to seem assured, I turned my mind toward what had been one purpose of my trip to Estonia [in 1926]: to find a suitable wife.

1. The name "Lepol," is derived from LEllep and POLysius.

2. The industrial-level kiln was built at the Heidelberg Cement Company in Rudersdorf. See Appendix 2 for photographs illustrating the work on the kiln. A "graduate engineer" named Maier helped Otto test and improve the kiln there. Otto later met him again in Argentina, where Maier worked as manager of a cement plant. (See Chapter 29.)

3. Otto mentioned to Renate repeatedly that he gained his doctorate as an "independent student" (independent of attending any classes). His PhD diploma exists in the Lellep Family Archives.

4. Renate:

   > Bernard Helming was Otto's most important friend as I was growing up. In my late teens, I watched Mutti preparing care packages to mail to her bombed-out sisters in Rostock and probably to the Helming family. Thinking of the Helmings' need to flee from Dessau in East Germany to Neubeckum in West Germany after the end of World War II, and remembering Bernard Helming's efforts as described above, Otto must have been led to speak repeatedly of their friendship when I was a teenager."

   Later, when Otto worked for Allis Chalmers, he invited Helming to help him and the company adapt his revolutionary traveling grate for the processing of taconite. During and after the war, Otto never failed to promote Helming and the Polysius Company whenever he could.

CHAPTER 22

Decision to Marry

1927–1930
Otto age 43-46: Lüneburg Heath and Dessau, Germany;
Riederalp Switzerland

When I was in Germany, it was customary, as it is now, to seek a wife via advertisement. My ad in the *Berliner Tageblatt* read as follows: "Graduate engineer 43 years of age is looking for a partner. Wealth not important." I received sixty replies! Reading the letters, I found that most of the respondents were unsuitable. I met the three most suitable women individually on walks in the beautiful, large park in the center of Berlin.

The best of the three [respondents] was a charming lady of appropriate age, a bookkeeper by profession and intelligent and capable, it would seem, from her conversation. She had only the usual common school education, but her innate ability was more important to me than her formal education. I met her on Sundays in Berlin or Dessau.

All my life, I had been occupied primarily with my work as an inventor. The attention and duties of courting a lady remained in second place. Wanting to see how I would get along with the lady from Berlin over a longer period of time, I was friendly with her for about two years, but my devoted work and testing of the Lepol kiln at Rudersdorf required my full time and energy, leaving me no time for her. She felt neglected.

OTTO'S ADVERTISEMENT IN ENGLISH

Little classifieds. *Life Reform.* Freiburg [Baden] April, Ostermond [Easter month] 1929[1]

Graduate engineer. Inventor and researcher. Age 44. Oddball, eccentric who's committed to his work, sacrifices most everything to it. Has inhibitions and weaknesses, nevertheless is creative and not without success. Reflective of Nordic brooding spirit, hates glamour but is ambitious. Socially timid, a life-affirming friend of Nature. Profession requires frequent displacements from home. Freethinking European, American citizen, long a resident of Germany. Materially secure. Dreams of intellectually developed life partner, modest home-maker, feminine, agreeable. Age, between 30 and 40. Reply to 657 *Life Reform.* Meet: Berlin.

Renate remembers: Sitting at the dinner table as a teenager, I heard the story of Otto's ad several times. Otto acknowledged his belief that no woman would be interested in a man of forty-five or older. He had no tolerance for inaccurate measurements in his technical work, but he allowed for playfulness or slippage regarding his age. At the time of the publication of the ad, he was actually forty-five.

I was given to understand that the paper's name in German was *Reform.* Its readers were forward-thinking, liberals—largely nudists and vegetarians. Kacy Peckenpaugh, our translator, notes that the German in Otto's ad is sophisticated, full of literary devices and clever turns of phrase. Charming though it is in English, the translation, in her view, reflects the facts but not the style and artistry of the original.

[Had we married], my life with the Berlin lady would not have been free from conflicts. I knew that she'd had a similar period of friendship with another person before me. She lived with her widowed mother in an apartment crowded with furniture and she liked to eat in costly restaurants, while I preferred simple but nourishing food.

[Further], during twenty-four years of ripe, unmarried manhood, I had arrived at the policy that my work as an inventor should not be hindered by the duties of family life. My lady friend could not accept this or excuse my attitude, and we came to a painful break in our relationship. I had never promised to marry the lady, though she expected marriage. When I broke off, I gave her a substantial financial settlement.

At the time, there was a small monthly paper, [*Life Reform*], published in Germany that encouraged higher ideas in intellectual life. It suited me, so I advertised my desire to marry there. I received twelve replies, three of which seemed worth a personal interview.

The third woman, Frieda Aina Brandt, seriously interested me. Her father had been born into a family of educated forest supervisors and first owned a large but unprofitable farm in East Prussia. After her father sold the farm, he became the proprietor of a wholesale store for food products in the city of Lübeck, in West Germany.[2] On her mother's side of the family, Frieda Aina's great-grandparents were Huguenots, members of a strict religious sect who [fled] to the Netherlands and Germany when they were persecuted by the Catholics in France.

Frieda Aina had been educated in a special school for the daughters of prosperous families. She helped her father in business for a while but later decided to enter a school that trained nurses for a large, city hospital in Dortmund. Frieda Aina worked as a nurse and at some point as a housekeeper, but her purpose in life was to be useful to humanity, and she found a job working and teaching in a school for the rehabilitation of city girls who had gone wrong with men.

I met Frieda Aina at the special school for the rehabilitation of girls. It was located in a hard-to-reach place preferred by people who liked the freedom of an undisturbed, almost uninhabited environment. Lüneburger Heide, the Lüneburg Heath, had its own beauty.[3] During Biblical times, the prophets educated themselves in such an environment.

For my visit, Aina took a day off from her duties. We went for a long walk in the peculiar, somewhat beautiful landscape. We

May 8, 1929[5]

Dear Miss Brandt,

I am the "eccentric" ["Sonderling"] who advertised in the April issue of *Life Reform*. Given your written response to me of April 11, I see that you are living an uncommonly rich life; one that is of interest to me. I would be very pleased to have the opportunity to know you as a wife and as a human being. I do not fully meet your expressed wishes regarding your desired partner, however.

I am a native Estonian. My hometown is Reval [Tallinn], but I am now a citizen of the United States. For the past two years, I have been living in Germany, where I have previously been a student. Currently, I am intensely engaged in the practical application of concepts I've developed related to cement furnaces. My work with a German global company (G. Polysius A.G. Dessau) is not without success. The company has staked 200,000 RM on my ideas. Recently, I have been unrelentingly focused on this most interesting project. [*Otto's personal ad in* Life Reform]

I may not be robust in terms of health, but no illness limits my activities. I have avoided tobacco and alcohol and could forgo meat in the event plant-based foods are available.

You dream of a harmonious, married relationship with a person who has also concluded that work alone is not ultimately fulfilling. An unforeseen opportunity can bring me to Hamburg. Should you still have an interest in the "eccentric," I would be pleased if we could meet. I would like to call you.

Respectfully,

O. Lellep

exchanged frankly the stories of our lives. We were experienced people: I was forty-three years old and Aina was six years younger.[4] Through our conversation, we rapidly got to know each other, and we were mutually attracted by the simplicity of our lives. As a cautious person, I could not promise Aina anything definite after a one-day visit, but we exchanged addresses and began to communicate by correspondence.

Frieda Aina left a serious impression on me, and I wanted to get more closely acquainted with her. Though I was working in Dessau on my doctoral dissertation, I wrote her a letter and invited her to spend a longer vacation with me in Switzerland's mountains. She accepted my invitation.

Frieda Aina and I met in Frankfurt and traveled together to Geneva, Switzerland. We made short stops in two cities on Lake Geneva, where we rowed boats and swam in the clear water. Deciding to spend a few weeks in a higher mountain resort in order to avoid noisy city life, we selected Riederalp, a village at a one-kilometer elevation near the Rhone Valley, opposite the Simplon tunnel and near the great Aletsch Glacier. A glacier is a slow-moving stream of ice that descends from a mountaintop to the deep valley below over a period of several hundred years. Scientific calculations show that the Aletsch Glacier took about three hundred years to travel from the top of the mountain to the deep Rhone Valley.[6]

Frieda Aina and I rode into the valley by railroad and bought food sufficient to last us several days. Loaded with heavy sacks of supplies, we intended to walk to a small settlement on the right side of the glacier, rest there overnight, and reach Riederalp on the left side of the glacier the next day. We wanted to avoid the easiest route and experience a walk over the ice at the widest part of the glacier.

It is dangerous to cross a great glacier such as the Aletsch, which has crevices, or fissures, and deep holes. One can fall a hundred feet into the ice without being able to get out. Like many other visiting guests, we hired an experienced local guide. He provided each of us with a strong girdle and securely fastened each girdle to a long rope. If anyone fell into the ice, the rest of us would be able to pull the person out. Our dangerous and difficult crossing required a few hours. When we reached the other side, we found the nearby Riederalp without difficulty.

22.1   Renate: [*"My mother and her sisters nursed soldiers who had been gassed in World War I, but Mutti told me that she left nursing and then served as head house-keeper in an east Prussian mansion. To offset her loneliness at her austere place of employment, she cultivated the friendship of a crow. When she bicycled to work, her pet crow flew above her, likewise accompanying her later in the day on her return home. Florence Nightingale had a pet owl, which may have inspired Mutti to form this consoling friendship."*]

I was glad to find that, [like me], Aina was able to appreciate long, difficult trips through high mountains and that she was also satis-fied with simple, home-cooked food. She was an experienced hiker. As a young girl, she had been a member of a group of *Wandervögel* ("ramblers") who sometimes walked as far as Sweden during the summer.[7] We did not like sitting near our small, rented summer cottage but preferred, instead, to see more of the splendid mountains.

The end of summer provided Riederdalp with mostly sunny days. Aina and I hiked often, even when the walks were dangerous. Our long hikes gave us excellent opportunities to learn about each other's past lives, and since we met almost no people, it was not difficult to take nice, naked sunbaths. Once, we came upon a herd of cows feeding on fresh grass, supervised by a woman who milked them twice daily and prepared the internationally known Swiss cheese from their milk.

Our little summer cottage was not far from the place deep in the canyon where the Aletsch Glacier melts and changes itself into a small river during warmer weather. Traveling from the high mountains, the river contains in its tremendous volume everything that has fallen into the ice over the centuries: broken pieces of rock from the sides of the steep canyon, whole trees, animals, and even men who have died in the ice.

Late one afternoon, Aina and I decided to explore the river. In the bottom of the canyon, we saw much running water melted from the ice, and our feet soon got wet. There were unexpected sights, such as the clothing of hikers and some cadavers of animals and birds, though we saw no human bodies. We wanted to see more and climbed with some difficulty onto the melting mass of ice. The running water had bored a number of holes and crevices into its ten-meter-thick mass, and the openings we'd seen when we walked the glacier weeks before had become wider.

We hoped to be back in our little cottage before evening, but we were inexperienced travelers from the flat country, and we lingered longer than we planned. Soon—almost suddenly—the narrow canyon grew dark. We were on top of the ice close to the end of the glacier, with many dangerous, deep holes and crevices around us. A fall into any of them would cause sure death.

A cold wind began to blow over the surface of the ice in the canyon. Aina and I had assumed we would return home before sunset and had not thought to take warm clothing with us, so we had to face some unexpected suffering that night. As brave sports, we decided to stay where we were. We thought we would run in place from time to time to increase our breathing and cause the burning of some fat in our young bodies to keep us warm. A normal girl would weep in this miserable situation, but Aina accepted the misery stoically—an indication of a desirable character trait.

For about seven hours, Aina and I remained in the darkness and freezing cold. In the morning, we climbed the steep walls of the canyon and went back to our little cottage. Our neighbors had noticed our absence during the night and planned to organize help to save us, but we had already saved ourselves.

Aina and I vacationed in Riederalp for four weeks. This summer vacation one thousand meters closer to heaven was a great idea. It freed us from the usual worries of humanity. For exercise, we walked into the valley twice each week and returned with all the necessities we bought there in rucksacks on our backs. Our room had a wood stove for cooking, we carried sandwiches in our pockets for lunch, and we easily found spouts of drinking water. We lived freely.

I was glad to see that Aina withstood the difficult trips without complaints, and we learned to know each other very well. I did not claim to have lived as a holy man, and Aina, too, had some excusable experiences in friendships with men. I had not yet promised marriage, though I was convinced that of all my former lady friends, she was the best—healthy, uncomplaining in difficulties, and free from expectations of perfection. I knew some ladies expected their male friends to show attention only to them, as had my lady friend in Berlin. [I was not such a man.] Looking back on my own life, I saw that I had almost always been in love with some idea about a new invention, first in nickel metallurgy and now in burning cement.

Aina and I traveled back to our usual work in Germany by train

22.2 A photograph of Aina and me taken by a professional photographer shortly before our wedding day

22.3   I asked the photographer to take a photo of me as a professional inventor. He stepped close to me, turned up the collar of my coat, and asked me to look important. This is the result.

and separated at Frankfurt. We had grown to be good friends and remained interested in each other, meeting from time to time on weekends. She invited me to visit her widowed mother and two sisters. She also visited me in my quarters at Dessau,[8] where I continued to work on my doctoral dissertation.

[In December of 1929, Aina and I married] after we were examined by our doctors and found to be in satisfactory health.[9] [This was accomplished] without great ceremony by a municipal judge, before two witnesses. I rented a car, and we took a little wedding trip ten miles into a beautiful area surrounding an old castle. For dinner, I arranged to have a meal served to us and our witnesses in our new apartment, located in a quiet section of Dessau, close to the city park.

[In 1930], our first daughter, Liisa, was born in Dessau. My forty-nine page dissertation was published in German—*Heat Transmission in a Combined Grate Kiln for Burning Cement*—and I was granted a doctoral degree in engineering [from the Technical University of Braunschweig].

22.4   Otto and Aina, c. 1929. [Renate: "Maternal grandson Mickle [Michael] Maher chortles about this photo. Before he took the shot, the photographer put into Otto's hand a high fashion magazine—one which Otto would never have occasion to hold, let alone to read."]

1.   In German, the ad read:
     Kleine auskünfte Die Lebensreform Freiburg [Baden] April Ostermond 1929

> Diplomingenieur, Erfinder und Forscher, 44 Jahre, Sonderling, der in seiner Arbeit aufgeht, ihr fast alles opfernd, hat Hämmungen und Schwächen, jedoch schöperisch und nicht erfolglos tätig, grüblerische nordische Natur, hasst Schein und will was sein, gesellschaftsscheuer, lebensbejahender Naturfreund. Berufsarbeit zwingt zeitweise zum Verzicht auf ständigen Lebensort. Freidendenker Europaer, amerikanischer Staatsangehöriger, längere Zeit in Deutschland. Materiell versorgt. Träumt von gesunder, geistig entwickelter Lebenskameradin. Gewünscht schlicht Hausfraueneigenschaften, weiblich, vertraglich. Alter 30 bis 40 Jahre. Aüsfuhrliche Zuschriften unter 657 an die "Lebensreform" Treffpunkt Berlin.

2. Renate:

> My mother's father's store was not an ordinary one. Its name was *Kolonialwaren*, meaning food from abroad (from "the colonies"). It was located around the block from where Thomas Mann situated his fictional Buddenbrook family. It sold more expensive goods than did day-to-day grocery stores.

3. Renate:

> At home, Otto and Mutti spoke of the girls' school she directed as being located on the Insel Fehmarn, an island in the Baltic, only as of 1963 connected by road and rail bridge to mainland Germany. The Lüneberger Heide, where I gathered they walked during their courtship, is located many kilometers south of the island, on the German mainland.

4. Frieda Aina was born in 1892 and Otto in 1884, actually making her eight years younger.

5. Otto's letter to Aina in its original German:

> Zementfabrik Guttmann & Jeserich, Post Kalkberge bei Berlin
> d.8 Mai 1929
> Geehrtcs Frl. Fr. Brandt.
>
> Bin der "Sonderling," der in der Aprilnummer der "Lebensrefrom" annoncierte. Nach Ihren Schreiben von 11 April haben Sie einen aussergewöhnten reichen Lebenslauf, der mich interessiert. Gern möchte ich Sie als Mensch and Weib kennen lernen. Allerdings genüge ich nich ganz Ihrer Specification des erwünschten Mannes. Bin geborener Este, Heimatstadt Reval, Estland, jetzt aber Staatsangehöriger der Ver. Staaten Americas. Seit 2 Jahren wohne ich in Deutschland (wo ich früher studierte) und bin mit der praktischen Durchbildung meiner Zementofenidee intensive beschäftigt. Arbeit nicht erfolgslos mit einer deutschen Weltfirma (G. Polysius A.G. Dessau) die für diese Idee 200000 RM riskiert hat. Die letzte Zeit is eine aufreibende "Hetze" von interessantester Arbeit gewesen. Gesundheitlich bin ich nicht robust, doch hinder mich keine akute Krankheit in meiner Tätigkeit. Tabak und Alkohol vermeide ich.
>
> Träume von einer ertragliche Ehe mit einer Persönlichkeit die auch zur Ansicht gelangts ist, dass die Arbeit alllein nicht das Leben erfüllen kann.
>
> Unvoregesehen Zufall führt mich nach Hamburg. Falls Sie noch interesse fur "den Sonderling" haben sollten, bitte ich um ein Treffen. Eventuell rufe ich Sie telefonisch an.
>
> > Achtungsvoll
> > O. Lellep

6. Renate:

> Though it seems she may not have mentioned it, I know that Mutti had already been to Riederalp, because some years before Otto and she had

become acquainted, she sent her mother a post card from this village. Perhaps she quietly opted for what she knew was Otto's preference.

Mutti loved swimming in the cool waters of the Baltic and later in the cold waters of Lake Michigan. The temperature of Lake Michigan was shockingly cold to me—far beyond what I could tolerate.

7. The *Wandervögel* was a German youth movement begun in the 1890s. It attracted young people who scorned materialism and were drawn to hiking, camping, and an alternative life that was simple and close to nature. It did not become a politicized youth group until the late 1920s, under Hitler.

8. Otto actually writes that he was in Neubeckum, but this is the post-war location of the Polysius Company. He must have been in Dessau.

9. Renate remembers hearing that her practical, frank parents married after confirming that both were free from any sexually transmitted diseases. They then signed a written agreement affirming that if no children resulted from the marriage and either party wished to part, husband or wife could leave, free from recriminations or responsibilities for the ex-partner. The medical proofs of Otto's and Aina's good health still exist in the Lellep Family Archives.

CHAPTER 23

Two New Inventions and the Loss of My Savings

1930–1936
Otto age 46-52:
Gerresheim, Heidelberg, New York, Los Angeles, Mainz, Hösel

I had accomplished my inventive task—the successful creation of the Lepol kiln [for cement production]. This brought me sufficient income, so I decided to continue my work as an inventor. Having studied metallurgy as my specialty, I [thought I would] try my luck with the metallurgy of the steel industry.

Aina and I moved close to Düsseldorf, the center of the industry. We rented a large, quiet apartment outside the noisy city, near Gerresheim, on the ground floor of a big, solid, stone house. We were surrounded by a one-acre garden, through which the brook "Düssel" ran. I worked on my experiments in a small hut on the grounds, and our daughter Liisa learned to walk in the large garden.

The Lepol kiln was a success—the Polysius Company sold it all over the world—but the large, heavy, preheating grate inside the upper end of the rotary kiln made it costly. I decided I would try to invent a simpler, less expensive cement kiln, with a metal preheater for raw mix pellets inside its upper end. [I knew] I could construct one in our little house in the garden, so I hired an assistant who could build the necessary equipment according to my sketches. After I successfully developed the small preheater and tested it in a plant in Heidelberg, I applied for a patent in Germany. When I offered the rights to the Polysius Company at a reasonable price, they accepted them.[1]

23.1   *[Birth certificate of Renate Lellep]*

My second daughter, Renate, was born in Heidelberg in 1932, during my experiments there. As a citizen of the United States, I had been investing in American stocks and bonds. I was satisfied with my life. While I was wholly preoccupied with developing my inventions, however, the price of stocks and bonds went down, entirely unexpectedly. I'd had mine managed by a friend in New York, a retired professor of Harvard University, and in 1932, in the crisis known as the "Hoover Depression," he informed me that the value of my investments had dropped from $75,000 to $25,000.

[Feeling that I must leave Germany], I boarded a ship and met my friend in New York. He showed me that some investors had lost even more than I, and that in extreme cases, some unhappy people had shot themselves.

[From New York], I traveled by train to see my best friend, Klaas, in California, but worry about the unexpected loss of two-thirds of my capital caused me serious indigestion and illness. Treatment by doctors brought no noticeable improvement, and I wanted to avoid bothering my friend with my ill health, so I rented a small cottage in a quiet suburb of Los Angeles. There, though I had some difficulty buying food and cooking it, my body responded to a simple diet of orange juice and fresh, [raw] milk that I let sour. After my health improved somewhat, I recuperated further by moving into a house where my food was cooked for me.[2]

As soon as a new idea began to occur to me, I noticed further improvement in my digestion, [so I began to work]. The possibility of using a shaking disc placed below the outlet of a rotary cement kiln to cool the clinker looked promising. [I experimented by constructing] a round, wooden disc, set horizontally on a central bearing. With a sudden push by hand, I could shake it. Pellet-sized gravel that I fed into the center of the disc completely covered it, then fell from the circular edge as [I shook it].

Traveling back to Germany, I lived with Aina and the children not far from Mainz, where I built a shaking, round, clinker

23.2   [On the back of this photograph, handwritten: "Pilot." An early prototype? Undated.]

23.3   [On the back of this photo, handwritten in German, "Birth of cooling invention." On the front, "Turu!" ("Market!"). Undated.]

cooler in a cement plant near the city. During the testing period, I constructed and installed three coolers of the same type in a plant in the Ruhr district. My model was much cheaper than the usual rotating cylindrical cooler, [so] the Polysius Company bought the rights from me.

The metal heat exchanger in the upper end of the rotary kiln—the small preheating grate—and the shaking disc clinker cooler provided sufficient income for my family to live as modestly as usual. [What next?] I had studied in Germany and had married a German wife. Both my daughters were born there.[3] Germany had become my second home. Although I was a citizen of the United States, as a free inventor and research man, I preferred to live in Germany where my inventions were better known.

I [thought I would] try my luck at improving the processes used by the steel industry [to create steel from iron]. Gutehoffnunghütte (GHH) agreed to cover the costs of the experimental equipment for my research and to assign me a capable mechanic to build it.[4] In exchange, I gave them permission to utilize any invention I developed without payment to me.

For a short period, Aina and both my daughters lived near Heidelberg, but we wanted to build our own house and selected a site near a beautiful forest of fir trees [a mix of deciduous trees and conifers] at Hösel,[5] a settlement between Düsseldorf and Essen. During the winter of 1935 we moved into our new home.[6] I bought a motorcycle and traveled daily on an excellent superhighway to GHH at Oberhausen.[7]

1. The Lepol kiln brought great success to the Polysius Company in the pre-war years, and the company was able to re-establish itself strongly after the end of World War II. It was later absorbed by Thyssen Krupp, existing now as Krupp Polysius AG.

2. Renate:
    Otto's approach to his digestive system and that of others followed the

lines of his thinking about furnaces, grates, and kilns. In 1964, as hospitalized Mutti was dying and my sister and I were raising our young children in homes far from our parents, Otto described and pictured Mutti's digestive problems in diagrams similar to his own technical drawings and discussions. The information felt cold and distant to me, lacking in affect, as if Otto were describing a machine. (See Appendix 1, Otto's letter of June 20, 1962.)

3. Renate:

    Both my sister and I were US citizens, born in Germany, and clearly so. In 2019, however, I found in the Lellep Family Archive, numerous documents related to Mutti's education and professional work—letters of recommendation, diplomas, certificates of training—indicating, it seems to me, her feeling of uncertainty about her own status.

4. GHH began in 1782 as an iron working company—Gute Hoffnung Hütte—when the Ruhr area was first developing as an iron manufacturing center. It later merged with two other companies to become JHH, gradually expanding into construction, manufacturing (steamships, railroad tracks, etc.), ore and coal mining. In 1873, again as GHH, the company began to produce steel. In the twentieth century, mergers, de-mergers, outsourcing, and reorganization left only some divisions with "GHH" remaining in the name. (GHH Fahrzeuge website, http://www.ghh-fahrzeuge.de/en/company/history/. Accessed November 29, 2017.)

5. Renate:

    Comparison of forests and trees was a theme in our family conversations, often discussed during our walks in the public forest adjacent to our large garden in Hösel. Otto and Mutti told us how they used to walk *Unter Den Linden* ("under the linden") in Berlin as they were just beginning to get to know each other. Trees figured in many of their conversations and memories: beech, birch, linden, alder, oak.

    Our parents' focus on trees is a family legacy—a practice. We surreptitiously placed Mutti's cremains among the roots of the Sequoia sempervirens of Muir Woods, and we dropped some of Otto's over an iron bridge and into a small stream in the woods of the Institute of Advanced Studies in Princeton. In Fort Meyers, Florida, where Otto died, his niece Alice Veinberg had a plaque made in his memory, marking a tree planted in his name. Some of the ashes of Otto's grandson Kevin lie in Moab beneath the "Purple Robe" planted above, and the ashes of his mother, my sister Lee [Liisa], lie in Moab, too, beneath a white, flowering Satsuma plum tree.

6. Renate has vivid memories of the house in Hösel and the garden. Enamored of the Bauhaus, which had moved from Weimar, Germany to Dessau in 1925, Otto had his home built in Bauhaus-influenced style.

Renate:

The house stood on at least two hectares of land. In the distant part of the acreage, beyond the sandbox, beyond the cherry tree where we sometimes had tea and cake, and beyond the rhubarb, my parents planted a vegetable garden where we grew carrots, cabbage, and potatoes. Prompted by teachers but also encouraged by Hitler Youth ideals, we neighborhood children proudly picked potato bugs off the plants and put them into empty tin cans—as I saw Cuban children doing in 1990. The observation of the children on a guided Food First trip to Cuba could not help but bring to my mind my childhood family farm, reminding me of my father's audacity: the far-sighted conservationism that prompted him to have our septic tank pumped out to flood the vegetable garden with fertilizer and stink. The smell reached the neighborhood and may have had people whispering, "Ach, diese Kinder sehen so Amerikanisch aus!" ("Oh, these kids do look so American!") We were already beginning to be seen as alien, and his act probably confirmed it.

7. Renate:

We all rode the motorcycle. On Sundays, Otto put Mutti onto the small backseat, which measured no bigger than a letter-size piece of paper. There, Otto settled Lee (Liisa) onto Mutti's lap. I sat within Otto's bony embrace on the front seat.

Sometimes, Mutti and Otto took us to the Essen River, where the water flowed black with coal. My parents wanted me to learn to swim, so Otto tied me to a fishing pole and put me in the water. I remember I didn't like it. I probably got the black water up my nose and cried. Only after becoming a camper in Berkeley's municipal Camp Cazadero in Sonoma County, under the redwoods, did I learn to swim. There, I advanced through all the Red Cross stages of accomplishment, including the lifesaving class. Only now, decades later, do I realize that the effort I expended to achieve that swimmer's goal made up for the shame or envy I had felt as a child in Germany, excluded as I was from the effort and fun of after-school activities like tumbling and camp-fire-singing. I was *nicht Staats angehörige*, not a "German" citizen. As an *Amerikaner*, I was separated.

*23.4   Otto: The house that we built in the very beautiful community
of Hösel, between Düsseldorf and Essen, one-third kilometer from the
railroad station. We lived there over five years, and I rode my motorcycle
to GHH daily.*

[Renate: "This is the house where Liisa and I grew up. Otto's study was
on the second floor, surrounded by many windows. From it, Otto used
to be seen looking out over our large Hösel property and the adjacent
dark forest. It was bordered by *der Kohlstrasse* (Kohl Street) on one side
and *der Rotenweg*, a pink gravel path, on the north. Hazel nut bushes
bounded much of our property. I loved harvesting these nuts in their
green, pointy jackets, well before they were mature. In a letter written
in the early thirties to Mutti, Otto described these hazelnut bushes as
a special feature attracting him to bid on the property. Mutti created a
rock garden just below Otto's great array of windows and invited me to
weed it at one pfennig per hundred weeds, thus teaching me numbers.
With these first earnings, I selected and purchased candy as colorful
as some of the flowers in her rock garden—a garden she later much
regretted having to leave behind, hardly confident that the German
officers billeted in our house in early 1940 would keep it up."]

CHAPTER 24

First in the World

1936–1940
Otto age 52-56:
GHH in Oberhausen, Germany

Between 1936 and 1940, I did research at GHH. As my first task, I attempted to eliminate the expensive and complicated Siemens Furnace that was [often] used in the production of steel.[1] [I wanted to find a way] to avoid dependence upon complicated heat regenerators by melting cheap steel scrap into valuable steel in a furnace heated with an oxygen flame.

My concept was to heat the furnace with the hottest flame that could be tolerated by the refractory materials, using coke-oven gas and oxygen, for example.[2] I planned to utilize the exit gas to melt broken pieces of iron or scrap metal, which I would load into a short shaft [used as an exhaust pipe.] [Again, I would use wasted heat—this time, melting the scrap metal into a pool of raw iron in order to create steel.]

Since it was inconvenient to try to feed a laboratory-scale furnace with scrap steel, I built a 200-kilogram-capacity, round furnace with a short, central shaft through its vault. [In my experiments], I used two tangential burners for natural gas and oxygen to heat the round space inside the furnace.[3] [There], I melted pieces of solid raw iron and [heated] the bath to about 1450ºC. I charged the shaft with a hanging bundle of scrap steel rods, 20 millimeters in diameter. After a while, the bundle of scrap melted nicely, like rods of ice in hot air, and the steel slid down [into the melted iron]. The exit gas on top of the steel was at such a low temperature that for a short time, I could place my hand in it without being burned.

It seemed to me the experiment had proceeded excellently. Unfortunately, [to my shock], the cold exit gas began to burn, even though it contained no combustible substances when it left the interior of the furnace. [I discovered the reason] for the disappointment of my high expectations [in an unexpected chemical reaction] inside the furnace. There, the natural gas completely burned with oxygen and was reduced to water vapor and carbon dioxide. When brought into close contact with the red hot rods in the shaft, the products of complete combustion partially decomposed the exit gas according to the following reactions: $Fe+CO_2=FeO+CO$ and $Fe+H_2O=FeO+H_2$. The precious steel scrap had partially burned and [instead of becoming steel, it was transformed into] cheap iron oxide!

I decided to build a larger melting furnace of 1000 kilogram capacity and heat it without regenerators, using a flame of coke-oven gas with oxygen. To make a bigger stream of oxygen available without building an expensive oxygen plant, I connected about seventy ordinary oxygen cylinders to a single oxygen pipe. The coke oven gas pressure was too low, so I increased it with an available compressor.

I used two assistants for my experiment. They charged the furnace with pieces of scrap steel and cast iron in weighed amounts, and we preheated it to about 1500°C during the night. One burner shot a theoretical flame of coke oven gas and oxygen onto the surface of the steel. Another directed a stream of excess oxygen into the furnace.[4] We observed the metal surface and inserted an optical pyrometer for measuring the temperature of the top of the bath through a single outlet, where we used a loop-shaped flame.[5] The control panel on the right showed the flow and pressure of oxygen and coke oven gas as they shot into the furnace, which was heat insulated on the outside.

[Once the experiment was completed], we removed the furnace's detachable roof and tilted it to pour out the melted steel.

[My experiment led me to conclude that] I could prevent the oxidation of steel scrap into iron oxide [in the process I'd developed if I sank] the steel scrap directly into the molten bath of raw iron and steel in the melting furnace. Further experiments with the furnace indicated that there were some economic possibilities [for industrial use]. One could [indeed] avoid dependence upon complicated heat regenerators and melt cheap steel scrap into valuable steel in a furnace heated with an oxygen flame. [The process appeared to me to yield better results than those obtained in the usual fuel- and air-fired, old fashioned, open-hearth regenerative furnaces, but] by many tests, other research men proved later that my idea was uneconomical because of the prohibitive cost of lining the furnace.

[I began to think about other approaches to steel production.] One system for refining raw iron into steel is the so-called Bessemer and Thomas process, named after its inventors. [Though it has some issues], the method is a work of genius because it uses simple equipment and results in a tremendous output of steel in about a quarter of an hour.

In the Bessemer and Thomas process, the furnace—the Bessemer Thomas converter—is preheated to about 1500°C and held in a horizontal position. Liquid raw iron is poured in while air is blasted [into the chamber] through numerous small holes in the converter's bottom. This burns out the carbon and other impurities, but because the process requires only about fourteen minutes, the converter operator must have an expert eye. Observing the character, color, and shape of the flame, he must recognize the precise moment at which the brittle, less-desirable raw iron is changed into strong, ductile steel. At that instant, he must pull a lever to turn the heavy converter, as big as a small house, into a vertical position. A horrendous noise is emitted and a white cloud of dirty gas rises from the top, as if a volcano were erupting. In the past, the heat from the flame escaped from the top of the converter plant and was visible for miles. In modern [oxygen-blown converters], the volcanic flame is directed into a large, vertical boiler where the heat generates steam for a power plant or other purposes.

A major problem with Bessemer's converter is [the great speed of the process]. [Often, the oxygen in the air blast burns out too much of the carbon, as well as some minor impurities such as phosphorous. These must be added back later in the correct percentages.]

[Inefficiency presents another problem.] In a Bessemer Thomas converter, the gas that burns out the carbon in raw iron is oxygen, yet the air blast contains only 21 percent oxygen (the active gas) and 79 percent nitrogen (the inert, inactive gas—an unnecessary ballast). Bessemer made the logically sound suggestion of using oxygen gas instead of air, but the gas was too expensive to be of practical use during his lifetime.

As an inventor, I considered it my job to make [the converter process for steel production] cheaper and better. At GHH, Dr. Lenning had already succeeded in using oxygen to enrich the air blown into a blast furnace, but if I could replace the air blast with an oxygen blast, I could greatly increase the output and lower the labor and general costs of conversion. I thought it would be profitable to use the gas even if it had to be bought. In 1930, a German company near Munich had been able to separate oxygen from liquefied air and had radically lowered its price.

My general rule in developing a new idea is to first try the process on a small scale. I knew the technical institute at Aachen had a small, high-frequency testing furnace of 50-kilogram capacity in the metallurgical laboratory. I succeeded in interesting an assistant professor, Dr. Schwarz, in my experiments, provided his efforts could be remunerated.

To begin, I insulated the side wall of my experimental furnace with a thin layer of magnesite. To introduce the oxygen, I installed in the bottom a water-cooled nozzle with a hole 3 millimeters in diameter. I melted lumps of raw iron in the furnace and preheated it to 1450°C, then blew oxygen gas into the molten bath from a steel container. [This worked] quite satisfactorily, converting the brittle, cheap cast iron into desirable, ductile, and strong steel. Dr. Schwarz and I danced around the furnace, [celebrating] the first oxygen-blown steel converter in the world![6]

Next, I constructed a small converter of 75-kilogram capacity, lined with magnesite and with a small water-cooled oxygen nozzle 3 millimeters in diameter. For many weeks, I experienced a series of difficulties in making the magnesite bottom and the water-cooled nozzle suitable for lengthy and practical use. The overheated iron oxide destroyed the magnesite insulation around the nozzle, and the nozzle itself—surrounded by melted iron oxide at about 2000°C—was always in danger of destruction. When I built a water-cooled steel bottom without magnesite insulation, I discovered it could withstand corrosion and I could attempt as many tests as I wished.

In one experiment, I charged pieces of metal steel scrap into the little converter. They burned with oxygen into liquid iron oxide, which filled the bottom of the furnace 12 centimeters deep and ran out through a hole in the side of the furnace. The temperature of the liquefied charge was around 1500°C. After this test, I saw one possibility for building a large oxygen-blown converter. I could use six oxygen nozzles with 3-millimeter openings and arrange a small, strongly water-cooled bottom of thin copper sheet.

[Arrangements were made] for the construction of a converter with 1,000-kilograms or 1-ton capacity for steel. As it was being built, I provided means for preventing human injuries. Beneath the converter, my assistants dug a hole half a meter deep and one-and-a-half meters in diameter, which they filled with broken pieces of limestone. If the bottom of the converter broke, the liquid steel, white hot at 1500°C, would [flow] into this hole.

When we tested the large converter for the first time, it failed. The thick, copper, water-cooled bottom burned through. White-hot, liquid steel [poured out], but it ran into the pit, so my two assistants and I remained free from harm.

I spent many days at home in Hösel thinking about how to build a converter bottom for an oxygen blast furnace. Since the results of my calculations showed that a 5-millimeter, intensively cooled bottom would be safer than one that was 15 millimeters thick, we [constructed a second version] made of a 5-millimeter copper sheet, 300 millimeters in diameter. For heat insulation of the copper plate, I smeared on a paste of magnesite powder moistened with linseed oil. It stayed on the plate, 3 millimeters thick, because of many hundreds of "holders," each 2 millimeters wide, 3 millimeters long, 1.5 millimeters thick, and inclined at 45 degrees. I also designed separate, very intensive water cooling for each oxygen nozzle.

The second, thoroughly calculated and well-designed copper bottom remained in perfect shape after thirteen tests, [and I was able] to invite three experts from the German engineering society to witness my oxygen-blown converter in successful operation.

[As I write today, in 1969, large oxygen-blown converters are in widespread use.] Imagine a lengthy container with a steel wall and narrowed opening on top, built with a basic lining of dolomite or magnesite. The inside volume of [a modern converter] of 300-ton capacity is huge—about four-and-a-half-times larger than the volume of liquid raw iron poured into it for refining. The total weight of a 300-ton loaded converter, including the metal, steel casing, and the weight of the thick lining may be around 500 tons, and yet such a heavy structure can be rotated around its horizontal axis!

1. For discussion of Siemens furnaces, regenerators, and Bessemer converters, please see the Introduction.

2. When coal is heated in an oven or furnace, its gas ("coke oven gas") is driven off and can be captured and sold. This was a common source of heat at the time of Otto's experiment.

3. At the time of Otto's experiments, natural gas wasn't easily available. It probably

did not become common until after the war. Further in the chapter, Otto unexpectedly reverts to referring to coke oven gas as the source of his heat.

4. When describing this furnace in his typescript, Otto actually offers a detailed explanation of diagrams he put in a paper he later wrote about his experiments, making references to "Figures 5 and 5a," as well as "Burner D, Burner E, and Outlet F." The passage is difficult because we do not have the paper or the diagrams. Thanks are owed to Dr. Roger Soderberg, whose explanations provided the basis for the editing.

5. This sudden and single reference to "a loop-shaped flame" is puzzling. Dr. Soderberg speculates that the flame may have come from a ring burner, similar to the circular burner on a gas stove. Otto may have aimed it down to heat the surface of the bath.

6. See Appendix 2 for Werner Oellers' literary account of Otto's aspirations and struggles to create an oxygen-blown process for steel production.

CHAPTER 25

Life and Work in Mexico

1940–1941
Otto age 56-57: Mexico

In 1939 or 1940, we [suddenly] received a telephone call from the United States consulate in Cologne. To my bitter regret, [I heard] a rough command: "Get out of Germany!" There were good reasons for the call. Hitler's soldiers had invaded Poland [in the fall of 1939]. Intending to overrun France, they had begun to march toward Belgium [in May of 1940]. The consul knew that the United States would enter the war and that I, as an American citizen, would then be taken prisoner.

I decided to travel to Italy, and from there by ship to the United States.[1] My wife remained in Germany for a while with Liisa, age ten, and Renate, age eight.[2] When Hitler's army marched into Belgium, I wired her: "Come with the children to the United States."[3] Fortunately, they found room on the last ship leaving Genoa for New York.[4]

After Aina, Liisa, and Renate arrived in December of 1940,[5] we moved into an apartment we rented in Allentown, Pennsylvania. Though they knew only German, the children entered a public school and soon learned to speak English.[6] I tried valiantly to find a paying job, but no one was willing to hire a fifty-seven-year-old man. Worry about the future almost made me sick. I did not want

G. POLYSIUS
Aktiengesellschaft

C
C
P
Y

DESSAU

Mr.
Dr.Ing.Otto Lellep,

Hoesel bei Duesseldorf.
-.-.-.-.-.-.-.-.-.-.-.-

January 24. th. 1940.

Dear Sir,

        We have pleasure in confirming that we have filed patents in Germany and abroad covering the following processes and installations which have been invented by you and developed by the aid of your collaboration in 1927 up to 1931. Furthermore, you have readily brought to our knowledge and assigned to us up to 1936 the inventions and experiences gathered in the line of the cement industry.

German patents:

466 298	530 035
508 462	551 919
515 172	578 935
526 451	630 819
528 808	660 486

and patent application : L. 79 725 V/80 c .

In compensation for the aforesaid inventions as well as for your collaboration we have paid you already RM. 379.000,-- (three hundred and seventy nine thousand Reichsmark), while a further amount of RM. 36.000,-- (thirty six thousand Reichsmark) will still fall due in the course of 1940.

        We are pleased to state that we are now as before on very good terms with you, and we are very sorry, indeed, that owing to actual political conditions you are compelled to leave Germany.

Yours very truly,

G. POLYSIUS.

Aktiengesellschaft.

Dr. Otto Polysius (Signed)

25.1   [A letter from G. Polysius]

to spend my investments, which, due to the sudden depression, had already dropped to one-third of their former value.

My position was critical when I spoke with an agent of the Polysius Company in nearby Bethlehem. He told me that the owners of a Lepol kiln in Mexico City wished to hire an engineer to investigate why it produced less cement than the same size Lepol kiln in other parts of the world. He recommended the most suitable man for the job, namely me, the inventor of the kiln. I accepted the offer of work. [Leaving the family in Pennsylvania], I traveled by train to Mexico City before Christmas [of 1940].[7]

English subjects had founded the cement plant in Mexico, so it had been designed in London and built by English engineers. The general manager of the plant was also an Englishman. The chief engineer was born and educated in Hungary.

I studied the kiln for two months, personally measuring how many tons of cement it produced per day, examining the details of construction, checking the properties of the fuel oil, and measuring the fuel use. I looked at the temperatures in the cintering zone, at the exit gases near the grate, and in the clinker. The raw mix and the clinker were chemically analyzed.

My measurements showed that the kiln was producing cement of normal, good quality and that the temperatures around and in the furnace were normal. Nevertheless, production was about 20 percent less than expected. Why?

As it turned out, the answer to my question was quite simple, though it had been overlooked by engineers in London, Mexico City, and Germany. Mexico City and its surroundings are located on a high mountain plateau, one kilometer above sea level, and everyone had neglected to consider the effects of the thinner air. The volume of air flowing through the furnace was correct, but each cubic meter of it contained less kilograms of the oxygen that generated the kiln's heat.[8] The output of men, animals, and even automobile engines is about 20 percent less in the thinner air of the high mountain plateau when compared to the output possible at sea level. Neither I nor anyone else could change these facts.

While I was in Mexico, my family was living in Pennsylvania. Aina had found a paid position as a nurse for an elderly, sick man.[9]

25.2   Portrait of Otto, taken in Mexico

I had a few good reasons for staying temporarily in the temperate climate of Mexico City while my family lived in the cold winter of Pennsylvania. As an expert from abroad, I received exceptional remuneration for my investigation of the Lepol kiln. The cost of living in Mexico City's better climate was less than in Allentown, and I found a clean, convenient apartment where I cooked my own food. In addition, I later decided to write a report about my metallurgical experiments and inventions at the Gutehoffnungshütte (GHH) in Germany.

I spent one of the most agreeable and enjoyable periods of my life in Mexico. Geographically, the country is located in the tropical zone, but the central Mexican plateau diminishes the tropical heat. Sunshine and irrigation contribute to creating an almost ideal climate. During the coldest month, in January, a little snow fell occasionally, but it was soon melted by the sun. I could walk outside without winter clothing.

[While I was in Mexico City, I explored the area]. The high plateau of Mexico is northwest of the country of the [Aztecs].[10] Because of its good climate, fertile soil, and sufficient irrigation, the [Aztecs] developed a relatively highly-civilized culture. When a small group of Spanish soldiers equipped with guns and gunpowder invaded, their behavior was barbaric, although they were Christians.

Through fraud and cheating the Spanish entered the capital city of the Mexicans, which at that time was on an island in the lake covering the lower part of today's Mexico City. They captured the native chief of the Mexicans and later killed him. The Spanish conquerors also stole gold, which angered the natives. All this was done in the name of the Christian god! We know, though, that during all wars, there are similar actions of brutal military power.

A great number of cultural objects related to ancient Mexican art and science have been collected in the rich museums of Mexico City. The most important museum in the country is located in the center of the city near an impressive cathedral and the large square before it. The museum contains the remarkable sculptures of the cultivated Mexican people who lived over five hundred years ago, in the period before the discoveries of Columbus and the Europeans. A large stone plate especially interested me. About two meters in diameter, it had been created by the scientists of that time as a calendar, indicating periods of the year.[11]

I can recommend the great University of Mexico for sightseeing and admiration. It was planned and built by the Mexicans. Because the climate is dry, some architects used the outside walls of buildings as an area for painting, but not in the usual manner. Before the walls were erected, blocks or tiles were painted and then heated or burned at high temperatures in order to fuse the colors. This artistic approach ensured that the paintings could withstand the corrosion of wind and weather for many generations.

[I also saw illustrations of the work of] the well-known Spanish writer, Cervantes: the world-famous story of Don Quixote, a chivalrous but impractical knight who traveled on horseback with his servant through Spain. The noble hero and his servant had a series of tragic but comical adventures that were pictured on the backs of chairs set around a fountain in a beautiful park in the city. These illustrations, too, were melted at high temperatures into the surface of ceramic tiles for the permanent enjoyment of generations of park visitors.

Not far from the center of the city, was a beautiful castle. Many years ago, a foreign king lived there. He was forced to govern the Mexican people against their will, and his rule came to a dramatic, sad end.

[I was not alone while I was in Mexico City.] The German colony had an important influence on life there. The large consulate handled vigorous trade between Germany and Mexico, and the Germans had founded an especially cherished "high school." The Germans were the most cultured people of Europe, and since the parents of the pupils had to pay high tuition for their children to attend, [it was possible to select] particularly capable teachers [for the school].

Through my wife Aina, I made good German friends in Mexico City. On her trip from Italy to New York with our children, she had become friends with a German family who lived there. The father was a German-trained druggist employed in Mexico City.[12] Aina gave me their address, so when I arrived in Mexico, I phoned and was cordially invited to dinner. That night, I was introduced to a Miss Luise, who taught German language and culture in the special high school.

On holidays and weekends, I enjoyed long, wandering trips in the area surrounding Mexico City with the druggist's family and their friend Luise. One sunny Sunday, the druggist and Luise invited me for a walk. We passed through a well-kept forest and then entered a Mexican village. The houses were small and quite simply built because of the moderate climate. Each sat on a small piece of land, planted mostly with tall, strong maize or corn plants.

The ordinary Mexican in the village fed himself mainly with the grains from the corn plant. Corn primarily contains starch, but it also has a little oil and even some protein, so it includes the main kinds of food needed by men for nourishment. [I believe] it is more complete in its composition than the rice eaten by the Chinese, Indians, and Japanese in Asia.[13]

The poorer Mexican families ground the grains of corn between plates of stone to make a flour. They then added water to create a paste that could be formed by hand into a thin, round patty. These patties were put onto nearby stones that had been heated by a wood fire, and in a few minutes they were baked into nourishing food. Created from home-grown corn, ground and made without any machinery, the patties provided the main nourishment for millions of simple people in the southern part of North America.

One Sunday, I took a taxi with Luise to the centuries-old, high pyramid not far from the city. Luise had promised and intended to marry a prominent man in Mexico City. She knew that I was a married man, so we became good friends without intimacy, and she became my tour guide. While we climbed the pyramid, she told me of the horrible, bloody, pagan ceremonies that had been executed on top. Long ago, pagan religious leaders governed the country, guided by a high priest. According to the laws of their religion, the peoples' god required sacrifices: human hearts cut from living men by the high priest, who stood on top of the pyramid in the sight of tens of thousands of native Mexicans on the large plain below.

On another Sunday, we took a taxi to the inactive volcanoes about thirty kilometers from Mexico City. Astronomy teaches us that our planet, the earth, is a spherical body with molten, white-hot material inside. Active volcanoes can throw out an immense amount of this molten material, which hardens partly into sand that can cover whole cities, as happened centuries ago in Italy not far from Rome. The large area around the volcano we saw, perhaps ten square kilometers, was covered with black, coarse lava—volcanic sand—empty of grass or vegetation.[14]

[I was aware of] an unusual [phenomenon] in the center of Mexico City. Every year, large, heavy buildings of many stories are sinking one millimeter or more into the ground. When the Spanish conquerors invaded about five hundred years ago, the small capital city on the island was surrounded by a sizeable lake. Many hundreds of years later, the lake dried out, and high, multi-storied buildings were constructed upon its muddy, soft bottom. The dirt eventually compressed, causing the sinking. No one seemed to know how to prevent this when I lived in Mexico City.

My apartment was located in the prosperous part of the city. On the top floor of a three-story house, it had a roomy living room, bedroom, bath, and a small kitchenette where I cooked my own food. The large buildings and institutes of the Mexican government were in the middle part of the city. A few magnificent streets also branched off from the center, offering some modern hotels and luxu-rious stores where it was possible to buy the kinds of merchandise available in large North American cities.

The prosperous people in Mexico City were a small minority. The largest part of the area around the center consisted of the simple houses of the average Mexicans, whose standard of living was much poorer than that of the average American. A considerable part of the population lived close to the state of poverty, with most people having just enough for food and clothing.

I visited the market place of the poorer people, which covered a considerable area. Narrow roads served for communication, with merchandise spread out on both sides for display, very often simply laid on the earth.

The necessities of life were primarily sold by women. I saw a number of them offering the most common food product: corn on the cob. A pile of cobs lay on the street by their sides. Other merchants sold potatoes and many kinds of vegetables, such as cabbages of different types, carrots, string beans or kidney beans, and peas in the pod. There was also a woman busily preparing and selling the most common food: the ground corn mixed with water and formed between the hands into a large, paper-thin cake. It was baked before our eyes on a heated iron plate. These were sold for a few cents each and were eaten by the buyer on the spot.

At the market, I also saw tables where fruits such as oranges, lemons, and many kinds of berries were sold. Very poor people could not afford such luxuries but everything that the common man or woman needed for daily existence could be bought inexpensively: household articles such as pots and pans, spoons, knives and forks, as well as simple clothing.

Of all the peoples of America south of the United States, the Mexicans probably rank first in education and freedom of life. Nowadays, Mexico is one of the best governed nations south of the Rio Grande. Now a mixed race of native Mexicans and Spaniards, the Mexicans have succeeded in freeing themselves from the Europeans [over] the past seventy years. They are developing their own culture.

[While in Mexico], after I finished my consulting at the cement plant, I began formulating my engineering report on the research I did at Gutehoffnungshütte (GHH). I wrote [in German] from March to May of 1941. The typewritten final report—"Steel Production in an Open-Hearth Furnace and a Converter While Using Oxygen Gas"—required forty-seven pages of text and included about seventeen sketches and forty-five photos.[15]

Once I finished writing, it was time to travel back to the United States to join my wife and two daughters [in California]. Regular mail service was not available because of the [imminent] war between the United States of America and Germany, so I put my report into the hands of the German consul in Mexico City. It was only some years later that I gave each of my daughters a copy of the report and my doctoral dissertation.

1. Renate remembers circumstances very differently. She recalls that Otto was not in Germany when he heard from the consulate, via a letter warning him that though his daughters were US citizens (born as they were to a naturalized citizen), they were in danger. "After June 30, 1940, we cannot guarantee them protection by the United States, and we urge you to have them leave Germany," the directive advised. Her memory is confirmed by Otto's letter to Aina dated May 26, 1940. (See Appendix 3.)

2. Renate: "Actually, Liisa was nine and I was seven."

3. See letter in Appendix 1 for an account of Otto's journey to the US.

4. See Appendix 4 for Renate's description of the family's flight from Germany and their new life in the US.

5. Aina, Liisa, and Renate came to Ellis Island on the SS Manhattan, arriving in July of 1940.

6. Aina hired a highly recommended school teacher named Mary Lichty to teach her daughters English.

7. Otto writes "Christmas of 1941," but given the timing of his work in Mexico and materials in the family archive, it must have been 1940.

8. Otto actually wrote, "The volume of oxygen flowing through the furnace was correct, but each cubic meter of air contained less kilograms of the oxygen that generated the kiln's heat."

9. While Otto was in Mexico, Aina and Renate lived in Germansville, Pennsylvania with Tom Keppler (or Kepplinger), an elderly farmer. Aina felt Liisa needed complete immersion in an English-speaking environment, so Liisa lived with a Whitaker family—found by Mary Lichty—on the other side of the Blue Ridge Mountains, in Ashville, Pennsylvania.

10. Otto inadvertently wrote "Incas" in his manuscript.

11. Renate: "Upon his return from Mexico, Otto brought as a remembrance of that country, a reproduction of the calendar woven into a blanket. This remains in our family."

12. Renate remembers a book of Hans Christian Anderson's tales for children that Otto brought back from Mexico for her and her sister. It was given to Otto for his two daughters by friends in Mexico, perhaps by the druggist and his wife? Published in 1938, the book is inscribed "To Li and Nate," from "Gudren" and [?] Madsen." Renate speculates that the two were active Socialists who fled Germany in peril of their lives. The book was re-published in Germany in the 1960s or 1970s.

13. Renate:
    This is true, but not completely true. Methods of milling and processing can increase or decrease the nutrient value of a grain, as is well described by Harold McGee, author of *On Food and Cooking: The Science and Lore of the Kitchen*. From ancient times, in Central and South America, corn, or maize, has been soaked in lye following the harvest. This *nixtamalización* releases the scarce niacin and makes it available for the body's use. The rural poor in Europe and the southern US adopted corn as a staple but prepared it without processing it chemically, unknowingly risking pellagra. Whole grain rice, in contrast, holds rich stores of thiamin in its outer layer of bran, and the nineteenth century removal of that layer by milling machines gave rise to the Asian vitamin deficiency disease of beri-beri.

14. A passage I deleted from Otto's typescript reads as follows:
    [Today, there are still active volcanoes.] A few years ago, newspapers reported that a small one issuing a smoky, dusty fire, appeared quite unexpectedly in the field of a Mexican farmer. It has remained active, and its lava and ashes gradually formed a mountain that is still growing.

    Geography teaches us that volcanoes are mostly located near the coast of the "Still" or Indian Ocean, the largest ocean on earth and often a stormy one. Many conical mountains, which could have been volcanoes some time ago, rise from its bottom. The highest and biggest cones rising from the Indian Ocean (sic) have formed the Hawaiian islands. There's a height of close to ten kilometers from the bottom of the ocean to the top of the mountains in that group. One of them has been an active volcano in my lifetime.

15. Apparently, Otto's report originally appeared in *Stahl und Eisen*, according to a summary of it found in the records of hearings held by the US Committee on Finance in 1967: "Between 1936 and 1940, for example, O. Lellep conducted experiments at Oberhausen, Germany with the use of pure oxygen

in a bottom-blown converter. While he succeeded in producing high quality steel at low cost, he found no way of preserving the service life of the converter bottom, and hence failed to come up with a commercially feasible process."

"Versuche zur Stahlherstellung im Herdofen und Konverter unter Benutzung von konzentriertem Sauerstoff, ausgeführt in der Gutehoffnungshüte A.-G., Oberhausen, in der Zeitperiode von 1936 bis 1940," published in Mexico City in 1941; cited in *Stahl und Eisen.*"

Hearings Before the Committee on Finance

United States Senate, Ninetieth Congress, First Session

On Proposals to Impose Import Quotas on Oil, Steel, Textiles, Meat, Dairy Products, and Other Commodities

Part 2; October 20, 1967; Page 878

CHAPTER 26

From Mexico to California

Spring 1941
Otto age 57: Los Angeles

I decided to travel from Mexico City to Acapulco by bus, and from there to Los Angeles by steamship. The zigzag bus ride from the high mountains through the hot tropical forest to Acapulco was interesting. On the coast, I enjoyed sun bathing and swimming in the ocean.

Arriving in Los Angeles, I looked up my life-long, Estonian friend, engineer Gustav Klaas. He lived in his own house in a suburb of Los Angeles with his eighty-year-old father, whom he had brought from Russia. All his life, Gustav's father had been a capable and skilled blacksmith, working in Crimea on the Black Sea, in the harbor of the Russian military fleet at Sevastopol. An elderly but strong man, he knew only Estonian and Russian. Despite language limitations and his age, he had managed to travel for many weeks by train from Crimea to Petrograd, by ship to New York, and again by rail to Los Angeles to the home of his famous son. He spoke with Klaas in Estonian.

Engineer Klaas built three houses in a beautiful area near La Jolla, in southern California. When I visited him in 1941, he had already completed two houses with help from his father and others. As an independent engineer using his own money, he hoped to earn a considerable profit.

For a few days, I had the pleasure of living in Klaas' home, which had a garden of orange trees in the best climate in the world.[1] From there, I traveled to San Francisco and to Berkeley, the location of the largest campus of the University of California system. My plan was to find a suitable position so I could earn money for my family. On the beautiful Berkeley campus, I looked up Dr. Duschak, a professor of metallurgy.[2] "You are Lellep," he said. "I believe I know your invention—there are two Lepol kilns operating in a cement plant south of San Francisco."

Professor Duschak's parents had been Czeck immigrants and his name means "person with friendly feelings towards other men." Through him, I found at least temporary work after a few days. He had good connections with the outstanding, rich industrialist [Henry J.] Kaiser and his main office in Oakland. Kaiser was planning on building a steel plant, and his chief engineer needed information about steel production in Germany. I was asked to translate some articles into English for him, from the German periodical *Stahl und Eisen*.[3]

I was particularly happy with the opportunity and found a room in a private home for students adjacent to the university campus, where I diligently translated the steel metallurgy articles. To maintain my good appetite and health, I climbed up and back a steep mountain nearby, every noon. The translation work took a few weeks, after which I was hired by Kaiser on a steady basis.

Following this happy event, I wrote to my wife and children and suggested that they take a leisurely trip from Pennsylvania to Berkeley, California with a friend who had a car. This would allow them to visit beautiful landscapes in the United States, such as the mountains of Colorado, Yellowstone Park, the Columbia River, and the great redwood forests on the western coast. The friend agreed to make the long trip in her car with Aina, Liisa (age eleven) and Renate (age nine).[4]

It was a pleasure to have our family together again after six months of separation. We decided to buy our own home in Berkeley.[5] After looking at a number of houses, Aina found one on a quiet street on the slope of a hill. From a window on the second floor, we had a splendid view of the San Francisco Bay, the Golden Gate Bridge, and other cities within a fifteen kilometer distance.

1. Renate remembers her father telling her several times that he planted an orange tree for her and one for Liisa in Klaas' garden in La Jolla.

2. In his memoir, the professor's name appears as "Dushek," but in a 1945 letter, Otto addresses him as Professor Duschak." I use the latter spelling.

3. The periodical was *Steel and Iron*. The request was made before the US had entered the war, prompted by the bombing of Pearl Harbor on December 7, 1941.

4. The friend was Mary Lichty, whom Renate's mother had first engaged as an English teacher for her daughters. Mary and Aina had become close. At eighty-seven, Renate vividly recalls:

    In the summer of 1941, it was Mary who drove us west, pausing at Hershey, Pennsylvania's chocolate factory (perhaps why I never became a chocoholic); Michigan's Kellogg and Post factories, whose boxed [cereal] samples with milk provided us every subsequent breakfast until California; and Madison, Wisconsin's Fourth of July fireworks. Mutti always respected my sleep, but crossing into Minnesota she gently woke me up, thinking I might never again have the chance to see the Northern Lights. On we went, to the Corn Palace in South Dakota; the Black Hills and Devil's Tower; and Yellowstone Park, where a bear followed me when I was carrying firewood to our cabin. Lii and I later decorated our various homes around the Bay Area with the gigantic pinecones we gathered in the Sierra Nevadas—from Jeffrey pines, I believe.

    How much Otto wasn't, couldn't, be aware of! And what a find Mary Lichty was. I wept a tear when I learned of her passing a decade or so ago.

5. Renate:

    Otto has actually collapsed time, compressing parts of 1941 and 1942. We arrived in Berkeley at the end of the summer of 1941. We rented an apartment on Hilgard Avenue, while Otto was translating the articles from *Stahl und Eisen* for Kaiser. We then moved to Los Altos (see Chapter 27) on Linden Street. We lived there for half a year. Otto had chosen Los Altos for the excellence of its schools. This was educationally a standout half year for me. Our fourth grade had a sand table, in which we sculpted Santa Clara County (now Silicon Valley), populated by birds, and trees, and plants that we made from paper maché.

    Equally vivid in my memory is hearing our teacher read aloud to us—*Blue Willow* by Doris Gates—the story of the daughter of a migrant family.

That's where I came into the English I am speaking now: the language I heard in the novel. I resolutely ceased speaking German in public and with my parents at home after hearing it.

The time was also significant because of the resonance between the story in the book and my life. Our backyard in Los Altos bordered on an apricot orchard, where I saw a migrant family working among the trees. I longed to join them, but I dared not.

As well, earlier that year, our fourth-grade dodgeball team lost our best player, Roxie, suddenly and without explanation. Her long arms and quick reflexes had been a terrific asset to our team, and we missed her greatly. It was weeks before we learned that she, with other Californians of Japanese descent, had been deported to concentration camps away from the Pacific Coast.

It was after the half year in Los Altos, in the summer of 1942, that my parents bought their house on San Mateo Road in the Berkeley hills—a short, curving, dead-end street between Indian Rock Park and John Hinkle Park. I wonder, now, what language my father used when he took me on walks in the Berkeley hills, blooming with brilliant, orange California poppies. He was trying to explain to the ten-year-old me—a girl intensely bent on passing as an enthusiastic patriot and unaccented, native American—the workings of the cyclotron on the campus below us.

CHAPTER 27

Hired and Fired by Kaiser

1941–1944
Otto age 57–60: Berkeley, Los Altos, and Fontana, California

My work at the Kaiser Company was very interesting. With his competent engineers, Kaiser was a genius in business and organization. The United States had entered the Second World War against Hitler and urgently needed to ship war supplies and soldiers over the Atlantic to Europe. Kaiser's [group] had discovered a method for building ships in an extremely short time, and capable agents in Washington [found ways] to provide him with the credit to finance his enterprises in the war industry. Almost every second day, the company could launch a transport ship with a capacity of 10,000 tons.

When Kaiser received an order from Washington to quickly build a plant for the production of metallic magnesium, construction began near Los Altos, California. [It was known that] the necessary ore, magnesium oxide, could be separated from ocean water because an Austrian, Dr. Hanskirk, had invented a new method by which magnesium oxide with hydrogen gas ($MgO+H_2O$) could be reduced to metallic magnesium at a very high temperature. Dr. Hanskirk had used the process on an industrial scale in Manchuria for the Japanese.

[After I was hired] and assigned to help put the production plant into operation, [our family moved to Los Altos]. My job was to use a rotating drum to produce round pellets about 1 centimeter in diameter from a mixture of magnesium oxide and carbon dust. After drying, these were [to be] reduced in an electrical furnace at 2000°C to metallic magnesium powder mixed with carbon dust and carbon monoxide gas.

In the plant, the temperature of 2000°C was [successfully] produced by heating carbon electrodes [requiring] 10,000 kilowatts, but the reducing hydrogen gas was replaced with much cheaper natural gas. In principle, this process was correct and possible, but apparently the inventor had not tested the feasibility of using natural gas.

We observed many unforeseen difficulties. The new plant actually yielded only a small fraction of the metallic magnesium needed for the war, and the expense was much higher than that incurred by the normally used electrolytic method. When production costs remained high, the unhappy inventor was fired by Kaiser. The commercial failure of his invention so depressed his mind and health that he died a few years later.

Hanskirk's expensive process remained in use for only a short time, though the plant did produce a powder of magnesium and carbon. This mixture was temporarily put into the bombs that ignited and destroyed the houses in German cities during the Second World War. After the war, when the plant was torn down, Uncle Sam lost at least $50,000,000.

During my experiments using the pelletization drum to create magnesium oxide from seawater, I broke a few bones in my right hand. In November of 1941,[1] I had to remain in the hospital for about ten days. Luckily, my bones mended and my family and I moved back into our house in Berkeley.

Kaiser's chief engineer in Oakland knew about my ability as an inventor, [so I could approach him with ideas]. Kaiser had decided to build a big steel plant in southern California near Fontana and had bought some deposits of iron ore not far from there. I suggested that steel could be produced more cheaply if we used reducing gas to

27.1   Portrait of Otto, 1943

Otto's ambivalent, sometimes pained view of Kaiser Steel, is reinforced in an article by Nancy Rivera Brooks that appeared in the *Los
Angeles Times* (February 9, 1987).

THE LONG WINTER OF KAISER STEEL:

*The industrial empire it once anchored is gone, and the firm struggles to
survive, beset by an internal battle for control and a hostile economy.*

For the war-weary populace of Southern California, the dedication
of Kaiser Steel's Fontana blast furnace a few days after the Christmas of
1942 was a patriotic extravaganza, even making the front page of the *Los
Angeles Times.*

College students sang. A young radio reporter named Chet Huntley acted
as master of ceremonies. And storied industrialist Henry J. Kaiser watched
as his bountiful wife Bess, sporting a large orchid, threw the switch to fire
up the blast furnace that Kaiser named after her in a sentimental moment.

With that, the first complete steel mill west of the Rockies roared to life.

"It was a glorious event," recalled Martie Hubble Bernhart, a Burbank
resident who attended the dedication with the Pomona College Glee
Clubs. "Bess came in like a gunboat—with that big bosom and those
huge flowers," she said. "And Henry J. with his big scowl, and he made a
speech. With that big scowl, he looked so tycoonish."

Those were the glory days of Kaiser Steel, founded by Henry J. Kaiser
to provide steel for his wartime shipbuilding efforts. Historian Mark S.
Foster called Kaiser Steel the "linchpin" of the powerful Kaiser industrial
empire that included businesses in aluminum, cement, electronics,
automobile manufacturing and health care.

The empire is gone now, although many fragments survive. Henry J.'s
massive Fontana steel mill was sold in 1984. And for Kaiser Steel itself,
survival has seldom been easy....

From the beginning, Kaiser Steel was plagued by limitations. When
Henry J. wanted to build a West Coast steel mill in 1940, he was opposed
by the Eastern steel giants and their supporters in Washington, said
Foster, a history professor at the University of Colorado at Denver who is
writing a biography of Kaiser.

Authorization and government financing for the steel mill finally came,
but not until three months after Pearl Harbor was attacked. And rather than
allowing the steelworks to be built on the coast as Kaiser wished, Washington insisted that the plant be constructed 55 miles inland to protect it from
Japanese attack. That resulted in higher transportation costs....

reduce the pellets of iron ore directly into raw iron, which could then be melted into high-grade steel in an electric furnace.[2] This would allow us to avoid the expensive construction and operation of a blast furnace and use of a complicated open-hearth furnace.

I suggested that we try this idea in Professor Duschak's laboratory at the University of California in Berkeley, where the professor could serve as a consultant for my work. I figured that at the time (1942–1943), research on a small scale for eight months would cost about $20,000 and that preliminary tests would show whether my plan was practical and sound. If so, I felt, the Kaiser organization could spend a hundred thousand dollars or more on larger-scale tests to reduce fifty tons of iron ore into sponge iron.

Kaiser's chief engineer accepted my proposal, and I began my research in the metallurgical department and laboratory at Berkeley, happy that I was near my family and not far from Kaiser's main office in Oakland. Because I proposed the project, I was deeply interested in its success.

As usual, I started on a small scale in order to reduce the cost, using less than 20 kilograms total weight of iron ore. A chemical engineer who was assigned to be my assistant built the necessary apparatuses, mainly of sheet steel lined with refractory material. Preliminary tests showed us the changes we needed to make.

My laboratory equipment consisted of two separate parts. In the first, natural gas mixed with water vapor and heated by electric energy was transformed into a large volume of reducing gas, as shown by this formula: $CH_4 + 2H_2O = CO + 3H_2 + H_2O$.[3] The second part of my equipment consisted of a shaft kiln that was filled from the top with iron ore pellets. These sank in countercurrent to the large stream of hot reducing gas as shown on the right-hand side of the preceding reaction.

I gave written reports on the tests to Professor Duschak and wrote the final one in my room at the Kaiser Company in Oakland. After many months of diligent work, I was ready to present my successful results to the chief engineer. Calculation of rentability showed that it was possible to produce steel more cheaply if the iron ore was first converted into sponge iron and then melted into steel ingots in an electric furnace, eliminating both the costly blast furnace and the large open-hearth furnace.[4] Based on my positive results, I detailed the profit obtainable on a large scale.

I hoped that the Kaiser Company would undertake experiments on a large scale, confirming my successful tests of the new process I had invented and for which I'd applied for a patent. I was thoroughly disappointed when Kaiser decided not to accept my suggestion. All my eager efforts and my invention were unrecognized, and my work of the previous eight months was lost![5] My unhappy feelings made me almost sick. I needed a vacation and went for a month to a quiet village on the shore of Lake Tahoe in Nevada.

In the meantime, the chief engineer selected a group of five engineers to undertake a study at Kaiser's large blast furnace near Fontana in South California. I was one of the five. We worked on the project for a few weeks and then a categoric order came from Kaiser: "All five research engineers are fired." Kaiser was a genius as a businessman but he hated research work.

1.   In his text, Otto actually dates his hospitalization as occurring in 1942, but Renate remembers visiting him in the hospital with her mother on the Sunday of the attack on Pearl Harbor. Otto told her that fan blades had injured his upper arm, causing him to lose the use of his hand. As her parents spoke in the hospital, they reacted to the news of the US entry into war "with relief, but also with regret." She explained, "Lend Lease had up to then been the US support for much-bombed London. The country was now entering a war that would cause the bombing of cities like Rostock, where Mutti's sisters Trude and Erika (with her husband Willi) had to live in the couple's basement after they were bombed out of their house. But Mutti and Otto thought the bombing of Pearl Harbor—drawing the US into a war already ongoing since 1939—would sooner draw the war to a close.

2.   Otto uses "raw iron" here and the more commonly used "sponge iron," below, to indicate the product produced by removal of oxygen from iron ore in the solid state.

3. Dr. Soderberg: "The formula should be $CH_4+H_2O=CO+3H_2$."

4. As a technical term, "rentability" appears in only one dictionary of the many I have searched, there defined as "profit or return derived from any differential advantage in production."(Dictionary.com)

5. Otto received no credit for his experiments and vision, but producers today do use sponge iron in the production of steel. From the Wellspring Steel website: "Sponge iron is a metallic product produced through direct reduction of iron ore in the solid state. It is a substitute for scrap and is mainly used in making steel through the secondary route. The process of sponge iron making aims to remove the oxygen from iron ore. The quality of sponge iron is primarily ascertained by the percentage of metallization (removal of oxygen), which is the ratio of metallic iron to the total iron present in the product." (http://www.welspunsteel.com/content.asp?Submenu=Y&MenuID=3&SubmenuID=60; accessed June 10, 2018.)

CHAPTER 28

No Patents and No Employment

1944–1945
Otto age 60–61:
Pittsburgh, Pennsylvania; Warren, Ohio; Berkeley, California

I considered the future: how and where could I work to earn money and support our family of four? The climate in California and our own home on the side of a mountain meant a great deal to us. My earnings had come mainly from my work as an inventor and my patented ideas. Since the industries using high-temperature furnaces for steel production were mainly near Pittsburg and Cleveland [in the eastern United States], I left my family in Berkeley and went to Pittsburg to look for employment there.[1]

Based on my four-year experience at GHH in Germany, I knew that the application of pure oxygen for the conversion of molten raw iron into molten steel would have an important future. In Pittsburg, I went to the manager of the research department of one large steel company and showed him my written report describing my work at GHH. I expressed my conviction that the application of pure oxygen in steel converters would have a big future.

The manager of research permitted me to see his laboratory, which was not far from Pittsburg. [Though] I'd had a second talk, with the director of research, and promised to demonstrate and repeat my successful process for steel production, as I had done at GHH, my suggestion seemed to the manager so absurd that he came close to throwing me out of his office. New ideas appear not only absurd but even offensive to some people. I felt quite sad at being unable to sell him the idea of making better steel with oxygen. Since he was absolutely sure of his own thinking, he was not willing to employ me.

I had another talk with a consultant of the Copper Clad Steel Company and found a position in that firm through him. The company had a steel plant in Warren, Ohio, not far from Cleveland. [I discovered that] its name did not correspond with its product. Actually, it bought cheap scrap iron and melted it into steel in a number of ordinary carbon electrode electric furnaces, adding alloys according to the wishes of its customers.

Since my job at the company was to learn the operation of the plant and make suggestions for improving or decreasing the costs of its processes, I developed the idea of converting one of the cheapest kinds of scrap iron into good steel by melting it in an electric furnace. I intended to use the chips obtained when steel is cut on a lathe. These thin, wiry, inexpensive chips have a very large volume per cubic meter, and I thought we could use a special press to compress them into dense briquettes weighing a few kilograms each. This would simplify the handling of the scrap and make for easy melting in the electric furnace.

I formulated the idea myself and mailed a description to a patent lawyer for a patent application. Then I gave a copy to the manager of the Copper Clad Steel Company. This infuriated him to such an extent that I was immediately fired. Apparently, the manager thought that only he, as the manager, had the privilege of patenting inventive ideas conceived in his plant. Most American engineers employed by a company *have* to give their ideas to the company if the idea is conceived during employment.

Professional Record:

Name: Lellep, Otto George   Location preferred: USA, Canada
Age: 60 yrs,but capable to work Will go out of town? Yes
Height: 5 ft. 7 in.   Languages: English, German, Russian,
Weight: 132 lbs.   Estonian, reads French
Married: Yes   Engineering Society: Member A.I.M.& M.
Children: Two in high school   Registered Engineer: Not registered
Citizen: Yes, naturalized 1923   Draft Status: Registered in 1941.
Religion: Student of Unity teaching

Educational Record:
College: School of Mines, Clausthal, Germany. Course: Metallurgical Engineering, graduated
1910 as Metallurgical Engineer. Wrote and defended Doctor of Engineering thesis concerning
own inventions in Institute of Technology at Brunswig, Germany in 1930. Degree granted.

Specialized Experience: Specialized in development and research of high temperature processes
and furnaces particularly for melting and refining of steel, nickel, burning cement. Unusual
attainments. Invented Lepol cement kiln saving for $2,000,000 worth fuel yearly. Pioneered
in industrial application of oxygen to melting, refining of steel. Has 17 patents, almost
all sold.

Experience Record

June 1944 to Nov. 1944. Attempted to interest Freyn Engineering Co., Chicago, Jones & Laughlin, U.S.Steel in Pittsburgh in his inventions of Bessemerizing iron with oxygen blast (US
2333654) and a process of increasing output in open hearth furnaces (p.applic.548222). Ideas
remain attractive, apparently profitable, but further development unfeasible during war.

1941 to 1944. Research and development engineer in H. J. Kaiser enterprises. Surveyed known
methods and patents concerning production of magnesium. Suggested a number of improvements
concerning carbothermic magnesium reduction process. Surveyed and reported on tried out
processes for production of sponge iron. Conducted sponge iron emperiments at University o
California testing his own idea. Analyzed and reported for Kaiser Company, Inc., on new
ideas and inventions concerning iron and steel. Kaiser Company letter available.

1940 to 1941. Returned from war-torn Europe. Took a year off. Traveled in U.S.A. and Mexic
Consulting work concerning his cement kiln in Mexico City.

1936 to 1940. Performed free lance research and development work without pay concerning his
own ideas in cooperation with Gutehoffnunoshuette, Germany, manufacturer of iron and steel.
Developed radical improvements in application of inexpensive industrial oxygen for production of liquid steel. Attractive business propositions followed successful demonstration
of process. Due to war, being a U.S. citizen, preferred to leave Germany.

1927 to 1936. Research Engineer and inventor in cooperation with G. Polysius Company, Dessau
Germany, manufacturers of cement mill machinery. Developed a group of own inventions con-
cerning a particularly economical cement kiln consuming 40% less fuel. More than 110 units
sold. The Lepol kiln saves cement industry about $2,000,000 worth fuel yearly. It brought
Polysius over $10,000,000 worth of business and made the inventor financially independent.
Polysius letter available.

1923 to 1926. Research Engineer with the International Nickel Company. Developed and sold
writer's invention concerning a simplified method of desulphurizing Monel metal matte.

1918 to 1923. Engineer with the Surface Combustion Company now in Toledo, Ohio, specifying,
designing, erecting and testing different types of industrial furnaces. Last two years
was Combustion Engineer in Mr. Lesley's cement mill.

1914 -- 1917. Officer in Russian Army. After being wounded was teacher in Officers' School
for mechanized transportation. Before the First World War worked as a Laborer in lead,
copper, and nickel smelters. Managed a lumber mill, surveyed peat industry for Estonia.

28.1   ["Professional Record," c. 1944]

Unemployed, I travelled back to Pittsburg and talked to a professor of metallurgy at Pittsburg University about an idea that I wanted to test in his laboratory at my expense. I would melt about 70 kilograms of steel in a small, electric arc furnace and refine it with a high lime slag. To speed up the process, I would agitate the steel bath with a slight amount of air blown through the porous bottom of the refractory material—porous magnesite, for example.

The professor in Pittsburg allowed me to test my idea provided I did the work myself. I also got to know the technical writer and author of a textbook on steel making in the United States Steel Company—as well as the company's patent lawyer. I was happy and satisfied to work in the friendly atmosphere I found in the lab and to have connections with the largest steel company in the world.

My tests showed that my idea was correct and possible to execute. It is easy to conceive of a new idea, to describe it on paper, and even to apply for a patent, but because of the innate vanity of inventors, millions of impractical patents have been applied for and obtained. Perhaps 90 percent of these "patents on paper" are impractical. Only thoroughgoing research, first on a small scale and then on an industrial scale, can establish what is actually practical. Unfortunately, the patent lawyer found a United States patent showing that the concept of agitating the bath through a porous bottom was not new. There was, therefore, no sense in continuing my experiments.

Meeting no success in my efforts to find satisfying paid work in the metallurgical plants in the eastern part of the United States, I decided to travel back to my family and my own home. There, in our own car, my wife, two daughters, and I made interesting, gratifying trips into the hilly, beautiful area north of San Francisco. We visited the famous and remarkable Muir Redwoods Park many times. The trees there are over one thousand years old and still growing. Once we stayed overnight in a tent near the park.[2]

[As it happened], a former salesman of the Polysius Company in Italy was living in California, and his California co-worker sent him to Argentina to see whether Lepol kilns could be sold there. He visited a wet-process cement plant in Loma Negra. Considerable savings could be obtained if the plant could be converted to the dry process, [using pellets and the efficient heating of a Lepol kiln].[3] The salesman gave me a sample of the wet-process raw mixture from Loma Negra [to see what I could do].

[I knew that the usual methods for drying the raw mix would be insufficient.] In large, industrial-scale filtration drums, the wet cement mixture falls upon a filtration cloth, beneath which a vacuum is maintained. After use of the ordinary commercial drum, 20 percent of the water remains. This would have to be lowered to 10 percent if the raw mix was to be made into the pellets used in the Lepol kiln.

Fortunately, I knew a professor at the university in Berkeley who was a consultant for cement production plants, and he allowed me to do a few preliminary tests in his laboratory. I found a filter four inches in diameter in the lab. Use of this reduced the water content to [the usual] 20 percent, starting from a 30 to 40 percent wet slurry.

Next, I made a beater by fastening a wooden handle to a thick rubber band. By beating the band of rubber upon raw cement filter cake,[4] I was able to further lower the water content from 20 percent to about 10 percent, making it possible to break the filter cake into pellets about 10 millimeters in diameter. These did not stick together and could be used on the preheating grate of the Lepol kiln.

We ordered a barrelful of raw mix from Loma Negra and filtered it on a small commercial filter in Oakland, [then used] rubber beaters. I sent a letter describing our successful test to the German manager at the Loma Negra plant. He wired immediately: "Come to us in Argentina." I was glad for the employment and accepted the invitation.

---

1.   For Otto's descriptions of his long, hard, unsuccessful struggles to find work in Pittsburgh, see letters in Appendices 1, 6, and 7.

2. Renate:

> My parents loved Muir Woods. I remember camping there when we were living in Berkeley. We were staying next to a creek, a very shallow stream, and Otto tried to make me a water wheel to put in where there was a little bit of rippling water. He carved the blades out of pieces of dry wood. He was so happy to put his hands on his knife. He used his knife for everything—even cut his fingernails with it. He always had a knife.

> The wooden blades of the water wheel broke apart, but Otto was trying to show me something that mattered to him, recreating the hydropower his brother had created long ago in an Estonian stream. He wanted to transmit something important to me, his offspring. But I was a teenager, trying so hard to fit in and be American. I didn't know or care that he was remembering his childhood.

3. For a description of wet-process and dry-process cement production, see the Introduction.

4. Renate: "Otto's description of his 'beater' evokes the image of the flails used in the harvesting of grain—not the 'beaters' of kitchen handbeaters."

CHAPTER 29

Discoveries in Argentina

1946–1947
Otto age 62–63: Argentina

The manager of the distant cement plant in Loma Negra had obtained a doctoral diploma from the Institute of Technology at Charlottenburg in Berlin,[1] working under a famous German cement specialist. He invited me all the way to Argentina because he knew from his reading that my invention, the Lepol cement kiln, was able to reduce the amount of fuel normally needed for burning cement by about one half. The cost of fuel in Argentina was high. A simple calculation showed that if I could substitute Lepol kilns for the usual wet process cement kilns at Loma Negra, the plant could save $1,000 daily, or $300,000 a year.

For the first time in my life, I used an airplane for transportation, traveling from California to New York, to Buenos Aires, and from there to Loma Negra. The settlement of Loma Negra consisted of more than one hundred small houses where the workmen lived. These were clustered near the cement plant. A little farther on, in a park, stood the beautiful, big house of the owner of the plant, who usually lived in Buenos Aires, or occasionally even in Paris.

I had been offered a good salary at the cement plant and accommodations in a guesthouse located in a nice park away from the cement dust.[2] For dinner each day, a servant brought me a nourishing, tasty soup with various vegetables and lots of the boiled meat of young bulls.

The day after my arrival, I met with the manager of the plant, Dr. Becker, and his assistant, Dr. Miretzky, who was the chief engineer. Because of the lack of industrial plants in Argentina, the large cement producers had their own facilities for the repair, or sometimes even the building, of their machinery. I was able to demonstrate the process I used at the University of California to remove excessive water from the filtered product. The broken pieces of the filter cake were easily converted into nice, round pellets when we shook them in a pan.

I wished to learn more at Loma Negra. How would the pellets behave on the grate of the Lepol kiln?[3] [In the days following], I constructed a small test furnace similar to the one described in my doctoral dissertation and used it to research the question. The test revealed no difficulties.

My income depended on the Lepol kiln, so while I was in Argentina, I [began to try] to improve it technically. Previously, we used a single fan to draw the exit gases from the rotary kiln to the grate. Unfortunately, the pre-drying of the pellets was insufficient, and the output of the grate was limited.

I discovered that I could improve heat utilization if I pulled the stream of hot gases coming from the kiln twice through the Lepol grate, using two fans instead of one. The first fan was designed to pull hot gas of 1000°C through the heating zone of the grate, [leaving] a temperature in the fan of around 400°C centigrade. The second fan received the 400°C gas coming from the first fan and moved it through the pre-drying zone of the grate. The exit gas temperature after the second fan was very low: only 100°C. In addition to better heat utilization, the double passage of gas through the layer of pellets reduced the amount of dust in the stack gas by about a third. I formulated a patent application and registered my idea with patent agents in Germany, the United States, and Argentina.

An inventor cannot sell his invention simply by having his patent applications registered. In order to convince my buyer, the Polysius Company, I had to demonstrate my new idea through actual tests. I began by making a construction drawing of a relatively small Lepol grate that would accommodate the double passage of gas through its pellets. The outside dimensions for the length, width, and height of the grate were .33 x 0.6 x 0.7 meters. After discussing my plan with the management of Loma Negra, I found them willing to build such a testing grate at their own cost in their well-equipped construction shop.

This was a very good [move] for me and the Loma Negra company, because the results from the use of the test furnace were convincing. The company anticipated reducing the dust lost through the stack by about one third and saving about $300,000 annually.

[I had many interesting experiences during my time working in Loma Negra]. I bought a Berlitz textbook for Spanish, and since I already knew English, Russian, German, Estonian, and some French, I learned to speak this language within a few months. To practice, I paid a clever schoolboy to walk with me. After three months, I discovered that I also understood the technical Spanish in books.

Dr. Miretzky, the assistant to the manager, became my friend. His father was a Russian Jew and his mother a Russian. He later became the general manager of the large cement plant and the auxiliary organizations connected with it. I also became friendly with an engineer, a chemist, and the master of the repair shop, most of whom could also speak English or German.

[I soon learned more about Argentina.] In terms of size, the country is the second biggest on the American continent, but the large fertile areas had too few people. Instead, a nourishing grass grew there, [eaten by] cattle and sometimes even ostriches. Elsewhere, there were immense, wide fields of wheat. The east had sufficient rain for agriculture, but the west was partially rainless desert. Catholicism had an important influence.

Although Argentina was nominally a republic, the land was usually ruled by generals—dictators who tried to please the big rich landowners and businessmen, neglecting the living conditions of the poor majority. The military generals and the owners of enormous estates often exploited the average inhabitant.

I became acquainted with an exceptionally rich man who owned three large cement plants; a substantial modern business house in Buenos Aires; a magnificent residence surrounded by a park; and a few small airplanes.[4] The peasants who took care of his cattle, however, lived in miserable shanties, built from wooden sticks smeared with clay.

Some [customs] of the Argentinian people were unique and enjoyable. Once each year, an *Asada* was celebrated at Loma Negra.[5] The owner of the plant owned 120,000 cattle, cared for in different locations by cowboys. About six bulls were killed for the *Asada*. Their heavy shanks were hung on solid steel sticks around a fire, where they baked. From time to time, the shanks were turned so both sides cooked, and after a few hours, the tasty, barbecued meat was well done.

About two hundred people living in the settlement of Loma Negra attended the *Asada*. In various groups, they walked up to the fire, pulled out their own special knives, and cut a large piece of beef, which was considered a special treat given by the owner of the cement plant to his employees and guests. Tables were set up nearby and a large number of wine bottles and drinking glasses were also provided.

The multi-millionaire owner of the cement plant, the manager of the plant, and some of their families sat at one table. I was included. Conversation became friendly and lively because of the wine drinking, and some people even made speeches. I sat at the table among them, drinking non-alcoholic beverages.

Since the Polysius Company in Germany had sold Lepol kilns to a number of cement plants in Argentina, I received invitations to visit and offer suggestions for improvements. Calera Avellaneda, a cement plant owned by a German, was walking distance from Loma

Negra. I visited it many times, and the manager, who was a German engineer, became my friend.

The owners of another plant, many miles away, near the frontier of Chile, also invited me to come and suggest improvements. The manager there was my friend and co-worker Maier, a [graduate] engineer who had worked with me in Rudersdorf near Berlin when we installed, tested, improved, and later demonstrated the first Lepol kiln.[6] To reach the plant, I took a four-and-a-half-hour bus trip to Buenos Aires and flew from there to Chile's frontier. Much of the land was uninhabitable desert, but near Chile, a river ran from the mountains and transformed the desert into a fertile land where oranges and grapes grew.

My friend Maier was a good-natured person, and we understood each other perfectly. At Rudersdorf, we'd had to overcome a number of deficiencies and mistakes in the first Lepol cement kiln. Maier's current difficulties arose because the owners of the plant had no technical training and were not willing to let him put his suggested improvements into practice.

Maier had married a teacher, an energetic woman whom I'd known at Rudersdorf. In Argentina they lived in the manager's house in the middle of a garden, growing grapes on tall, supporting, wooden grids. This was the Spanish method of grape growing. As the plants grew in the warm or hot air, away from the colder ground, the grapes became fine tasting and sweet. I was invited to eat as many of them as I liked.

After ten days in the west, I flew back to Buenos Aires, where I spent a few days learning about the capital city [and more about the country]. I stayed in an old-fashioned but clean hotel, four stories high. All the rooms were arranged around a narrow, central courtyard, with windows that opened onto it. I ate at a good, modern restaurant.

Though the majority of the Argentinian people lived in very modest or even quite poor conditions, Argentina was a very large and prosperous place. In the harbor, I noticed vigorous activity.

Large steamers were loaded with frozen meat or wheat—the country's primary exports. Imports consisted mainly of machines, autos, and luxurious articles from all over the world. Education seemed to be adequate. Practically all the people could read and write, and there were at least two universities in the country.

Most of the inhabitants of Buenos Aires lived in modest houses outside the prosperous center of the city, but along the richer streets I saw stores with all kinds of luxurious merchandise and a number of good, modern hotels and restaurants with all types of food. One of the widest streets in the world ran through the city, with well-built, high, modern houses on each side. I also found a very beautiful park. Because of the mild climate all year round, [it was permanent home to] a large number of cats who were fed by ladies who took walks there.

I bought a few small presents before my flight back to Berkeley, where my patient wife Aina had been living with my daughters [from 1946–1947]—the whole year I was busy in Argentina.[7]

After I arrived home, I wrote a long letter to my good friend Bernard Helming, in Neubeckum, Germany, describing my new invention and its industrial advantages. Industry in Germany was to a large degree destroyed during the Second World War, however. [Unable to buy from Polysius], the Loma Negra plant attempted to purchase the new Lepol kiln from a small American firm in Los Altos, California. While I was in Argentina, I'd loaned the firm's agent $1,000 [to advance this possibility], but unfortunately, the firm fell into financial difficulty. It was unable to fill the order, and I lost my money.[8]

1. Charlottenburg is now a neighborhood in West Berlin.
2. Perhaps this guesthouse was in the same park as the owner's home? This is unclear in the text.

3. Renate: "'Behave' is usually used for living creatures. Here, Otto anthropomorphizes the pellets. He animates them. In fact, he *lived* with pellets, in Estonia, Germany, Argentina, and the United States."

4. Is this perhaps the owner of the plant in Loma Negra?

5. *Asada* translates as "grilled" or "roasted."

6. Otto writes: "a diploma engineer."

7. Renate:

    In writing "my" daughters, not "our" daughters, Otto is not denying Mutti's importance. He often acknowledged gratefully that she raised the two of us. Rather, his choice of pronoun reflects *his* sense of responsibility for the persistence of his lineage and bloodline. After all, my parents both married with the explicit, expressed desire to procreate and raise offspring, as they stated in their pre-marriage agreement.

8. Renate:

    As described in Chapter 30, the Polysius Company relocated to Neubeckum after the war. While writing this paragraph, Otto must have been remembering the time immediately following World War II, when Polysius was facing the hopelessness of trying to resume production in Dessau, in the Soviet sector of then partitioned Germany. In the post-World-War-II world, not knowing anything of Polysius' possible production capacity, Otto seems to have made the risky loan of $1,000. He wanted to support, somewhere, the purchase of one of his "offspring," for at home and in at least one letter, he spoke of his inventions as *meine Kinder* ("my offspring").

CHAPTER 30

New Industry for Minnesota and Michigan: Taconite and Allis Chalmers

1948–1964
Otto age 64–80: Wauwatosa; Milwaukee;
and Allis Chalmers in Carollville, Wisconsin

Shortly after I arrived [back] in Berkeley, I attended a large national meeting of engineers in San Francisco. There I met Mr. Puerner, assistant manager of the furnace-building department of Allis Chalmers, the world-renowned firm in Milwaukee, Wisconsin. After I told Mr. Puerner about the work I had done in Argentina, he phoned his manager at Allis Chalmers. He asked if I would be willing to work at the company. I expressed my willingness, and I flew to Milwaukee the next day, where I met Mr. Puerner and his chief, Mr. Woody, the department head.

After a general orientation in Milwaukee, I had to work out a fixed and clear agreement between Allis Chalmers and myself. I felt that my research, development, and testing work with the Lepol kiln at Loma Negra and my patent applications in nine major industrial countries gave me a strong position. I expected that my primary income would be from licensing fees for the Lepol kilns sold in Europe, the United States, and Canada, so I agreed to a relatively modest remuneration as my monthly salary. I gave Allis Chalmers exclusive rights to sell the kilns covered by my patents in the United States, Canada, and Japan and reserved the exclusive rights for sales in Europe for the Polysius Company. Both firms had the rights to sell in South America and Australia.[1]

I soon discovered that Allis Chalmers was especially interested in pelletizing and burning finely ground, concentrated iron ore. Minnesota and the Upper Michigan Peninsula had large deposits of low-grade iron ore called taconite.[2] This ore contained only 25 percent iron, but an ore concentration plant in Minnesota could process it into a high-grade powder with an iron content of almost 65 percent. Raw iron is, of course, used for producing steel, which is needed for the building of ships, autos, and other necessities of the civilized world. The concentrated powder was high enough in iron to be used for steel, but its form made it unsuitable. It would have been blown out of a blast furnace.

My extensive experimental work over a period of many years— research in the United States at the Giant Portland Cement Company; tests in my workshops in Egypt, Pennsylvania and at Willem's house in Tallinn, Estonia; and the large-scale experiments at the Polysius Company in Germany—had given me practical experience helpful for transforming the raw mix powder of the cement industry into stone-hard, clinker pellets of Portland cement.

Tests in the laboratory of Allis Chalmers showed that the powder of concentrated iron ore could be converted into iron ore pellets by about the same method I'd used in the cement industry. Once I'd obtained a handful of the finely ground ore, I easily produced pellets one centimeter in diameter.[3] These I dried at a low temperature and burned in a laboratory furnace at 1400°C until they became beautiful pebbles as hard as stone. I was particularly

happy about this little test because it gave promise of great industrial development and success.

I gave the new product to Puerner and told him that the production of such pellets was just as easy as the pelletization of cement. I
also showed my beautiful iron ore pellets to our department chief, Mr.
Woody. He was not interested. "Stop your tests," he said. "I have a better method." His idea was to produce the pellets on a briquette press.

I was working under the direct supervision of Puerner, an
assistant to Mr. Woody, and Puerner had nothing against my desire
to work out drawings for a test furnace that would burn 70 to 100
pounds of iron ore pellets at about 1350°C. [In the end], I was
allowed to build the testing equipment because Mr. Woody soon met
a few difficulties in his plan to produce moist iron ore pellets on a
briquette press.

I first produced moist iron ore pellets in a small rotating drum
like that used for concrete mixing in the building industry. My
furnace was designed so that it could pre-dry the pellets at about
300°C before the application of a hot flame at 1350°C. During the
test, I measured the flow of gas and air into the furnace, as well
as the temperature of pellets of different thicknesses. My previous
experiences in Germany and Argentina helped, and I found that a
temperature of 1350°C in the layer of the pellets yielded successful
results.

Mr. Woody was finally won over to my method, the success of
which was confirmed by my lab tests. He gained support for the
production and burning of concentrated iron ore pellets from the
president of the Allis Chalmers Company, but then we had to choose
between two possible means of production: Dwight Lloyd's method,
invented fifteen years earlier,[4] and the grate kiln system that I'd
invented in Estonia in 1926 and had fully developed in cooperation
with the Polysius Company.

Since the Dwight Lloyd method had become well known in the
United States, Mr. Woody had decided we should try it first, but I

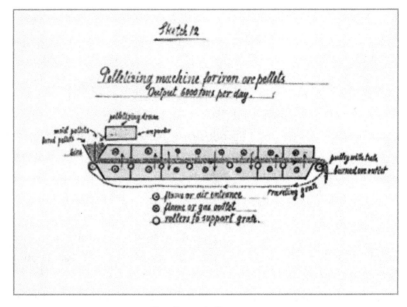

30.1   Sketch 12: Pelletizing iron ore

formulated patent applications for my technique of heat hardening, or burning, the pellets. I saw the positive economic possibilities of partially recovering the heat in the cooling section of the grate and utilizing it for preheating the air in the drying section.

The decision to produce high-grade pellets of concentrated iron ore was very important because the United States alone consumed over 100 million tons of iron ore a year. Mr. Woody planned to use a meeting of engineers and businessmen connected with the iron ore industry to demonstrate our method of heat hardening the iron ore pellets. [In preparation for the meeting in Duluth], the best drafts-man in our department had to make a clear drawing showing how the wet pellets could be formed in a rotating drum and later turned into stone-hard pebbles. I had the job of burning good pellets and packing them into about twenty sample glasses.

The meeting in Duluth was interesting and proceeded as planned. My samples and Mr. Woody's report showing the drawing of the grate provoked lively interest among the mining and metallurgical specialists. I took particular pleasure in distributing the twenty sample glasses of pellets and explaining how I had made them.

After the successful meeting in Duluth, the basic industries department of Allis Chalmers had to decide where to build a special research and development plant to produce a ton of good iron pellets per hour. There was no place in the Allis Chalmers plant in Milwaukee. Mr. Woody found a spot in Carrollville, about twenty-five miles from the plant in Milwaukee, on the shores of Lake Michigan, but it seemed to me costly for our engineers to have to [drive] back and forth every day.[5] I wrote a memorandum to Mr. Woody suggesting that a place closer to Milwaukee be found. Irritated by my suggestion, he came out of his office and in front of all the other engineers tore my suggestion to pieces and threw it into the waste-paper basket. "There it is," he said and returned to his office.

I was painfully humiliated in front of the other engineers. What should I do? According to my contract, Allis Chalmers had to pay me $6,000 if the Lepol kiln, the so-called "grate kiln" in the United States, could be developed and put into operation on as large a scale as I hoped. Should I complain to the president of Allis Chalmers? If I did, Mr. Woody would probably fire me and I would lose my $6,000. Mr. Woody's rough and brusque character was generally known. I decided to forget the sad incident because I handled my problems mostly with Mr. Puerner, his assistant, who was a tactful person.

At the time, I was over fifty years old. Mr. Woody wanted to hire a younger engineer who would obey his will without protest. He selected Mr. Stowasser for directing the work in Carrollville and sent him to [the University of Minnesota in] Minneapolis for a year to find out why the pellets of magnetite (Fe_3O_4) hardened at a white-hot temperature. The university had a large, special department for the study and development of an economical method for converting taconite (the low-grade iron ore containing 25 percent iron) into a desirable, high-grade concentrate with close to 70 percent iron.

30.2   [From A-C Views, *April 8, 1952: "Object of interest here is a model of the Taconite pellet heat hardening pilot plant which the company is building on its Carrollville property. It probably will be ready for operation in June or July, according to G. V. Woody, manager of the Processing Machinery Department, which will supervise the project. The pilot plant will be able to turn out one to two tons of heat hardened pellets an hour from filtered magnetite concentrates which will be brought in by rail from the Mesabi iron range. After hardening, the pellets will be shipped to a blast furnace for testing. Shown with the model are, left to right, Dr. O. G. Lellep, consultant; W.F. Stowasser; and W.J. Hartwig, all of the Processing Machinery Department."]*

Stowasser worked under the direction of an assistant professor and at high magnification found that small crystals grew into larger ones, and the larger ones in turn grew together on the cold, polished sides of the burned pellets after they were heated in an oxidizing flame. The hardening of iron ore pellets at white-hot temperatures had been observed before, not only by us, but also by a Swedish professor, Tiegershold, who had published an article about his work in Stockholm.

Our job at Carrollville was to transform the powdery iron ore we received from the Minnesota ore concentration plant into strong, stone-hard, round pellets about three-eighths inches in diameter—a lucrative raw material for the production of molten iron in the blast furnaces of the steel mills. Methods and means had to be invented and developed to produce the pellets on an industrial scale.[6]

At the plant, we had to design, build, and install everything we needed: the equipment to move the powdery ore from the railroad cars into the building and from one machine to the other; a pelletizing drum to transform the ore into pellets; a mechanical sorting screen to separate the pellets that were too small and return them to the pelletizer until they could reach the correct size; a traveling grate cintering machine with three sections to dry, cinter, and cool the stone-hard pellets; and the transporting belt onto which the cooled pellets could fall and be carried to the storage pile outside the building. All the equipment was powered by electromotors.

To my surprise, the manual labor at the Carrollville pilot plant was performed not by common workers but by graduate engineers. Mr. Woody selected them as workers for two reasons: they performed all kinds of dirty work without complaint, and they were outside the labor unions. Unionized workers were allowed to do only one particular job, such as carpentry, machine building, or blacksmithing. In the United States, they were also paid more than the young engineering graduates, who performed all kinds of manual labor and learned to use such simple tools as hammers, chisels,

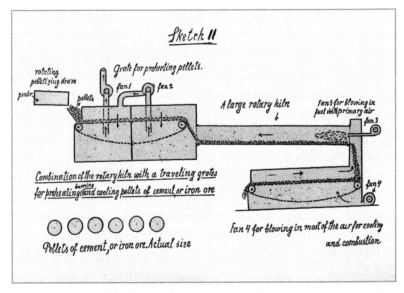

30.3   *Sketch 11: Rotary kiln with traveling grate for cement or iron ore pellets*

drills, files, shovels, or oxyacetylene welding torches. By the time the taconite-loaded cars pulled up to the plant in Carrollville, the moist iron ore concentrate was frozen. The engineering graduates had to break it up; carry it into the building; thaw it to make it suitable for the transporting belts and pelletizing drum; and screen and feed the heat treatment grate or kiln.

We had to overcome some difficulties at the plant, especially during the cold winter months. The experiment building was fairly large, without any special equipment to keep the workers, all engineering graduates, comfortably warm. Some heat became available when we had the grate or grate kiln system in operation, but the newly invented equipment did not necessarily work as expected. When the equipment was idle, as was necessary during the reconstruction or repair of the machinery, or when something had to be discarded and replaced with an improved device, we had to work in heavy winter clothing at freezing temperatures.

Mr. Woody speeded up the plans and building we were doing. To be safe, he invited Stowasser and me to his home on a Sunday to talk about the production of moist pellets, the arranging of a number of transporting belts, and the cintering grate. This discussion took place in a quiet, friendly manner.

Following about six months of experimentation in Carrollville, it became obvious to us that a large, industrial-size grate should be built. I'd discovered how the gases flowing through the different sections of the grate should be directed in order to produce a high-grade product with the lowest fuel and general cost. After a few changes and improvements in the equipment, the Carrollville engineers were prepared to demonstrate our system to buyers from the mining plants of Minnesota and the [Upper]Michigan Peninsula.

Mr. Woody was pleased to show these experts, and visitors from other countries, how perfectly the Allis Chalmers grate fulfilled its purpose. Our relatively small experimental grate successfully produced one ton of pellets per hour, at a development cost of around one million dollars the first year.

The Allis Chalmers agent in Duluth found a substantial mining concern in Minnesota that was planning to build a large plant there. It would buy the large ore crushers and wet grinding mills made by Allis Chalmers, but because Allis Chalmers had never made a roasting grate for any purpose, it cooperated with a firm in Cleveland, Ohio.

Five engineers from Allis Chalmers, including me, traveled to Cleveland to discuss the Minnesota project. We decided which machinery was to be delivered by the firm in Cleveland and which was to be built by Allis Chalmers. The two firms worked together on the plant, but it was the Cleveland group that built the large grate for heat hardening the pellets.

The industrial-scale experimental plant built by the two firms produced 750 tons of pellets per day. After the tests there proved successful, a large plant was built in Minnesota near Lake Superior. It had an output of 1,500 tons per day, and it remained in permanent operation,

Latest Practice of Burning Cement and Lime in Europe

By

O. G. LELLEP

Consultant, Pyro-Processing Section

ALLIS-CHALMERS MANUFACTURING COMPANY

Presented Before

AMERICAN INSTITUTE OF MINING AND METALLURGICAL ENGINEERS

New York, N. Y.

February 16, 1954

30.4   *[Cover of Otto's talk in New York]*

using a single grate and no rotary kiln for the drying, burning, and cooling of the pellets. The total expenditure may have been between five and ten million dollars. The establishment of this successful industrial plant—a great technical achievement—was managed by the mining interests in Minnesota. I can only admire the persistent courage and daring of this group of capable Minnesota men.

According to my agreement with them, Allis Chalmers had the right to utilize in the United States my patents covering what was called, in Europe, the Lepol kiln. In the United States, this method for efficient heat use became known as the "grate kiln system."

1. Renate:

    Otto has not mentioned our family's move from Berkeley, California to cold, flat Milwaukee in the Midwest. At the time, Lee was admitted to the University of California, Berkeley as a first-year student, and she remained on the West Coast for a year. Mutti engaged herself with the International House and Settlement Service. I entered Wauwatosa High School as a senior.

    Despite the counselors who advised me to register for higher level classes, I signed up for both business math and drafting, considering them "more practical." Our lifetime friend Elfriede Friese an immigrant from Germany, advised me to apply to Oberlin and Bryn Mawr, but a major in Occupational Therapy (OT) at the University of Wisconsin looked like the practical route. Otto had frequently told me: "For the first time in my life, at Allis Chalmers, I've earned my way with a regular job as an employee with paycheck."

    For more about Elfriede, who was an extraordinary woman and a dear and wise influence on our lives, please see Appendix 14.

2. Dr. Roger Soderberg explains:

    There are several oxides of iron. FeO is ferrous oxide. Fe2O3 is ferric oxide, common iron "rust," with the mineral name "hematite." Fe_3O_4 is a mixed-valence oxide of iron. It is magnetic (lodestone), and the mineral name is "magnetite." The great open-pit mines in the northern Minnesota iron range in the first half of the twentieth century contained almost pure Fe_2O_3, hematite. When this source was exhausted in about 1950, the industry had turned to more plentiful taconite, a low-grade ore containing Fe_3O_4, magnetite. This is what is currently mined in Minnesota. It is ground up, and the magnetite is separated magnetically and then baked into pellets that blast furnaces can use.

Renate further notes:

> Otto is here referring to Minnesota's Mesabi Iron Range, an area just south of the Canadian border. At one time, there were more than one hundred mining pit operations in or near the town of Chisholm (now the home of the Minnesota Museum of Mining). We have in Otto's papers (the Lellep Family Archives), an oversize postcard of the large taconite plant near Hibbing. The Hibbing Taconite Company still mines millions of tons of iron-bearing ore for its production of iron ore pellets near Chisholm. [See online resources for Hibbing Taconite Company, Hibbing Mine, Minnesota Museum of Mining, and Mesabi Iron Ore Range.]

3. Otto's experiments were not confined to the laboratories of Allis Chalmers. Renate:

    > I remember our home in Wauwatosa, where I lived with my parents my senior year of high school. Mutti adapted to a clumsily designed, flimsy house in Wauwatosa. She used to say that the house had *eine sehr unglückliche Tür*—"an unlucky door"—a poorly designed layout in which four doors opened in and out onto a floor space of just a square meter. My sister and I were then becoming aware of tailings pollution—the ore waste of mines. I suspect we harassed Otto a bit about the tailings dumped into Lake Superior from the mining of "his" taconite.

4. Prior to the invention of the Dwight Lloyd method, ore mixed with lime was burned in great pots. This produced unsatisfactorily uneven results, with the upper portions remaining unsintered and the lower portions fusing into nonporous slag. In Dwight Lloyd machines, materials were sintered on articulated grates that moved continuously, like conveyor belts. The patent for the invention seems to have been filed much earlier than "fifteen years" prior to Otto's writing. There is record of a Dwight Lloyd patent issued March 17, 1908, for "a process of treating ores." A patent was reissued June 23, 1914 ("upon application for reissue filed August 9, 1910") for "an apparatus for calcining, desulphurizing, agglomerating, and sintering ores and like materials." (Case Text: "Dwight Lloyd Sintering Co. v Greenawalt," accessed August 16, 2018. https://casetext.com/case/dwight-lloyd-sintering-co-v-greenawalt)

5. Renate:

    > The encounter with Mr. Woody occurred after gas rationing had ended, and Otto may well have been thinking of the well-being of the poorly paid engineers, but he must have also been concerned about the waste of gas and energy required by the commute to Carrollville. Otto was consistent in his commitment to conserving and effectively using energy. Any time I wanted to light a fire in our American fireplace, he chafed at the waste of heat going up the chimney.

6.   Renate:

Otto was sixty-four the year he needed to commute to Carrollville. He got exhausted by driving, because of the concentration he felt it required of him. One day that summer, he drove up to a major highway and waited to cross. After a long wait, as he told it, he decided, "I've waited long enough," and he pulled out. The accident that followed was not a bad one and he was not injured—it didn't shake him up too much—but that day, he knew he was no longer fit to drive, and he gave up his license.

I was at home between jobs then. I had learned to drive, but Mutti had quietly anticipated the need for her to drive Otto to Carrollville. Born 1892, Mutti had learned to drive at age 63. She took three courses of driving lessons, trying to get ready. In the early fall, she and I drove to Cape Cod to see the fall foliage. We spent a long time in a big parking lot there practicing her driving, and after she got her license, she took Otto to Carrollville each day.

After my college graduation in 1954, in preparation for my first job, Otto had accompanied me when I went to buy my own car. It was a Hillman Minx, a very tiny British car that had to be started by crank. I was strong and was able to master the technique at the time of purchase. I could start the car successfully during the summer, but in the cold Wisconsin winter, I found I didn't have the necessary strength. That crank would really yank an arm. I began to count on the early morning milkman to crank it up for my drive to work at Lakeview Sanitarium on the far side of Madison's icy and windy Lake Mendota.

Of course, I had to learn to change a tire before I drove the car, and Otto had to see me do it.

CHAPTER 31

The Lepol System and Portland Cement

1950s

Otto in his 70s: Wauwatosa and Milwaukee, Wisconsin[1]

According to my agreement with them, Allis Chalmers had the right to utilize in the United States my patents covering what was called, in Europe, the Lepol kiln. In the United States, this method for efficient heat use became known as the "grate kiln system."

Since the system guaranteed a practically dust-free operation with the lowest fuel consumption in the world, the Marquette Cement Company of Milwaukee decided to purchase one. It intended to erect a plant in the center of Milwaukee, where limestone and shale, the necessary raw materials, could be cheaply delivered to the plant in barges. The finished product, Portland Cement, could also be transported to the customer at low cost due to the central location of the plant.

Allis Chalmers found it more profitable to build pellet burning equipment without the participation of the Cleveland firm that initially supplied the large grate for heat-hardening iron ore, but it had no experience burning cement in such a system. In order to learn, the company planned to build an experimental plant at Carrollville with a grate kiln based on the Lepol kiln.

The Lepol-kiln-based system consisted of four parts: a pelletizing drum; a pre-heater for the pellets that was about 40 feet long and 11 feet wide; the rotary kiln, which was 10 feet in diameter and 83 feet long; and the cooling grate, which was about 60 feet long and 10 feet wide. Elaborate tests were organized, and the hope was to produce 700 tons or 14,000 bags of cement every twenty-four hours. In the currency of 1971, the cost of the building and the machinery amounted to over a million dollars.

I was able to be particularly helpful in this project due to my many years of experience in Germany, but the European design of the kiln was not quite suitable for conditions in the United States. For this reason, over one hundred sheets of kiln drawings were redesigned at Allis Chalmers. Fortunately, friendly cooperation between the management at the Polysius Company in Germany and the cement experts at Allis Chalmers was possible.

The Polysius family had lost all their property when the Russians [Soviets] took over the eastern part of Germany, including Dessau, where their original machine-building plant was located. After the Second World War, one member of the family died as a prisoner [of the Soviets] and the other members were forced to flee to West Germany. They took a few Lepol kiln drawings with them when they left, and they were able to sell cement kiln equipment temporarily from a cheap cellar room in Beckum. Later, the company office was moved to a modest house in Neubeckum. Due to wise and energetic management, the enterprise prospered and grew rapidly.

Bernard Helming, my life-long friend, served as the very competent chief engineer at Polysius in Neubeckum. He came to the United States to discuss his experience with the leading men at Allis Chalmers. The cooperation was profitable for both sides, as European ideas were related to the extensive experience of the Americans.[2]

Allis Chalmers built the Marquette Cement Company's plant in Milwaukee, but it was the first it had ever constructed, so it was only natural that a few errors occurred. These caused considerable extra cost during the design and building of the plant. The manager during the first year of construction and operation was a young and inexperienced engineer who was not able to help Allis Chalmers. Work definitely improved when Mr. Howe, a new, experienced plant manager, was appointed.

My tests at Carrollville had opened up possibilities for new industries in Minnesota and the Upper Michigan Peninsula—the industrial-size kilns for heat hardening iron ore pellets that were built there were able to cinter iron ore concentrate at the remarkably low fuel consumption of only 155 calories per 1 kilogram of magnetite ore pellets and 260 calories per 1 kilogram of hematite ore—but, [as later applications proved], they also gave cement-production companies greater options for fuel efficiency.

1. Otto gives no indication of the dates of his Milwaukee work on cement production, but an early photograph of "the first ship unloading at the Marquette Cement Manufacturing Co." held by the Milwaukee Public Library is dated September 22, 1956. (Milwaukee Public Library, Marine Collection)

2. Otto's text reads "extensive practice of the Americans," which we can guess might mean their "experience."

CHAPTER 32

Looking Back

1971

Otto age 87: Milwaukee, Wisconsin

In 1948, [when I was sixty-four] and started working at Allis Chalmers, the advantages of using iron ore pellets for the steel industry were unknown. Given how important the pelletized iron ore concentrates became, the $6,000 for which I sold the rights to all the patents I developed during my years of employment there was a pittance.

In the United States, my patents and ideas for the Lepol kiln are mostly utilized under the name the "grate kiln system" and development is ascribed to Allis Chalmers. Rights to my patents gave Allis Chalmers access to business in Minnesota, Michigan, and some foreign countries—and to definite success. Due to the remarkable talents and energy of my friend Glenn Hanson, one of the company's capable sales managers, the grate kiln system with double passage of the rotary kiln's exit gases through the pellets on the preheating grate has found world-wide application. In 1971, grate kilns based on my patents at Allis Chalmers produced 44,000,000 tons of iron ore pellets. (See Appendix 2 for the company's description of the grate kiln system.)

Most of the patents in the world do not lead to success, and relatively few are beneficial to humanity. The majority of the inventions covered by my patents in the United States, West Germany, Western

32.1   *The Carl Lueg Memorial Medal*

32.2   *The presentation of the Carl Lueg Medal in Dusseldorf in 1960. The presenter, Dr. Schenck, stands at the left; Professor Durrer and I (nearest the viewer) face him.*

Europe, and other industrial countries, such as Japan and Argentina, did not profit me. But I cannot complain.

I was the first person in the world to demonstrate that steel could be made in an oxygen-blown converter of 1,000 kilogram capacity. Though I earned no money during my four years of research at Gutehoffnungshütte when I invented the process, and though it seemed that all my work was lost when Hitler moved against Belgium and France [in 1940] and I had to flee, the German Society of Steel Engineers [Stahlinstitute VDEh, verein Deutscher Eisenhüttenleute] honored me and Professor Durrer at their annual meeting in 1960. They gave us the golden [Carl] Lueg Medal in recognition of our invention of the basic oxygen steel making process. (See my publication in German: "Production of Steel in Open Hearth and in the Converter Using Concentrated Oxygen.")

After sixteen years of work at Allis Chalmers Company, I retired of my own will in 1964, when I was 80 years old. [During that time, I did not forget the Polysius Company]. Of all the places in Europe—other than my birthplace, Ripsi, in Estonia—I most cherished its seat. It was at Polysius in Dessau—now illegally occupied by the Russians [Soviets]—that I carried out one of my most useful and profitable ventures as an inventor.

I still vividly remember when Bernard Helming and I worked arduously to prevent moist, raw cement pellets from cracking into dust, I during the day and he during the night. We worked for five days, which I mention again because my friendship with him began during that time in 1926 and has continued to this day. Bernard Helming is my lifelong friend.

My first German patent covered the single-pass preheating grate, and when the patent for it expired, the Polysius Company needed the improved, double-pass Lepol kiln. I was glad to be useful to the younger generation of the Polysius family and to again meet Bernard Helming, who had been promoted to chief engineer. The company and I worked out and signed a new agreement, to our mutual satisfaction. It

32.3   My friends of fifty years: Bernard Helming and his wife [Anneliese Helming]

specified that payment to me would increase at the same rate as the cost of living in the United States. This figure is officially published each year in Washington, DC. I had learned to introduce this cost-of-living specification after making the mistake of selling my patent rights to the Allis Chalmers company for a single, fixed sum.

The Polysius Company has been generous in paying my royalties, and I have visited there several times. After I was hired by Allis Chalmers in 1948, I arranged a leave of absence and traveled by steamship over the Atlantic Ocean. Karl Otto Polysius, [the owner], met me on my arrival and took me by car to Neubeckum.

In 1954, when I returned again, the company occupied only a small portion of a low building. Over [the following] fifteen years, this facility grew gradually in length and height until it consisted of ten stories, including the one below ground. [Moreover, by the time of my last visit in the early 1970s], the little city of Neubeckum had become too small to hold the Polysius Company and the many cars of its employees. A second building, about the size of the first one, was erected in a village half a kilometer away.

32.4   *When the Polysius Company first started in Neubeckum, it was in a small building about one-quarter of the size of the lower building in this photo.*

32.5   *From 1949–1971, the company grew, as shown in this photo. An additional building had to be constructed in a nearby village.*

The remarkable growth of the Polysius Company was based on its very capable management and on the world-wide sales of the Otto Lellep fuel-saving combination of the rotary kiln with the double-pass preheating grate. At this point, over 350 grate kiln systems have been bought in Germany, Italy, Austria, France, Spain, and England. While the primary market has remained in Europe, where fuel costs are high, the kilns have also been bought in Jordan, India, South Korea, Japan, South Africa, and South America. Each year, Polysius-built kilns covered by the Lellep patent put out about sixty million tons of cement. The larger units cost around ten million dollars and produce up to 200 tons or 4,000 bags of cement per day.

Today, the Polysius Company builds other efficient and technically progressive equipment. It employs about a thousand people in West Germany [the Bundesrepublik Deutschland] and elsewhere in Europe. By far, the majority of the stock is in the hands of the giant Krupp Company in Germany. Only one member of the Polysius family, Jochen Polysius, holds about 28 percent of the corporation's stock.

The equipment produced by the Polysius Company has been copied by manufacturers all over the world. The largest competitor is the Lurgi Company in Germany, which uses the simpler and cheaper straight grate [and which has] a licensee that is building the equipment in the United States.

I can modestly say that my inventions of the single pass and later, improved double pass grate kiln for burning cement and iron ore are outstanding, economical, fuel-saving pieces of industrial equipment serving people in many parts of the world. The benefit can be estimated with credible accuracy in the case of both the Lepol cement kiln and the Allis Chalmers pelletizing machinery. Polysius' Lepol kilns have a yearly output of about 50,000,000 tons. The grate kilns based on my patents at Allis Chalmers Company produced 44,000,000 tons of iron ore pellets per year during 1971.

According to the cement industry's data, in 1929, before the introduction of the Lepol kiln, Germans and other Europeans consumed

1,780 calories per kilogram of cement clinker when they burned dry process cement. According to our official tests at the Rudersdorf cement plant, the Lepol kiln reduced this figure to 1,015 calories per kilogram. One kilocalorie is equivalent to 1.8 BTU per pound, therefore, making a very conservative estimate, we can assume that the 350 Lepol cement kilns are now saving at least 382 calories per kilogram of cement clinker burned. Calculating the cost of coal and the savings made possible by a Lepol kiln burning one ton of cement clinker, I believe that the 350 Lepol kilns in the world save humanity $71 million annually.

I sold to Allis Chalmers the rights for three US patents related to heat hardening pellets on a straight grate and one patent related to the heat hardening of iron ore and the burning of cement on a grate kiln. Based on information from Glenn Hanson at Allis Chalmers, the thirty-six straight gates and the grate kiln system together produce 69,000,000 tons of heat-hardened pellets. Steel industry use of my inventions results in higher output and fuel savings in blast furnaces. We can feel justified in valuing these benefits to humanity at one dollar per ton of pellets.

The annual benefit resulting from use of Otto G. Lellep inventions in the cement and steel industries is, therefore, as follows:

Straight grate in steel industry	$65 million
Grate kiln in steel industry	$20 million
Grate kiln in cement industry	$71 million
TOTAL	$156 million

My patents covering the burning of cement and the system for heat-hardening iron ore pellets in the United States have been quite profitable, securing my life in my old age and enabling me to contribute to the Boy Scouts, the education of Estonian students in the United States [the Jüri Lellep Fund, established through the Estonian

Students Fund in USA, Inc. (ESF)], and my daughters, Liisa and Renate. Having earned more money than I needed, I am happy that my inventions of the single pass, and later the improved double pass grate kiln for the production of Portland cement and iron ore pellets, save humanity millions of dollars yearly. Civilization needs creative work that serves others.

Now, as a father and grandfather, I can be satisfied. The Russian Revolution of 1917 brought me to the United States of America. Thus I had to learn English and was happy to become an American citizen. Liisa and Renata grew up, finished studying in the public schools, and continued their educations in Madison and Ann Arbor.

Both my daughters have married outstanding scientific professors, one of whom works at the University of Western Michigan in Kalamazoo and the other at Dartmouth College. Liisa has three boys and a daughter, Renate has two boys and a daughter. My grandchildren are growing up in prosperous, beautifully located homes.

My wife Aina and I had a twenty-five year marriage, during which we never said a harsh word to one another. Aina had an excellent character—peaceful, tolerant, and helpful. She was easy to get along with and was a good caretaker and educator of our daughters.

When I was eighty years old, in 1964, after my good wife Aina died, I made an airplane trip around the world, starting in southern California, stopping for a few days in Hawaii, then flying to Tokyo where I remained over a month. I stayed in Hongkong for ten days and also visited free China on a seven-hour auto trip. I went through Bangkok into Thailand, then to Bombay, India for two weeks. I stopped in Beirut and Athens for about four days each and went from there to Köln and Neubeckum in Germany. My chance to see and experience Japan, China, Thailand, India, Lebanon, and Greece made this a very pleasant trip.

Having now reached the age of eighty-four years, I thought it high time to inform my children, grandchildren, and friends about my long life. [In this book], I have described how my childhood toys

32.6   Aina and I were proud that both of our daughters were studying at the University of Wisconsin, Madison. One Sunday, we traveled by car to see them.

32.7   Lisa age 23 on the left, Renate age 21 on the right.

32.8   A photograph also taken in 1968. Seated from left to right, the Maher family: Professor of Anthropology Robert Maher; his son Michael [Mickle]; his mother; his daughter Eva [Eve]; me, my daughter Lisa, Robert's wife; their sons Kevin and Mark.

were technical products—self-designed, self-built, and [self]-oper-ated—and I have recalled my interest in the growing of [crops] and the production of different objects in Father's mill. I've remembered my student days in Tallinn and Germany, where I studied technical literature concerning new industrial developments and learned of the progress being made in transportation and manufacturing.

Observing life in the enormous country between Petrograd and the Ural Mountains, [I saw that] national development depended strongly on how much a particular country understood about [the need to] replace human power with machines powered by steam or electricity. Inventors create and develop these useful machines. They direct the materials of nature and the work of other people to best benefit humanity.

32.9 A photograph taken in 1967. Seated from left to right, the Fernandez family: Professor of Anthropology James Fernandez, my grandson Lucas, my granddaughter Lisa, and my daughter Renate—wife of James Fernandez. (My grandson Andres was born one year after the photo was taken.)

[Thus, I became an inventor, and here I will end my story]. It is the history of a man born in Estonia who grew up as a patriotic Estonian on a farm powered only by a water mill, who attended five schools in Estonia before beginning studies in metallurgy in Germany, who knew people of four nationalities during his student years (Estonians, Russians, Belgians, and Germans), who worked in five countries, learned four languages well and used two additional languages temporarily, who fought in a dangerous battle, and who earned his living as a professional inventor specializing in large-scale, industrial furnaces.

32.10 [My lifelong friend Gustav Klaas, in 1958]

32.11 My daughter Lisa.

32.12 [Otto taking a photo of Aina, 1952.]

32.13 Climbing the Acropolis in Athens on a hot day.

32.14   *Aina and Lisa.*

32.15   *Aina with her first grandchild [Kevin Maher].*

32.16   *My granddaughter Eva [Eve Maher] about age three, showing her pet cat.*

32.17 *[Renate: "However late Otto actually married, he had throughout his adulthood aspired to marry and create Lellep offspring. He wanted children, as did Mutti, who enjoyed motherhood so much that she urged me, 'Even if you never marry, do become a mother.' Before their marriage, Mutti said that she had asked Otto if he had any 'outstanding children,' meaning offspring out of wedlock whom, she said, she 'would be pleased to raise.' Apparently, Otto knew of none who had been conceived. I see in this photo Otto realizing his parenthood, practicing parenthood amidst the family—the Maher family and me—that he so desired."]*

32.18 [Renate: "Left to right: Alice Veinbergs (Otto's niece, daughter of Otto's brother Jüri), Otto, and the Fernandez's Asturian friend Sofia Rodriguez in Cangas de Onis, Spain. After Mutti's death, Otto moved to Fort Meyers, Florida to live within the sphere of Alice's attentions. Alice was his support and traveling companion on at least his last trip around the world. Sometime between 1972 and 1974, at the end of one around-the-world trip, Otto stopped in Cangas, Spain to pick up a tuxedo a tailor was making for him. He needed it for a grand reception in New York, planned by members of the Estonian community in his honor. Upon Otto's arrival in New York and before the event took place, the tuxedo disappeared, forcing him to urgently look for one off the rack—hardly an easy task given his bony, 109-pound frame in his last years."]

32.19 [Portrait of Otto at age 86]

A Daughter's Afterword

Renate Lellep Fernandez

One

I remember when we heard the news of Gandhi's death in 1948. My father, my mother, and I were at dinner, sitting around the kitchen table in Wauwatosa. My sister was probably away, studying during her first year of college in Berkeley. This was during the time when Otto was employed or had lab access at nearby Allis Chalmers.

On hearing the news, Otto wept. I don't recall his having ever wept in my presence, before or subsequently. As he aged, his blue eyes faded and tears formed in response to dry eye, but his only real tears were for the loss of Gandhi. Not, I think, because Gandhi died by an assassin's bullet, but rather for the man and his principles. Otto had repeatedly expressed admiration for Gandhi's modesty, non-violence, and appreciation of handwork such as spinning.

I saw my mother's tears just three times. They flowed the morning after Kristallnacht—the Night of Broken Glass, November 9, 1938—when she told me (age six?) that our physician's piano "had been thrown out of the window" of a high-rise apartment in Dusseldorf. Our physician was Jewish and a woman—a tall woman with hair cut like a man's. Mutti had deliberately chosen her because, Mutti said, she had had to transcend the limitations placed upon her as a woman to excel. The second time, soon after VE day, her tears flowed when she told me she had learned (probably from her sisters) of the passing of a dear friend, a violinist, Toni Von Hofen, who lived in Mainz on the Rhine.

The third time I saw my mother cry was on VJ day, when Lee, our friends, and I were blowing bubbles. We were dipping our loops into a commercially sold bubble-blowing mix that celebrated the end of the war with Japan through an image of an atomic bomb that was printed on the label. Mutti was crying for the civilians who died from the bomb. As she imagined the suffering in Hiroshima and Nagasaki, I'm sure she was remembering all the suffering men she treated as a nurse during World War I, or perhaps she was recalling her brother Theo who was gassed while he was painting warships and who later committed suicide in Stockholm as a result.

Two

On two occasions in the early 1970s, my sister Lee and I visited Otto in Fort Meyers, Florida, where he was living with his niece Alice. We took our young offspring.

Otto would sit in the shade of a tree on the Sanibel Island beach, watch the gulf waters, finger the broken shells that compose the substance of that crunchy beach, and run his long, thin fingers along the bare, chubby legs of the youngest of his descendants, my son Ripsi—now called "Andrés" but originally named for the farm on which Otto was born. With his fingers, Otto would read the toddler's young flesh—read it as his fingers read the underside of a leaf hanging over the walkway of Corkscrew Swamp, the coldness or density of a bridge railing while he gazed upon alligators below, and the solidity or crumbliness of concrete underfoot at Corkscrew Visitors Center. His "work was done" but his need to read and understand the substances of which the world is made never left him.

A Final Note

Frieda Aina (Brandt) Lellep

Renate Lellep Fernandez

My mother, Frieda Aina Brandt, born in 1892 in Germany, died in 1964 in Wauwatosa Wisconsin. Some months or years before she died, she had let me know that she wanted to have Theodora Kroeber's "Poem for the Living" read at the rite that would be held for her at Milwaukee's Social Service Center. She had volunteered at the center since we'd moved to Wisconsin in the late 1940s—a time when she and Otto were welcoming Estonian refugees into our home. These refugees were professionals, too old to be able to resume their careers in America. I remember my parents sadly saying of one man, "the only work he can find is filling chewing gum machines."

[Renate: "Frieda Aina standing so tall in her senior years in Wauwatosa, Wisconsin, at the door of the last house she ever lived in. Otto may have taken this photo to pass on to her sisters in Rostock before her last trip to Germany, a homeland 'no longer quite my homeland,' she said to me. 'I'm no longer the German I was, nor quite the American I've long worked at coming to be.'"]

POEM FOR THE LIVING
Theodora Kroeber

When I am dead
Cry for me a little.
Think of me sometimes
But not too much.
It is not good for you
Or your wife or your husband
Or your children
To allow your thoughts to dwell
Too long on the dead.
Think of me now and again
As I was in life
At some moment which is pleasant to recall.
But not for long.
Leave me in peace
As I shall leave you, too, in peace.
While you live
Let your thoughts be with the living.

Otto G. Lellep

Otto died at age 92, in Fort Meyers, Florida, where he was living with his niece, Alice Veinbergs. At his funeral on October 21, 1975, a friend read a poem she translated from Estonian.

> We do not want
> to be a silent, forgotten page
> in the book of history.
> We want to reach for a star.
> We want to walk always
> toward great goals.
> We want to live and write
> in the book of history.

𝕮𝖍𝖊 𝕹𝖊𝖜 𝖄𝖔𝖗𝖐 𝕿𝖎𝖒𝖊𝖘 | https://nyti.ms/1H5KdDe

ARCHIVES | 1975

DR. OTTO G. LELLEP, ENGINEER, INVENTOR

SPECIAL TO THE NEW YORK TIMES   OCT. 20, 1975

Dr. Otto G. Lellep, a retired mining and metallurgical engineer, who specialized in energy-efficient furnace construction design and held patents in his field, died Saturday in Fort Meyers, Fla., where he lived. He was 82 years old.

1 Dr. Lellep was born in Estonia and studied there and in Russia and Germany. He was sent here by the Kerensky Government in 1917 to contract for the construction of metal-I smelting plants in Russia. Cut off by the Revolution, he became a United States citizen and did research for the International Nickel Company and at Columbia University, and received two patents on nickel smelting.

Returning to Estonia, he developed in the nineteenthirties a cement rotating kiln. He also pioneered in the use of oxygen in liquid iron conversion to steel.

In the nineteen-fifties he developed with the AllisChalmers Manufacturing Company in Milwaukee a pelletizaItion method for making cement and an efficient method for burning iron from taconite, a low-grade iron ore.

Surviving are two daughters, Lisa Maher of Kalamazoo, Mich., and Renate Fernandez of Princeton, N. J., and seven grandchildren.

The text of the obituary contains one error: Otto G. Lellep was 92, not 82, when he died.

APPENDICES

APPENDIX 1

A Selection of Otto's Letters

In preparation for work on Otto's memoir, Renate gathered all available copies of his letters. Several had been boxed up by her sister Lee, and they emerged as work on editing was approaching completion—we had thought. In the English selections below, we have preserved Otto's language and style. Translations from German were done by Renate. Her name and Liisa's have been left as Otto wrote them—"Nate" (pronounced "Nah-te") and "Lee."

The originals of these letters and many more may be accessed in the Lellep Family Archive.

> Milan, Italy. 10 Febr. 1940
> At the Gutehoffnungshütte A.G.
> e.g. Director Lemnnings in Oberhausen
>
> Dear Director.
> I hereby write to report the research results related to the use of oxygen in the production of steel. You have kindly promised to contribute 10,000 RM towards my expenses.
> I wish this to be credited to the account of my wife, Frieda Lellep, who lives in Hösel, near Düsseldorf. Please credit the gold to her account at Deutsche Bank in Düsseldorf.
> My address in America will be c/o A.J. M. & M. Eng. 29 W 39th St, New York City
> Sincerely,
> O. Lellep

[Penciled letter] Mailand de. 10 Febr. 1940 [Mailand = Milan, Italy]

An der Gutehoffnungshutte A.G.
z. H. Herrn Director Dr. Lemmings in Oberhausen.

Sehr geehrter Herr Direktor.
Hiermit verpflichte ich mich Ihnen über de Forschungs-
ergebnisse in Verbindung mit Anwendung des Sauerstoffes
bei Herstellung des Stahles schriftlich eing..... Bericht zu
erstatten. Sie haben freundlichst versprochen zur Deckung
meiner unkosten RM 10000 beizutragen. Ich trete diese
Somme an meine Frau Frieda Lellep wohnhaft in Hösel
bei Düsseldorf, ab und bitte das Gold an ihr Konto bei der
Deutschen Bank in Düsseldorf zu über führen.
Meine vorläufige Anschrift in Amerika ist c/o A. J. M & M.
Eng. 29 W 39th St. New York City.
Hochachtungsvoll
O. Lellep

[Otto's letter in pencil, except for marginal notes p8, p10. In
another's penciled hand, numbered small at bottom left of page (cen-
sor's sign?) 3805, 3232, 3239, 5232 etc.]

My dear wife, Otto Feb 28th 1940
Hotel Park Plaza, New York, 50-58 West Seventy-Seventh
St. New York
"At the Gateway to Central Park" [Heading on stationary]

My dear wife,
I mailed you my last letter from Genoa, Italy—about
2 weeks ago. Since that time my life has been full of new
impressions and I am happy to say mostly of the very agreeable kind. In Genoa I enjoyed the famous Riviera with warm

sunshine, palmtrees, blue sky and blue Mediterranean sea.
The formalities of getting on the ship were a little tedious—
waiting for hours in a long row (*Reihe*) with third class people
for passport control. Our trip from Genoa to Gibraltar in the
Mediterranian was most satisfying. The weather was perfect
like the day before on the Riviera. 3 days of southern climate
had made me like reborn.

Margin note: *This hotel looks prosperous from outside. But it is filled mostly with poor people.*

Margin note: *Bitte weiter schicken an: Frau Dr. Lellep, Hoesel bei Duesseldorf. O. Lellep. ["Please forward to..."]*

I felt happy and full of pep like a boy of 20 years. The
environment and milieu on the ship *Manhattan* was on the
whole very satisfactory. The third class has the rooms of
former tourist class. The actual third class rooms were closed
and empty. At our round table ate 5 persons—among them 3
with highest education. All were American citizens and had
to leave Europe for the same reason as I did. There was Mr.
V.P. Vilbert 27 year old correspondent of the Associated Press
(*Korrespondent eines amerikaknischen Nachrichten* bureau)
coming from Paris. A broadly educated, very agreeable chap
with whom I became a friend. There was another young
German American who had studied medicine in Innsbruck.
Further a German American decorator and painter (60 years
old) who had been visiting at Krefeld. A Polish American lady
of 35, wife of a Danish baker from Chicago with pretty face
and good table manners. Further an inoffensive quiet man.

We had at our table a harmonious company and felt like a
big family. Although I had the passage in the third class but
our food and table service corresponded about to German
first class hotels. The main dishes consisted, as usual of
meat—but on special request I could obtain all the vegetables,
salads and fruit I wanted and that without any extra charge
(*Sonderpreis*). The English kept us at Gibraltar for about 12
hours and searched the ship for German export goods. The
passengers with German passports were also controlled, but
none to my knowledge was taken to the shore.

My happiness took an end during our passage of the Atlantic. As you know I am extremely sensitive to the sea sickness. On the whole there was not any storm except one day. But during the whole week the ship was shaking slightly and I did not feel well. Really seasick I was only one stormy day, but during 5 other days I had to remain in my bed—mostly reading American periodicals or books. Every time I tried to get up it became worse. But remaining in bed I felt pretty satisfactorily.

Friend Vilbert came to visit me often in my cabin and remained at my bed for long hours. We had most interesting talks on politics, sociology, war, problems of education etc. This young Gentleman took me in his confidence. His mother is a professor of sociology in the cultured New England part of USA. He himself felt dissatisfied with his reporting job. He is told to report on superficial, trivial things—while in his heart he wants to do serious work. The boy seemed to have talent and has been editor of his college newspaper for 5 years during his student years. He hinted about his unhappy marriage. I tried to console him telling him what kind of big talks in public life are waiting on him as newspaper reporter in a free country.

In our sleeping room we had 3 German Americans and a catholic priest from Poland. There was one 72 year old sickly, grouchy musician who quarreled with the priest, who left our room. I also had some disagreeable arguments with this man about keeping my reading light going in the night.

After arrival in New York (9 days on the ship) I took the train for Bethlehem, Pa. Mr. Hoffmann met me at the station. [Renate: "Was Mr. Hoffman perhaps a representative of the Polysius Company?"] I spent 2 days with him having big talks about business and politics. He took me twice to dinner to his landlady where we ate German specialties, where we drank German beer. Very decent agreeable people. In the evening the short wave radio apparatus was tuned in on *Deutschland-sender*, Germany and everybody heard with enthusiasm.

Margin note: *This letter was written in New York but mailed from Washington on my way to the South. Starting from March 15th American Air mail service between New York and Lissabon will not any more be controlled by the English. You can use this airmail route via Italy 7. Ministrialrat Fritsche.*

Decent people are living mostly outside of cities and are commuting to business office on their cars. The landscape where Mr. Hoffmann is living is almost as beautiful as in Hoesel and I arranged a 7 kilometer hike through the country the day after my arrival.

In order to learn whether and how I could proceed with research work Mr. Hoffmann arranged me to meet his friend professor of metallurgy in Lehigh University. Mr. Doan and the world famous research authority on steel making Mr. Hearty of Bethlehem Steel Company. I told them confidentially about my results, which interested them. However my work is at least temporarily hindered by the fact that Americans do not believe (as the Germans do) that industrial oxygen can be produced cheaply. I also visited 2 times while in Lehigh cement district my old friend Mr. Dewson and his wife and had sweet friendly talks on many aspects of life and work. Dewson has remained a subordinated small salaried engineer and blames his boss (general manager of the plant). Poor chap! An honest and agreeable fellow! I went together with him and his wife to his church Last Sunday and met also his preacher.

Came back to New York and looked up Elfriede. She lives now 733 West 183rd Street. New York

Margin note: *To avoid British censorship of your letters mail them to our good friend Mme Z. Giampiccolo. Eich-mammary and Co. Via Giovanni Morelli, Milano, Italien. She will mail them me.*

As her apartment [Elfriede's] did not have any telephone I went to her room 8:30 in the morning. She had not yet come in from her night work of nursing sick people. Her room was small but orderly and modern. I let her get some sleep and met her later at lunch table. We talked for an hour or two. We were glad to see each other. She does not look so bad, but the youth is gone and her hair is quite grey. Apparently this fine girl has had some disheartening, sad experiences. I did not ask confidential questions.

Besides nursing some sick people in the night, she is taking care of some children in the afternoon. She had not yet got any regular job corresponding to her capabilities although she has tried hard to find one. There are 10 million people jobless in USA. Her work has been always only temporary. Says that she had to live often for $40 per month! Counting every penny! That's really very hard!

I have decided to take a vacation somewhere in the South. Have not decided yet which place exactly. My friends in Washington will help to choose. I intend to spend there a few weeks and then go to Washington to settle my patent matters. Use my old address A.J.J. and M. Engineers.

I am feeling fine and wish you and children would feel the same way. Too bad you could not have all these experiences together with me. Anyhow we belong together! Heartily greetings to everybody!

O Lellep

Margin note: *Have received your card-letter dated Feb 8th. Please inform me whether you received the nuts from Italy. Did Kaasboertje send you something?* **

** [Renate: The above letter is cautious and lacking details regarding *Manhattan's* arrival. Otto has not yet been advised to get his US citizens (his daughters) out of Germany. The reference to "nuts" seems to be some sort of code. Since our Hösel property was surrounded by hazel nut trees, there would be no need for us to receive nuts from Italy.]

[On an envelope in the box holding this and various letters, Otto wrote in pencil: "10 photos of Otto G. Lellep father's burial place with iron monument of Jesus and a favorable inscription from poem

"Kalewipoeg" characterizing father's character. In front is the large cross on the grave of my oldest brother Hans, who died in Germany. But the daughter of Hans, Else, married to Punin brought the body to Wiljandi and buried it on father's grave."]

Aufschriften vorne ["Inscription on the front"] Oma rahu aman ma teile. ["My peace to you/My peace I give to you."] Jüri Lellep. Die sechs Söhne und drei Töchter zur Welt brachte. ["Six sons and three daughters born to him."] Mari Lellep zweite Frau nach Liisas death. ["Mari Lellep the second wife after Liisa's death."] Aufschrift hinter Jesus, unten ["Inscription behind Jesus, below"] Kanget meest ei koida koied ["A strong man is not downed by moths"], Pea ei kinni rauda paelad ["The head does not stick to the iron straps"] From Epos Kalevipoeg *[the Epic Kalevipoeg]*

Pittsburgh, Pa.
Nov. 21st 1944

My dear Aina.

Usually my letters describe my doings or events in professional or business life. Everything in my letters has been usually and mostly concerned my own person. I have neglected you and children so often, yes, most of my life. I am and have been a selfcentered, typically introvert (as the psychologist say) person. My attention to this fact was called by reading a good, long article in the magazine "Your life" the backnumbers of which I am going to mail you.

Today I am somewhat in a "blue" disposition. It is a wet, cold rainy day. All my efforts to find a suitable position have been in vain. (But I know tomorrow the disposition will be positive and I will proceed in writing letters applying for positions in my specialty). It does not do me any harm, to the contrary, it may make me feel better to confess in my "sins" of having been a selfcentered introvert.

Selfcentered is not exactly the same as a narrow minded selfish person. I have not cared much for selfglorification, the pettier personal comforts and smallish social vanity. But I have deified always my work, the same as the Christian missionary, author Buck's father in the famous novel "The good earth" in China. As this missionary in the name of an abstract Gods service neglected the closer and warm human contacts, the same way I have neglected you, children and my professional friends for the sake of my technical dreams and inventions.

In these inventions I saw human progress and benefit. Sure my inventive work has benefited humanity, the Lepol kiln saves the cement industry 2 million dollars yearly. I certainly am proud of this benefit. But this benefit is only of a material character, enabling us a higher material standard of living. We all like a comfortable living as: Beautiful, well-equipped houses, tasty, healthy and variegated food, {????} for enjoying nature, leisure, fine arts, traveling and good climate in suitable countries like California. But I am not ashamed to confess to you that chasing ardently after inventions and thus endeavoring to better our more material standard of living and especially the material standard of humanity I have missed practically entirely the intimate family life with you and children. Even my best friend Klaas wrote me sometime ago: "Why do you write all the time about yourself. Tell me also something about your family."

Yes my dear Aina, I have sinned against you and children during 15 years of our marriage. All the time you have been an uncomplaining sufferer. God forgiv me and bless you for all your goodness. I married you for your good character, which is more important than so many "acomplishments". Sometimes in my selfish blindness I expected from you accomplishments and was irritated when I did not find in you ability as an engineering secretary. But how could I expect from you all the accomplishments being myself an extremely onesided "crazy" inventor neglecting my holy duty as husband and father. I know you wept sometimes, never complaining. God bless you and help me to better myself at least in my ripe elderly years.

See back of this. [Further text unavailable.]

Nov. 23rd 1944

Today is American Thanksgivings day. Yes, despite
extremely poor chances for a 60 year old man to get a
profitable job, despite our lost (or almost lost) fortune in
Germany, despite the probability of a moderate inflation after
the war—we can be thankful to God being better off than
say 60 million of American families who have no savings, to
mention decidedly better off than 400 million Chinese and
400 million Indian inhabitans, much luckier than 16 million
homeless Germans or two to three times as many Russians
and Poles. In the worst case we will have less comfort, but we
probably never need to go hungry or live without a house of
some kind!

I am now preparing application letters for possible
employment to 4 Research institutes in my speciality

1. Bottelle Institute, Columbus, O.

2. American Rolling Mill, Middletown, D.

3. Mining Experiment Station, University of Minnesota.
Besides that I am applying for

4. Special work through the New York Engineering Societies Employment Bureau.

Each place requires its special application forms, letters
and references. I hope to get all this very tedious work
finished this week. When these letters are finished then I will
see and try what are the possibilities of developing a few of
my smaller inventions which do not require big capital for
development.

Your man is hunting some kind of income. His chances are

A—work outside his specialty bringing say 100–200 d. per
month.

B—Work in his specialty may bring twice as much

C—But a well chosen inventiv idea based, or partly based
on my previous research experiences may bring us a little
fortune as a few of my previous invention have brought.

And Pittsburgh the centrum and Metropolis of the steel
and allied industries is the place to find out about special
work and actual facts about developing own ideas.

Apparently my Work remains my main interest in life. Out
of work or performing uninteresting low paid work I would

be unhappy and a newsance [nuisance] at home. Or a 60 year old man must change his life habits! You may have some hardships to live in good house without a man. Please tolerate this situation a few weeks or months more until I feel sure that nothing profitable is gained by my living and trying to find something here. Present the children some useful thing from me too but you buy them!

With love for you and children   Otto

⚬————◆————⚬

Pittsburgh, Pa   Sep. 10th 1945
[Aina's birthday was September 11]
Dear Aina,

Your letter of Sep.11th is cheerful and full of confidence. And the birthday celebration was apparently pleasing for yourself as for the girls. Fine! . . . [Discussion of the garden.]

A few words about my work. Any honest and decent man ought to work. In my particular case, I was fortunate to combine my work and hobby profitably developing or looking for inventive ideas. In the period from 1921 to 1940, I succeeded to develop about 17 inventions and earn over $200,000. That is many times more than an average engineer earns. The war destroyed the well established business connections Polysius and GHH (Oberhausen). The advanced years hinder to find corresponding business relations in the USA. A 60 year old man is utterly out of luck to find new employment, especially now when lots of young engineers are looking for jobs. True, the endurance and energy with my 60 years is less than 10 years ago. During the warm season there were up to 50% of days when the will power and energy was lacking to do anything. Now with the cool days I hope finally arrived it is better and I can work up to 6 hours dayly. Since 4 weeks when I started again cooking for myself there has been no digestive disturbance.

I believe perhaps the best bet for me in the time being is to follow up a number of my inventive ideas. It seems fairly sure (based on my former experience) that if I investigate by mental analyses and small scale experiments from 5 to 10 well selected ideas I may find one idea which will be profitable and practical for the steel industry. The idea I was following up in Somerset and during the first weeks in Pittsburgh looked impractical and I abandoned it. (This was the idea of refining of molten iron in the cascade furnace.) Now I am busy with the next thought: speeding up refining of steel in electric furnace by agitation of molten steel with a gas. While the first mentioned idea involved only a trifle in experimental costs (about $30) the present idea will require at least $100 or even $400 for preliminary tests depending how much the industry is going to contribute with technical equipment, help and working facilities. I am now looking for a firm which would support these experiments to some extent.

In general, American steel industry is not sold for doing research or development work to such an extent as the German industry was. They are becoming research conscious in the coming generation, but then we may be dead. Pittsburgh is the place to try my luck with the ideas. Here is the biggest centrum of iron and steel, here are most of the experts in this live, here is the best and biggest library in this specialty. In Berkeley, I could not do the job.

[Long discussion of their securities and sources of investment advice.]

You are a good wife and mother. Wish to pat your back and give you a kiss.

Yours, Otto

Pittsburgh, Oct. 9th 1945
Dear Aina,

Just received your good letter of Oct 7th. I owe you and the girls my answer since many days. There was nothing cheerful or hopeful to report and it is in human nature to keep indifferent or discouraging events for ourselves. I decided some time ago to think and calculate less about my idea how to speed up refining of iron and steel. It looks more expedient to find out what is the opinion of the experts about my idea and more important to find out: is there demand or market for this particular brainchild.

Margin note: *I am writing to Verhoeven brothers. They may know whether German Verhoeven is alive but hardly more. Do not be afraid to write to anybody about anything in free America. Censorship is abolished. There is no Gestapo or GPU. [The forerunner of Russia's KGB]*

I also was looking for a place where I could test or try out the idea on small scale. The opinion of the experts is not always unmistakable. For instance, the best German cement burning expert Prof Kühl of Technische Hochschule Charlottenburg [Berlin Institute of Technology] took in 1927 a negative attitude toward our successful Lepol idea. But just the same, talks with the experts are useful as they often give new viewpoints or mention industrialist, manufacturers or other experts who can clarify the situation.

Last week, I succeeded to contact the Manager of Research at Jones & Laughlin Steel Corp. Mr. Work, with whom I have had conversations and talks formerly also. In a larger discussion of the situation it became clear that J & L has not much sence to apply my dear brainchild. Consequently, they were also unwilling to let me experiment in their plant even essentially on my own cost. This was a bitter disappointment for the father of the idea. But disappointment and hindrance provoke extra courage and sometimes a false sence of youthful power and ability. Under such a feeling I went into a restaurant and ate my lunch, forgetting that I was yet excited. There followed a little digestiv disturbance which hindered me to work for 2 days. My digestion is in good shape again but this silly boy of 61 years has apparently not yet learned how to behave! I think there are other steel plants with other processes where my idea would suit perhaps better. I decided to explore further.

Next I attempted to get an interview with Prof. Fitterer, Head of metallurgical department at Pittsburgh University. Through his contacts in the centrum of steel industry he ought to know. Finally, after visiting his office 3 times, writing him a letter and phoning his secretary 6 times, I reached the man today. We had a friendly talk about for two hours. Nobody can give a definit opinion about an untried new technical idea. He did not grasp it quite and some of his objections were not to the point. On the whole, he was skeptical. One good thing came out of this visit. Dr. Fitterer is prepared to let me experiment in his laboratory at small cost provided that there is demand for my invention. He can give me the names of two leading persons in top electric furnace companies where I could find out more about the question: is there demand or market for my invention? I am going to get interviews with these people next. Both are in Pittsburgh. But it takes time and repeated effort to reach key men. As you see from this letter, this type of work I am doing now can be done only in the centrum of steel industry.

[Discussion of investment advisors.]

Margin note: *Nate's two letters and Lee's letters are unfortunately not yet answered. I am the guilty party. Will write them soon. Have been again so busy with my thoughts.*

⌐——◆——⌐

Pgh Jan 7th 1946
Dear Aina.

I am apparently born to live as an "Einsiedler" ["hermit"] and enjoy the independent life in my crowded living-bed-room with adjoining kitchen.** I had last week days of hard physical work. I built a new 80 pound heavy melting furnace. Carrying this heavy device from one room into the other, hammering and doing the brickmason work makes me bodily tired in the evening. But after a short rest period at "home" I cook and eat my dinner and that goes after the following time table:

Peeling potatoes and cleaning vegetables . . . . . 5 minutes
Cooking my dinner, setting table 10
Eating 20
Washing dishes 5
Preparation, eating and housework for a full meal 40

And in the morning I have sometimes tea and grapefruit
and lots of good ideas in the bed. Then the breakfast is eaten
in the kitchen and lunch packed there too.

Let me know what did you decide concerning your sinus.

Yours cordially,

Otto

** Renate: "Otto knew himself to be a loner. Even on family vacations, as to
La Palma or to Little Deer Island, he sought lodging for himself at a goodly
walking distance from the family's lodging."

[in pencil] Wauwatosa Jun 20, 1962

Dear children

A few days ago mother and I went to American Express
to plan a two week vacation together in Hawaii to start end of
February. Mother had been recently and is even now quite active.
She took me every day to Allis Chalmers and back home, or to
my dentist. However, she felt a little pain sometimes in the bowels. After some urging she went to our family doctor Mrs. Fisher
who arranged immediately a thorough X ray investigation at the
Milwaukee most modern $2500 X ray apparatus, operated by a
very capable radiologist Dr. Marks. He made a so beautiful and
clear 9 picture study of the bowels as I never have seen before.
After the doctors presented a diagnoses, we with mother went to
see the X ray pictures at "Doctors Hospital." The pictures show in
a number of projections a stricture in the colon [thick intestine].
See sketch [in margin]. Whether the deformation or growth is
cancerous, or not, is not known. In any case the stricture has to
be cut out and the ends of the colon put together again. Mother

will go to "Doctors Hospital" in Milwaukee tomorrow. Dr.
Fisher selected a surgeon with reputation whom she will assist
personally. Mother will have a private room. After a few days of
preparations the operation will take place perhaps during the latter part of the week. Although mother has an operation, but she
takes the risky unavoidable event with most remarkable courage.
She despises the agonizing postoperative feelings and asks not to
be bothered during that time. I will keep you informed by phone,
or wire, any day after 7 in the evening. The doctors and I will take
good care of mother.

In sorrow your Father
*(A Copy went to Fernandez (but no evidence of having been
received))*

------◆------

O.G. Lellep, 3990 – 4th Street, Riverside, Calif. Oct. 2ned 1964

Dear Lee and Renate and your families–
A few days ago I had my 80th birthday. It was an agreeable surprise to receive from the *Geschatfuhrer* (President-
Manager) Karl-Otto Polysius and from the Board of Directors
(*Aufsichtsrat*) of the Polysius Co at Neubeckum the enclosed
letters recognizing my admirable cooperation with this company since 37 years. In case you keep a file about life-history
of your "old man" these documents belong into this file.

To celebrate my 80th birthday I am going today to my oldest
friend G.P. Klaas to spend a week end. We are friends since 58
years back. His address is 926 Marine View Drive, Vista, Calif.

My experimental work at the California Portland Cement
Co. at Colton and Mohave in South California is proceeding
with my dedicated cooperation. I am going to formulate a
patent application on the idea in USA which involves about
20 pages of [legend ? light?] text and 3-4 drawings.

I feel fine!

Otto

O.G. Lellep, 4723 Neubeckum, W.Germany, Jahn Str.20
June 3 1968

My dear daughters, sons in law and grandchildren
I was very glad and happy to receive from Lee a family
picture and a letter inviting me to come to visit you all this
summer. This letter will inform you what my situation is here.
Despite my very soon 84 years I have here at Neubeckum quite
interesting and fairly active life. Our mutual mine and Bern
Helming's invention preheating lime for basic oxygen steel
converter, on which we worked 2 ½ years and spent substantial
sum of money did not succeed commercially. Our estimate
of profit to the steel companies was not recognized by steel
experts or not found sufficient to apply the idea on big scale.

About 4 weeks ago the manager of research division at the
largest steel company in Germany [Thyssen] Professor Dr.
Kootz talked me about the great newer idea of simplifying
the steelmaking by changing the present intermittent process
of converting in oxygen-blown converter into a continuous
process. The French governmental owned research company
Irsid has been busy on this new continuous process since about
4 years, so have also the English steel people. To my knowledge
the Germans and Americans have not yet done anything
outstanding in this line. The Irsid Engineers have demonstrated
this process in their experimental plant and have patented
it in France. The findings were published last fall in Spanish
language in Montevideo, South America. [next page missing]

O.G. Lellep, 4723 Neubeckum, W. Germany., M. Luther Str. 5
Oct 21, 1968
Dear Lee, Bob and children
Have received your letter of Oct. 12th. I appreciate the 4

photos Bob and yourself took during my enjoyable visit to your big house, garden and swimming pool. Lee looks like a young pretty girl in the water below the rubber boat loaded with all the children and myself. Your snapshot of 8 persons comprising 3 generations is interesting. On the wall in my room hangs the large size picture of Renate's family made by a professional photographer. Below it hangs the small size view of your 8 person family. The small size gives an entirely wrong impression. I wish very much to have yours, a large size about 13x9 inches to hang side by side with Renate's family. I would gladly pay the professional photographer. After say 15 anybody in your family would be very happy to see how they looked when they were 15 years younger.

I am pleased to know Bob's mother is out of hospital and is living in her house with daily help.

According to Newsweek the USA tries, or plans to finish the bloody war in Vietnam.

At present in 85th year of life I stopped my practical inventive work and am attempting to find out in what country I should live starting with 1969. My personal income tax in Germany would be excessively high and wish to inquire how much this tax would be in USA—when according to my Trust agreement in the Marine Bank in Milwaukee I pay most of my income to the Estonian students.

2. No, I did not get the Fairless award sponsored by the US Steel company, for which I was only one of the three candidates. Not I, but my very good friend, formerly at Allis Chalmers R. Fran started to get it for me. My inventions and work is very little known in USA and very much more in Europe especially in Germany. Allis Chalmers Co gets all the credit for the very large about 15 iron ore pelletizing plants based on my patents and producing at the present time yearly 26 million tons of the hardest, dust free iron ore pellets in Minnesota, peninsula Michigan, Canada, Sweden. I am not sore, because "the prophet is usually not famous in his own country". I am quite satisfied when unexpectedly the German Iron and Steel Society granted me during 1960 the biggest award with gold medal—because the first oxygen-blown steel convertor in the world was developed by your father and demonstrated in the

Gutehoffnungshuette after 4 years of experiments in 1939. You lived at that time in Hösel. You Lee were not yet born when I discovered the Lepol kiln idea in Estonia and Polysius Company built it in Dessau during your [Lee] birth. Now 330 very economical Lepol kilns for burning cement have been sold to all 5 continents by the Polysius Co in Germany.

With cordial good wishes for you all
Otto

<hr />

My dear daughters and your husbands, April 16th 1969
O.G. Lellep. 3416 Booth Str., Milwaukee, Wis. 53212
My dear daughters and your husbands,

This morning I happened to read the 4 page article "the Healing Touch of Attention" in the April number of *Readers Digest*, starting on page 175. I notice to my regret the negligent attitude of some university professors to this most successful periodical in the world, which appears in 28 million copies in 13 languages of the world. What does it make so successful? I believe one reason is it helps most people to improve their bodily, or mental health and to make the readers more healthy and happy.

Thinking back on my own long life I have to confess I was relatively successful in my very interesting profession as inventor, saving for the cement and steel industry and the consumers around $100 000 000! But I did not sufficiently pay attention to your dear mother and you both personally. This frank confession makes me feel better.

Your old father Otto

APPENDIX 2

Photographs from "Contributions Toward the Development of the Lepol Kiln in Heidelberg: Dr. Ehrhart Schott and Otto Lellep"

The photos below are from a piece that is undated, with no named author. It appears among materials posted online by the Heidelberg Cement Company. The translations of the photo captions are by Renate. (Accessed on October 25, 2020: https://www.hc-museum. de/sites/default/files/assets/ document/9d/29/a12_2015_ lepolofen.pdf)

For more references to the research kiln Otto built in Rudersdorf at Heidelberg Cement, see the Heidelberg Cement blog by Dieter Kramer: https://blog.heidel-bergcement.com/en/cement-industry-on-the-cutting-edge-for-150-years

(Accessed October 25, 2020).

The research kiln today [2015] with further additions.

Photo 2 (page 4): [Dr.] Otto Lellep with Phillipp Hoffman during a trial run of the kiln, ca.1931.

Dr. Ehrhart Schott standing next to the trial kiln in Leimen, ca. 1930.

[Dr.] Otto Lellep standing next to the trial kiln at the cement works in Leimen, ca. 1931. [Renate: Otto is probably standing at the control panel.]

Probably [Dr.] Otto Lellep's research kiln at Adler's Cement Works, in the industrial park of Rudersdorf.

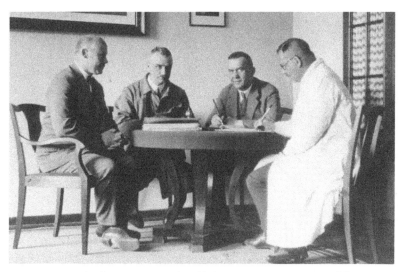

Meeting of colleagues, upper level kiln commissioners, in Karlshorst.
(Dr. Jahns; Director, Engineering DoctorWecke; Dr. Spiegeberg;
Dr. Ehrhart Schott) ca. 1930.

The new Lepol kiln II in Leimen, 1961.

APPENDIX 3

The story below appeared on the front page of *Kölnische Zeitung (Cologne Newspaper, Morning Edition)* on December 30, 1938. It is what John McPhee calls "the literature of fact," written by a literary—not a political—columnist or journalist.

Werner Oellers was a neighbor and friend of Otto's and of the entire Lellep family. His story is clearly based upon Oellers' personal knowledge of Otto and his efforts to create an oxygen-blown process for the production of steel. An actual factory for production had not by then been built but in his memoir, Otto does mention three experts from the German Engineering Society who viewed the successful operation of his large-scale, experimental furnace.

Oellers was a literary author who worked freelance and for newspapers. He has been described as having opposed the Nazi regime, a view corroborated by Renate. She recalls her mutti telling her that Oellers had taken his young son, Renate's playmate, for a walk, risking his own and his family's life by the frankness of his words opposing the Nazis. Like most young people at the time Oellers' son participated in Hitler Youth activities, from which Renate was excluded.

The Inventor

By Werner Oellers
Translated by David Kretz

Doctor G. stood at the window of his office, on the second floor of his country house, which he had built years ago, and looked into the brightening morning. The eastern sky was turning red. Rising up from the horizon, the dark fire soon flooded a quarter of the celestial dome. The park's defoliated trees and bushes stood in front of it like black, fantastic latticework. Most likely, there would be rain.

The Doctor had not slept all night. The work of thinking, if one had once caught the obsession, could not be terminated at will, as little as a heartbeat could be when one lay down to rest.

The Doctor reclined his elbow on the window handle and cast a fleeting glance at a letter in the middle of his desk. He knew its contents by heart already, and yet he felt himself driven, again and again, to read: that the new experimental plant, and with it the needed quantities of oxygen, was ready and that the management of the factory was expecting him, the doctor, for a large-scale experiment.

For a moment, a smile of almost moving purity and clarity passed over the strict and haggard face with its deeply indented temples, but only for a moment. What was it now that he had claimed to have invented? Was it the thought of blowing pure oxygen through the converters, which took up the raw iron from the blast furnaces to turn it into steel, rather than blowing impure air? In order to increase the efficiency, improve the quality of steel, to keep the pesky nitrogen out? This, in order to obtain a higher quality steel at the old or even lower costs?

Yet many had already had this thought. It was as old as the converters themselves and thousands of hours and nights of the best brains might have been spent brooding over it. "Spend your time on something better!" a university professor had counseled him. "Otherwise, you'll wrack your brain for nothing."

The Doctor had traveled to foreign countries and fished for information among steelworkers of high repute. Those reputable people had smiled. "Keep your hands off it," they had said. "There is no material that can withstand the insane temperatures that must occur in the process." And another, standing next to the first, had added: "Not to mention all the other difficulties."

The Doctor had returned home with these reports. There, he long and often stood at his window, looking over the park, just as he did now, in the red sunrise, to think it all over once more. How many hours and days of how many weeks and months might he have stood there? For three years? Then, at one point he had suddenly sat down and started to calculate. How much would the oxygen cost? What temperatures would result? Could they be reduced? How would the chemical processes in the steel bath run down? What new conditions would present themselves? Would there be new phenomena at the jets? In the converter hulls? Would dangerous gases develop?

Every question had given rise to several new ones and each of the new ones gave rise to yet new ones in turn. The Doctor had heaped equations upon equations, filled page upon page, mountains of pages, with calculations based upon his slide rule and logarithm charts, all done according to the orders and degrees of higher mathematics. Eventually, he had begun to design an experimental plant. He drafted and discarded, and drafted again and discarded again. In between, again and again, he had stood at the window. The strict, brooding intellectual's face in the window had become a familiar sight to all who regularly walked the path at the edge of the park.

No, there was no point in recalling all of this—not yet, not today. Nor did he want to recall how he had traveled here and there with his drafts and calculations to find only shaking heads and a thousand counter-questions and perhaps, at times, also a smile that hid much underneath.

Yet he needed to be trusted. He, who did not own a thing, except his knowledge of the laws of nature and the tenacious strength of his spirit, he needed help for his work that might cost thousands—and might be all for naught. So, he had sat down to examine open questions, to clarify and solve, for days and weeks; then he had departed again.

How could he forget the festive day when the sun rose upon his toils and efforts, the day on which he found someone with faith and trust in his project. True, he had found some for himself already, in the faith his wife and friends placed in him. If this had been a blind, inexpert faith, placed in him more than in his work, it had nonetheless given him new strength and in mysterious ways encouraged him and driven him further. Now, however, power's aid had joined itself to faith. "You can conduct the experiments in our factory" the steel mill's director had told him. "You will be provided with all that you need."

That had been one of those rather rare, festive days of life in which the entire world seemed abloom. Nothing had really been achieved so far, and yet how strongly did it feel like an achievement to him! The funds for a research expedition had been granted to him, for a march through difficult terrain full of obstacles on the edge of which, somewhere, he suspected a treasure. Would the direction be right? Would he be able to reach the threshold of the wilderness—through expected swamps, high-piled mountains, through jungles and primeval forests? Would he find the treasure in its suspected place? For he knew well that neither he nor others were meant to create; he was only to search, and find, and transform what was already present, albeit hidden. Believing himself to know what he could expect from Nature, in constant awe of its mysteries, he was driven to search.

Thus, the Doctor had started to build an experimental plant. Every day he drove from his country house to the far-away city, where the air is smoky and sooty; where a forest of smokestacks, chimneys, towers, and scaffolds rises up, and glowing snakes of steel strips are shot through crashing, wheeling machines; where the stompers roar and the converters thunder; where colorful sheaves of fire magically illuminate the night; and Nature's enormous forces are channeled, transmuted, and bundled until, through ever new channeling, transmutation, and bundling, they give rise to well-ordered shapes of strange things: airplanes and locomotives, armored cruisers and automobiles, typewriters and vacuum cleaners.

In this monstrous, coordinated chaos, the workshop and the laboratory of the Doctor had now become an unknown, mysterious, and dangerous land, such as emerges when pure oxygen is let loose into a furnace of a-thousand-and-a-half degrees Celsius with the pressure of several atmospheres.

After indefatigable works of calculation, consideration, and drafting, the Doctor had decided which questions to put to Nature. His specific questions drove the plant's design; its operation posed them. Only by "Yes" or "No" would Nature answer.

Yet Nature was unruly. She raged wrathfully that someone dared, once again, to intrude upon her secrets. In her fierce fury, she shouted one "No" after the other into the Doctor's face. She threatened dangerous eruptions and seethed like an uncanny, bubbling volcano. One day, the foaming lava had flooded the entire apparatus and, in a sudden rush, had destroyed it utterly. The Doctor and his helpers had been able to save themselves from the raging forces only at the last moment, and not without getting caught by a few splashes of steel hurled at them.

After a sleepless night, the Doctor now recalled these events as he stood by the window, looking into the morning as the dawn's early, red light started to pale. Now and then, his glance touched upon the letter on the desk, and from time to time a slight, clear smile returned to his stern face. He had been quite a burden on his wife back then, when he had thought the mountains of his yearlong calculations and drafts had been thrown over by a higher force and he himself had been cast under a spell of impotence. It must have been a miracle that he did not give in to despair and some strength remained in him to believe and to continue to work. No one, not even he himself, could say how it occurred that one day, when, following a mysterious necessity, he sat down at his desk again and started, once more, to calculate and draft. The motivation had barely come from himself. And yet he knew that he now found himself face to face with Nature, in the position of a pedagogue facing a child who is hard to reach, headstrong, and withdrawn, yet within which immense forces are slumbering, both good and evil. Only through unspeakable patience, through humility and the awareness of his own inadequacy, and only through ever-renewed efforts to grasp and understand could he help awaken and order the good forces.

Thus, he had built another experimental plant. Again, he had worked out the questions that he wanted to pose in the experiment; again, his questions had been answered in the negative. But now the answers seemed less harsh, and one day, it happened that neither a "Yes" nor a "No" was returned, but rather an evasive, ambiguous answer, as the Pythia used to give, with a quiet smile, to those seeking her counsel. At this, the Doctor, too, had smiled and begun to narrow his question even further, and yet further, and further.

Life came into the house. He was startled a little by the loud, boisterous, children's voices suddenly rising from the kitchen. He looked at his watch, took the letter from the desk, and left.

It was raining when he pushed his motorbike out of the garage fifteen minutes later. His wife came out to the street with him. She had put an apron over her head against the rain and nodded at him with a smile as he started the machine. He knew then that he had not been able to conceal from her what he had so persistently tried to keep secret. She still stood at the same place, one hand lifted, waving at him, never minding the rainfall, when, from the road, he turned back once more to look towards her.

Her smile and distant waving remained with him, strangely dispensing warmth, as he sped over the splashing road through the rain. The ever more congested road began to demand an increasing share of his attention. All thoughts of his work and the last three years' labor fell away him, until, eventually, nothing remained but an everyday motorbike rider, making his way through the thicket of people and vehicles, his eyes and ears wide open.

Only when the breath of the steel mill blew in his face, steaming and hissing, red-glowing and flaming, and the inclined lifts rose above him, and the beats of the cyclopean gas machines let tremble the earth, did the Doctor's old obsessions and restless anticipations overcome him again. He felt as if his heartbeat followed the rhythm of the machines and glowed in the hellish heat of the foaming steel. And yet, he still saw in the distance, on a forlorn country road, a woman in the rain who waved at him with a smile, a fluttering apron over her head.

Then, everything happened as if in a dream. Only a few images from the thrilling preparations later remained with him: how the dumper hopper high up in the air floated towards them with the raw iron; how the glistening broth gushed into the gaping mouth of the lowered converter; how the converter slowly erected itself into its working position; how the eyes of the director, filled with a strange tension, were looking for his. Then the oxygen was released into the iron soup. It roared and foamed under its violent, consuming jets, and meter-high flames burst forth from the gigantic mouth of the converter.

The Doctor felt the others looking at him from time to time: the director; the engineers; the yellow-skinned, weather-worn faces of the workers. Yet he did not move, gazing only at the colors of the flames. He was surprised to note how calm he felt suddenly, having, to the contrary, expected in himself a turmoil like the one he had caused in the boiling iron. He felt a great joyfulness inside, true; and yet he remained quiet and pensive.

Suddenly, the color spectrum of the flames seemed to indicate that the load was done. But was it well cooked? The workers with long-shafted dippers ran to take samples. Oh, what the poor steel had to endure to be recognized: slow-cooled steel, or steel quickly "refreshed" in the water-bath, steel at all temperatures. Big machines stood ready to break and bend, to pierce and press, to pull and fold, to wring and hammer it, measuring with precision all the forces it could bear. Quickly, a sample bar was thrown into the mouth of the tearing machine to see how elastic the steel would be; how grained and fibered it would be; how far it could be stretched; and what attacks would beat it. Slowly, the force was increased, and though no change was visible in the bar so far, they all stared as if mesmerized by the machine tearing with uncanny force. The finger of the manometer trembled, climbing higher and higher, yet before it had climbed high enough, they heard a soft crack. The steel had torn.

A sudden terror gripped the people's faces. as if they had witnessed an ungraspable misfortune. Some, it seemed, dared not turn towards the Doctor. But those who looked at him with pity and sadness saw that he smiled. A clear, happy smile had appeared, strangely pure and a little hapless, on the furrowed face. The Doctor, too, could not have said what made him smile at this dire moment, yet he felt in himself a great calm and laughter.

"What do you say?" asked the director standing next to him.

The Doctor turned toward him. Neither now nor later knowing how these words came to him, he said, "Before it holds its own, it seems the steel itself wants to know how much force I myself can endure before tearing. I should think in half a year we will be ready."

The director walked with him as the Doctor left the factory hall. It was still raining. The two men shook hands and nodded at each other, smiling. The Doctor mounted his motorbike, and while the director looked pensively after him, sped on across the factory premises towards his country home.

APPENDIX 4

May 26, 1940:
Otto's Letter to Aina

[Renate's translation of Otto's letter in German]

OG Lellep c/o American Institute of Mining
in Bethlehem, Penna., May 26, 1940

My dear Aina

As of my most recent letter to you of April 27, much has changed. In that letter, I had proposed your coming with the children to America since the war seemed to be one of long duration. And that possibilities of getting out through Italy seemed increasingly dangerous. I cabled my decision to you, including the fact that I had paid for three passages for you on US Lines. Apparently as a result, on May 11 the Stuttgart Consulate and the Washington State Department received from you a telegram "impossible for her and children return USA before June 1." Concerned about these travel costs I informed you on May 13 "Telegram received Advise soon as possible pay tolls to USA Lines sending ten dollars Brenner Pass 40 Genoa to all, good luck."

The Great War had begun, and I thought you and children would already have arrived on American soil. I started looking around for where our family might find lodging. In this world, unfortunately, one must take the moneybag into account. In Germany we were living at least a middle-class life; here our standard of living is less favorable. We had considerable income resulting from my inventions as well as

interest and security from capital investments. This income
and security disappears the moment we are no longer in
Germany. Thirty thousand dollars here can't pay what thirty
thousand DeutschMark could in pre-war Germany. From our
earning of our capital investments we could at best reside in a
hut while satisfying the hunger of our four-head family. We'd
have to adjust ourselves to living a far less convenient and
comfortable life than in our German home. That would be
the worst-case scenario should I be unable to find income-
producing employment. So, I have been looking around to
find out how my oxygen-ideas might here be valued.

Especially in regard to steel production, Bethlehem Steel
Company produces five times as much steel annually than
did GHH. Unfavorable for me. In Germany about 40% of
steel is produced by the Converter method, here only 3%. My
invention pertains only to steel produced by converters, hence
would apply to only an insignificant part of steel production
here in America. Moreover, German technical professionals
are impressed by the low-cost economics of oxygen's use in
steel production, while here (because of some large industrial-
ists' self-serving propaganda) the professionals consider
oxygen's cost too high. [Nevertheless], any correspondence
with willing producers of cheap oxygen in Germany has
become impossible. On top of that, my invention is not yet
ready for mass production. Therefore, Bethlehem's professional says to me "Not interested." This bitter news saddens
me. My consolation is that some day other firms, especially
a German one, might regard my invention as significant.
Whether I'll have the luck of being alive when my invention
comes into flower remains questionable.

Here, in Bethlehem, Mr. Hoffmann of Polysius corporation (Dodson Building, Bethlehem Penna) is helpful. As also
Prof. Doan, who teaches metallurgy at Lehigh University,
is pleasantly inclined toward me. Both of them have helped
me get in touch with steel professionals. But a gigantic firm
like Bethlehem Steel is like a feudal kingdom. Certainly not
with the king himself, not even his ministers. Yet I know that
it would be worthwhile for such "ministers" to be aware of
and evaluate my oxygen-ideas. Unfortunately, it turns out the

current minister is no professional technician, but rather, the well-seated father-in-law of the king. And for this expert of the "minister" I'm nothing but an unwanted competitor. But the real issue is that my oxygen-idea is for the America at this time not suitable. Naturally I do know that I could undoubtedly be useful in some way to the American steel industry. To demonstrate that capability to American industry at this time is, however, no easy task. Naturally my best experiences have been with cement and to some extent with nickel.

Only after having found no response by the steel industry here to my oxygen ideas will I offer my readiness to serve in some other capacity. That I will do only in order to obtain some sort of income to support my family upon and after its arrival. But it will take a long time before I find a suitable position according to my capacities. I haven't lost hope but do realize that this is far more difficult than I had been able to imagine during my vacation. Moreover, there are the facts that a 56-year-old man cannot render the workload of a youngster, and this is a man with a "nervous" stomach.

I've searched further for how and where the family might reside; city rentals do show up but only on long noisy streets, and there are sufficient houses to purchase, but there are no rentals on the outskirts of the city, and none for lease. How could we purchase a house when I don't know where I'll be working? In the worst case, one can make a living arrangement. For example, out in the countryside along a fast-flowing stream there is a house attractive for the family, but at 18km from the nearest town, no nearby stores, and a with a village 4 km away. What there is nearby is a one-room schoolhouse where all the children of all eight grades study together under one teacher.

Meanwhile, the situation of Germany's victory in Holland, Belgium, and France has shifted. Up until now the Blitzkrieg has been successful, and should Germany be successful in securing the English coast and the nearby countries, its victory will be assured. The Italians are also planning to join the German effort. One sign is that the big passenger ocean liners are no longer leaving port. And the media reports that Italy is no longer issuing transit visas. Americans have not needed to get through customs into Italy, and perhaps you with the children might yet get through.

In view of these difficulties about getting out and of finding a place for us to live in America, and in view of the likely German victory, I have cabled you "Italy apparently prohibits transit. Stop. Outlook for work and house poor. Stop. Upon quick peace agreement I return. Stop. By foreseeable war of long duration you come here. Stop. Swiss credit bank 270 dollar. Stop. Heartfelt greetings. Otto"

You know my views regarding freedom, whether here or in Europe. Here, to speak any word in German is unwelcome, even dangerous. But in war, matters swing, are uncertain, to be decided, maybe, next week, as to who will have the long-term victory. Should Germany win and reorganize Europe, Germany is the most suitable for continuing my work of research and inventing. We are rooted in Germany. You'd notice that once you spend some time here in America. But as long as the war continues: I cannot get a pass for over there.

A war of long duration means deprivation and misery for the whole world and especially for Germany. For this eventuality, try to get to America. Consulates will give you advice on how to get through. For travel expenses you have 270 DM in Bern. Can send more if necessary. The whole world is now in turmoil, making it impossible to give any advice. Should you, counter to your desire, have to remain in Germany, I will try to send food packages.

Any letters from you have stopped coming through. The last one was from April, if I remember rightly. It's of course my fault that I, an American citizen, have married a German wife and that the two of us, with our children, are suspended, pedaling between two worlds. I wish our separation would end soon, even if we have to live here on very limited means. I address this letter to you in Hösel, and send a second one to the US line Genoa. You are going through very difficult times getting together all the necessary paperwork for departure and the difficulties of getting through Italy. Should luck prevail to get aboard the *Manhattan*, you need not telegraph. The line will do it. I will meet you at the ship. You poor woman, and the dear children.

Receive my best greetings. Otto

Margin note, in English: *Meet you in the port of New York. Send word to Polysius Corp Bethlehem PA 4221. Financial consults G.C. Cox bureau 70 Pine St NY and German Secretary Miss Herrmann. Elfriede's address 733 West 135th St NY. She has no telephone.*

Margin note in German, first page: *Now only for the first time, do I notice how good we had it in Hösel. Our home in Hösel, I would not like so easily to lose.*

Memories of Germany and the US

1940 and 1941
Renate Lellep Fernandez: Age 8 and 9

In the spring of 1940, Mutti received the directive from Otto and the US consulate in Stuttgart urging her to leave Germany. At the time, she was housing German army officers in our Hösel home—to my pleasure, as I, age seven, enjoyed sitting on the men's laps, making an album collection of the glossy, wildlife photos that accompanied their cigar purchases.

Mutti had to get us out of Germany without the helpful presence of Otto. He was away and had given her to understand that as a naturalized US citizen, he was not allowed to return to help us leave. Germany had invaded Poland on September 1, 1939, and Europe was at war. We do not know what US regulation or policy prevented Otto from returning to a war zone, though Germany itself was not yet at war with the US.

Alone, Mutti made all the arrangements for departure. As the wife of a naturalized US citizen and the mother of offspring born in Germany but of American citizenship, Mutti felt herself vulnerable to the possibility of being forcefully separated from Li [Liisa] and me. We were age seven and nine, our brown hair and blue eyes making us look "Aryan" to those Germans believing in racial purity. Mutti knew we would soon be nubile and therefore attractive as candidates for *Neugeboren*—Hitler's program recruiting girls to become young unwed mothers of his future fighting forces "conquering the world." (*Deutschland, Deutschland Über Alles* was the song that was spinning in my head.)

Monetary transactions were encumbered or blocked in Switzerland, and ships intended for Atlantic crossings were being canceled, overbooked, or mined at sea, but Mutti prepared to leave Germany. She was most concerned for our safety. Were she to be forcibly separated from us, she hoped we sisters could yet make our way through France, over the Pyrenees, across the Iberian Peninsula, and out of Lisbon to America. To that end, she prepared tags for us to wear around our necks stating our father's name, "Otto Lellep," and the address of our destination in America—the one he gave us. Before we left, she also bought Liisa and me *hakelstiefe*—boots whose lacing passed through hooks (*hakel*). I supposed she'd selected them in the event we sisters were separated from her, and the two of us would have to hike out over the Pyrenees to ship out of Lisbon.[1] The boots were very impressive, if heavy, footwear.

It was well into June before Mutti could arrange for us to make our way across the densely guarded Brenner Pass and into Italy. Men in military uniforms were posted every hundred meters along the pass, probably because people were fleeing the war zones. The train paused and our papers were checked, but I was looking at the families in the meadows making hay. One woman had a growth around her neck that made her look to me like the witches I'd imagined and heard mentioned in fairy tales.

We arrived early in Nervi, since absorbed by Genoa but then a sweet village of orange and lemon trees, just above cliffs that guarded the narrow beach below. We remained there several days longer than expected because the ocean liner's departure was deliberately delayed in order that refugees from Eastern Europe who were booked for passage might yet arrive. By or during that time,

Mussolini must have allied with Hitler, joining the Axis powers. I did not know this. It may have happened while Mutti secluded Li and me on a tiny, narrow beach, shaded by the cliff, forbidding us to go into the sunlit water. At the time, I think, Mutti was trying to manage her way through officialdom to enable us to board the ship. Can you imagine everyone's anxiety, those who had booked passage but were grounded and those still trying to make their way to Nervi?

Some refugees did manage to arrive. The ship—the *Manhattan*—was the last commercial passenger ship able to leave from the Mediterranean for the United States. When it finally departed, it was triply loaded. Once we were underway, people in thick crowds leaned over the rails, spending most of the day watching the water. I learned much later they were anxiously looking for mines and submarines. My sister and I, however, had a happy time racing throughout the many fancy rooms on the various levels and up and down the grand staircases.

On a hot, July day, Mutti succeeded in getting herself and us onto Ellis Island. Li and I arrived wearing the only footwear we had—our Hakelstiefe. Our address tags, which Mutti had draped around our necks each day before we even left Germany, had somehow disappeared.

Mutti got our trunks and baggage and made a tight enclosure for us to sit in, strictly instructing us not to move. She left to attend to our papers. I remember anxious people milling about, but I sat quietly, enjoying the stained glass, rose window in Ellis Island's great hall. Somehow, we got from the island to a high rise in Manhattan. I do not recall the moment of our meeting Otto, but I remember that he took us to a cafeteria—a Horn and Hardart's. He pointed out that we were to take a tray that we could push smoothly along the shiny steel rails, while selecting from the single servings of food set out on glass shelves along the rails. I buttered cracker after cracker and ate so many I developed a stomach ache.

Otto had found a rental in Allentown. Mutti hired a highly recommended school teacher named Mary Lichty to teach us English.

I was learning with great urgency and anxiety. In the meanwhile, my mother heard me shouting in German in my sleep—four-letter words I must have absorbed from our gardener back in Hösel.

While Otto was in Mexico, Mutti and I lived in Germansville, Pennsylvania with Tom Keppler (or Kepplinger), an elderly farmer. Mutti felt Li needed complete immersion in an English-speaking environment, so Li lived with a Whitaker family—found by Mary Lichty—on the other side of the Blue Ridge Mountains, in Ashville, Pennsylvania.

Mutti was a highly trained, experienced nurse, but it was impossible for her to gain certification in the US. Instead, she had found two job possibilities: one in an orphanage, where she could use her nursing skills, and the other working for an elderly farmer, Tom Keppler, whom she could help as a practical nurse and housekeeper. She took me to see the orphanage, then let me choose between the two possibilities. Made to realize that, like the orphans, I would unable to spend much time with Mutti, I chose the elderly farmer, "Old Tom."

Tom Keppler was an experimenter and innovator who, in his adolescence, lost one hand in the course of experimenting with explosives. Every Sunday, his descendants descended upon him to make a big chicken dinner, starting with his live chickens. A vegetarian, I closed my eyes whenever I had to go out through the kitchen, having to pass the big, wooden tub of chicken guts and feathers the Keppler women were discarding as they prepared for dinner. Mutti helped, as well. One day, self-blinded, I missed my way, and to my horror stepped into that mess. That was probably the first time that I vocally expressed myself in a four-letter word in English. I cleaned myself up at the hand pump outdoors, which so sharply contrasted with the ordinary plumber's faucet that I used to turn on in our Hösel kitchen. For the first time, I saw how water could be drawn from the ground. "Americans are so practical," I said to myself. I could see how things worked! I loved working that pump. Of course, that was Otto's influence.

Every night when I went to bed, the spatial arrangement of the house required me to pass in front of Old Tom. He was always sitting in his big, well-worn, easy chair, with his heavy, black, iron safe adjacent to him. He once showed me how he could spin the golden dial to open his safe with his only hand, but he did not use this hand to shake mine goodnight. This disappointed me. It was our family custom, and also German custom, that one shook hands upon going up to one's bed. A polite child, I'd learned to shake hands or to curtsy as appropriate in many contexts in Germany. I had to struggle to de-condition myself with Old Tom and in my classroom at school.

It was in Pennsylvania that I was introduced to life in America. I was happy with so many of my experiences: the party gift of a little cardboard box suitcase of animal crackers—I could carry the box here and there by its string handle; the beautiful sunsets, seen from the hill Mutti and I climbed, in contrast to the flat land where we walked in Hösel; and Old Tom's outdoor handpump that I worked with much satisfaction.

---

1. I learned many years later that people like Lisa Fittko were known for conducting refugees over the Pyrenees to the relative safety of Lisbon. I am guessing that Mutti was hoping we could find our way to such people, should the dire need arise.

APPENDIX 6

Reference Letters for Otto

December 23, 1944

The following letters are related to Otto's time in Pittsburgh and his attempt to find work at the Bureau of Mines in Colorado

Mr. Parry is introducted to Fieldner. He interesting in good mountain climate works in put my country : gas penetration, oil shale industry etc.

305 Roup Avenue
Pittsburgh, Pa.
Phone: MO 2619

December 23, 1944

Mr. V. F. Parry
In Charge Bureau of Mines
Golden, Colorado

Dear Mr. Parry:

      You may need in the future assistance or help. Enclosed please find my experience record and a few references. To help you and serve at the same time our country during the war time, I wish to make you an exceptionally favorable offer explained in the following frank statement.

      You may find my records quite satisfactory (an application for civil service was mailed last summer to Mr. Fieldner) except my 60 years of age. The higher age limits our bodily capacity, we are also slower. But our experiences may be richer and according to impartial scientific tests the old people can have keen minds and their capacity and willingness to learn may compete with younger ones. To my surprise I found recently that the chances of employment for a 60 year old man are exceedingly poor despite the much publicized shortage of manpower.

      I do not expect from you any extra favor, but feel that the Bureau of Mines, as a Governmental organ, could try to employ for the duration older professional men who are in surplus and in many cases not only willing, but anxious to work. This would release younger men for more strenuous war work.

THE UNSHAKEABLE FAITH OF AN INVENTOR

In my personal case this war has almost destroyed my European investments. But I am glad to be safe and alive in this adopted country. I do not feel justified to retire consuming family's savings as long as I feel capable to work six hours per day. Productive work which seems possible in your organization would make me happy.

Considering the abovementioned unfavorable employment chances for a 60 year old man, I am prepared to forget my former very substantial earnings as a free lance development engineer and inventor or my $450 monthly salary in Kaiser enterprises half a year ago. You do not need to take my chances. I offer my help as volunteer to your organization without any fixed salary for a month. You can pay me or not according to your own judgement - whatever I am worth to you in competion with the younger set. Any inventions made during the employment would be credited and assigned to your department.

The type of work I am willing to perform shall suit your conditions. I feel quite at home as helper in overalls to experiment with gas generators, retorts or furnaces, or as engineer for solving problems in process, combustion or furnace engineering, or to collect, analyse and summarize most recent data on the modern profitable Estonian oil shale industry, or to act if desirable only as a consultant.

Mr. V. F. Parry　　　　　　　Page 2　　　　　　December 23, 1944
In Charge Bureau of Mines

Although my best results have been achieved when working independently on own initiative, I am perfectly willing to be directed by you for the best interests of the Bureau.

Writer's keen desire is to help you and thus help our great country by working at your very interesting and promising problems.

Yours sincerely,

O. G. Lellep

OGL/cla

I gave Klaas as reference to Bureau of Mines. OG

UNITED STATES
DEPARTMENT OF THE INTERIOR
BUREAU OF MINES
Golden, Colorado
January 8, 1945

G. P. Klaas, Consulting Engineer
c/o Braun & Company, Engineers
1000 Fremont Avenue
Alhambra, California

Dear Sir:

We are considering the employment of Mr. O. G. Lellep on development work in connection with complete gasification of coal. Mr. Lellep has given you as a reference and I shall appreciate it if you can express your opinion regarding his probable adaptability to our work.

We have a small laboratory in Golden, Colorado employing about 14 persons who conduct investigations on gasification and carbonization of coal. We are somewhat crowded as to office space. Mr. Lellep may be engaged on a part time basis and I am wondering if he will fit pleasantly into our group.

Any information you can give me will be appreciated.

Very truly yours,

V. F. Parry
Supervising Engineer
Subbituminous Coal and Lignite Section

But the pay in Bureau of Mines in Golden Colorado is exactly the same as here! Only the climate is better here. Has it sense to change again? Tell me what would you like better! Naturally I do not know whether Bureau is going to engage me because Klaas letter was delayed. In hurry Otto.

C F BRAUN & CO
Manufacturers and Constructors

Alhambra, California.

C O P Y
※※※※※※※

January 30, 1945

V.F.Parry, Supervising Engineer
Subbituminous Coal and Lignite Section
U.S.Bureau of Mines
Golden, Colorado.

Dear Sir:

Your letter dated Jan.8 concerning the employment of
Dr. O.G.Lellep has only today reached me. The delay was caused
by my leave of absence.

I have known Dr. Lellep for almost forty years and I
can recommend him as one of the ablest engineers for research
and development. His many-sided knowledge and experience is
eminently suited for this kind of work.

His most prominent engineering characteristics are:
--the ability to approach a new problem systematically thru
preliminary study of component problems,
--the resourcefulness in devising means for inexpensive testing of components before tackling the main problems,
--the disapprobation of haphazard and expensive large-scale
trials, before all factors are clearly defined and thoroughly understood,
--a wide experience in metallurgical and ceramic processes,
furnaces, fuels,refractories. All backed by solid theoretical knowledge,
--an intimate knowledge of laboratory and industrial techniques and materials.

As to his ability to fit pleasantly into your small
group I would say that Dr. Lellep is a man of simple tastes,
cooperative, entirely free of jealousies and intrigues, hon-
estly devoted to his engineering tasks.

This letter may be too late to be of use to you.
Should you, however, desire more detailed information about
Dr. Lellep's past work, I would gladly supply it, having par-
ticipated personally in some of it myself.

Very truly yours,

G.P.Klaas
Engineer-Consultant.

Sorry! Someone slipped in our office. Instead of mailing
Mr. Parry's letter to me, they held it until I visited the
factory today and picked it up.

APPENDIX 7

Letter to Professor Duschak

December 5, 1945

In 1945, Otto wrote to Professor Duschak, metallurgist at the University of California, Berkeley, who had earlier helped him find work at the Kaiser Company.

THE UNSHAKEABLE FAITH OF AN INVENTOR

1338 Cordova Road
Pittsburgh 6, Pa.
December 5, 1945

Dr. L. H. Duschak
In charge of Metallurgical Dept.
University of California
Berkeley, California

Dear Dr. Duschak:

I should have written you a long time ago remembering the good time and admirable co-operation while working in your department on the beautiful campus of your great University. I think California, and Berkeley in particular, is one of the most favored spots on this troubled earth ball. Therefore, I keep my family living on a quiet street of your city, and maybe some day I will come back there myself. I left the good city looking for broader opportunity to serve the industry of my specialty: The iron and steel mills. Unfortunately, perhaps, only 1% of steel production capacity is located in California. I spent one half of 1944 attempting to interest steel people in a number of my inventive ideas. I found insufficient interest to begin actual experimental work during the war. Therefore, after many vain attempts I took employment. Here is one grave difficulty. The employers consider men of 61 years as so much human scrap.

The Director of research at Jones & Laughlin was earnestly willing to engage me for his most interesting laboratory and pilot-plant. But the legal department vetoed the plan because I had twenty-two registered inventive ideas for steel industry which might have interfered with J. & L.'s ideas. So I engaged myself during the first half of 1945 for moe or less regular combustion engineering and partly metallurgical problems at the Copperweld Steel Company at Warren, Ohio. This plant was a wasteful war baby, but to their credit, they managed to produce during the war years over one million tons of electric furnace steel. Since July I am again "free lancing" looking now in peace time for an opportunity to investigate and develop some of my own ideas.

The hot months of July and August I spent in the cooler high Allegheny mountains. There I carried out a number of gram scale experiments attempting to desulphurize or desiliconize molten pig iron. The tiny furnace was heated by electric arcs generated by the conventional welding machine. Yes, do not laugh, dear Professor. Certain quite interesting results can be found and studied even by inexpensive "shoe string" experiments. Since the last six weeks I am in a "happy honeymoon" disposition. (The biggest fool is an old fool!) But it looks as if I have hit a little promising and simple thing. The objective remains desulphurization or desiliconization of pig iron in the ladle by a more efficient and better controlled method than the present purification with soda or iron scale during filling of the ladle. Soda as desulphurizer becomes inefficient and expensive when you want to eliminate in the region from 0.05% to 0.01%. For years I have had the thought to speed up the slag-metal reactions by controlled agitation of the bath. For weeks I hunted in this "iron metropolis" for laboratory facilities to experiment with a 10 kg capacity iron ladle. After a dozen wrong places, I finally

To: Dr. L. H. Duschak   December 5, 1945

discovered a metallurgical laboratory in a local university. According to
rules I am prohibited to mention names. I built into the bottom of my
ladle, heated at the top with a 13 kw electric arc, a porous graphite block
with almost invisible pores. Nitrogen gas can be easily pressed through
this "gas disperser" and molten metal while it remains impenetrable for
molten iron. The metal can be agitated with slag to any desired degree
from zero movement to a most violent "explosive" boil. The first two experiments have been made with high lime and flourspar slags. Sulphur went down
rapidly and better than with soda. Next I will test CaC_2 as desulphurizer
as Bureau of Mines did. Carbon is a most perfect "refractory" for high
temperatures under reducing condition. It maintains its strength, is not
wetted or corroded, not by metal nor by slag. Porous magnesite or mullite
as gas dispersers will be tested for oxidizing air blast and desiliconization.
The amount of gas required seems to be fifty times less than in Bessemer
process. The application of the idea may be limited, but even if a single
blast furnace could apply this invention the "human scoop" could earn an
honorable and sufficient income. I am going to find out what are the practical and economical possibilities of this thought. It may be a lame duck,
though it does not look as such in the present stage of investigation.

The laboratory I am working in has three experimental arc furnaces
and the transformer capacity is 150 kw. The professor in charge is grabbing
numerous machine tools, cranes, welding machines, heat treating and other
equipment from surplus military materiel and is getting all this allegedly
without payment. The same procedure may suit your laboratory.

Work keeps my health in quite a satisfactory state and the family at
Berkeley is thriving.

I wonder why Kaiser did not get the Geneva Steel Plant. If he gets it
I may attempt again to do some work for them.

The number of young students in the after war period may increase
tremendously and I hope you will find lots of satisfaction in teaching and
consulting work.

Let me express my sincere appreciation for all the good active help
and assistance received from you while in California.

                                                        Yours gratefully

                                                O. G. Lellep

OGL/vef

The ACL System
for Burning Cement Clinker

The
ACL
System

Orto Lellep

FOR BURNING CEMENT CLINKER

One of Opa's inventions

ALLIS-CHALMERS **A-C**

More Efficient than any other Rotary

What is the ACL*ˣ⁾* System

The ACL system for burning cement clinker is a low dust loss, high efficiency process.

In the ACL process, raw mix is formed into pellets. Pellets move from pelletizer to kiln in a uniform thick bed on a traveling grate.

The traveling grate is totally enclosed — there is no place for dusty gas to escape.

Appropriate baffle in the housing channels gases through bed of pellets on grate at end closest to kiln. Partial calcining and dust reclamation takes place in the first pass through grate as hottest gases (A) are drawn through bed of pellets to B.

Gases are moved from B to C through dust collectors, then drawn through the feed end of the grate which is loaded with moist pellets. Drying and final dust filtering takes place as gases pass from C to D.

Kiln gases are efficiently filtered and heat efficiently transferred to material.

Lower Dust Loss

In the ACL system, all gases pass through the traveling bed of pellets twice. This double pass reduces dust loss below 1% of weight of feed without an additional dust-collecting system. Valuable processed material is saved. Dust loading of exhaust gas is lower than from any other known kiln system.

Lower Fuel Consumption

Fuel consumption for ACL systems now in operation averages 600,000 btu. per barrel (365 lbs.) of clinker. Conventional long dry process kilns range from 750,000 to 1,000,000 btu. per barrel.

Lower Power Consumption

Because of an unusually small volume of exhaust gas and low static pressure (averaging 6" w.g. for each pass), the ACL system requires about 2.3 kwh per barrel of clinker for operation of the kiln department. This is about 1/3 less power than required by kilns using other pre-heating systems.

Less Space Required

The entire ACL system — grate, kiln and cooler — is about 40% shorter than the conventional kiln installation. The totally enclosed traveling grate is about as high as the average kiln feed end housing. No unusual structures are required.

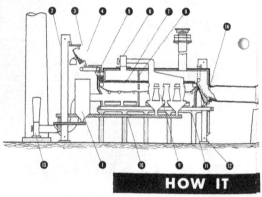

HOW IT

Materials Specially Treated

Dry mix is fed at a uniform rate into pelletizer where water is added at an average rate of about 12% to form pellets. Pellets, varying in size from ¼ to ¾ inches in diameter, are discharged in a continuous flow into a feed hopper which delivers a uniform depth of pellets on a traveling grate.

A six to nine inch layer of pelletized feed is moved slowly by the traveling grate from C to A where feed discharges into the rotary kiln. Clinker from the kiln is cooled in an air-quenching cooler . . . oversize clinker is broken by a built-in hammermill.

2

x) Allis-Chalmers-Lellep

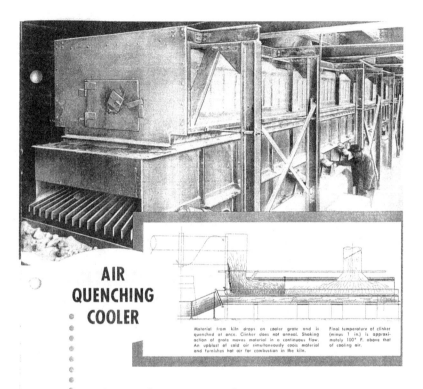

AIR
QUENCHING
COOLER

Material from kiln drops on cooler grate and is quenched at once. Clinker does not anneal. Shaking action of grate moves material in a continuous flow. An upblast of cold air simultaneously cools material and furnishes hot air for combustion in the kiln.

Final temperature of clinker (minus 1 in.) is approximately 100° F. above that of cooling air.

SAVES Fuel Costs • Grinding Costs • Power Costs

The Air-Quenching shaking grate cooler, developed by Allis-Chalmers more than 20 years ago, isolates and captures the hottest secondary air above the cooling clinker and returns it to the kiln.

Recovery of Hot Secondary Air Improves Combustion

A movable baffle located in the air housing above the cooler grate separates the hottest air from the lower temperature air. The return to the kiln of this highly pre-heated air promotes proper combustion and maximum fuel utilization.

Rapid Air Quenching Improves Grindability

Because clinker is cooled rapidly, not gradually, it possesses favorable grinding characteristics. Capacities of grinding mills have been increased by as much as 10% through the use of an Allis-Chalmers Air-Quenching grate cooler.

Lower Pressure Fan Requires Little HP . . . . . .

The uniform, relatively thin bed of material on the grate, resulting from the reciprocating motion of the cooler, requires only low air pressure for penetration. A fan and motor using only about ½ hp-hr. per barrel of clinker does the work. Further power economy is realized by the absence of auxiliary conveying equipment.

7

ALLIS-CHALMERS is the Largest Builder of Complete Cement Manufacturing Equipment in the U.S.A.

and There's a Reason

Since the turn of the century, Allis-Chalmers has led the way in rotary kiln development ... has engineered many of the major improvements in kiln design and performance.

For example, air-cooled kiln feed and discharge ends save rebricking costs and kiln shell distortion. Allis-Chalmers kilns' true circle, all-welded construction insures best lining fit, long refractory life. Improved kiln gears apply driving force uniformly. Floating-type riding rings provide flexibility, ample support and proper weight distribution.

In addition to the unequalled experience gained in designing and building hundreds of rotary kilns, Allis-Chalmers offers the most complete pyro-processing research and testing facilities available anywhere.

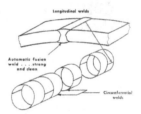

Longitudinal welds

Automatic fusion weld . . . strong and clean

Circumferential welds

Air-Cooled Feed and Discharge Ends Keep Nose Brick in Place

There's no end warpage in a kiln equipped with air-cooled ends. Cooling air circulating around kiln ends along underside of nose casting keeps kiln ends cool, prevents distortion. With fewer shutdowns necessary to replace end brick, production loss is greatly minimized. Substantial savings in bricks and labor are also realized. Another advantage of air-cooled ends is the fuel economy made possible by the positive air seal.

6

ACL System

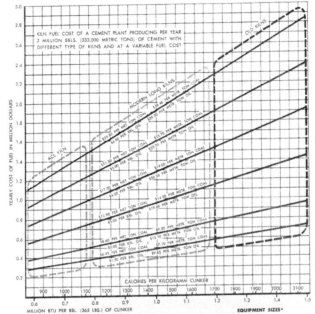

ACL System

MILLION BTU PER BBL. (365 LBS.) OF CLINKER
CALORIES PER KILOGRAMM ARE EXPRESSED IN LOWER HEATING VALUE AND BTU PER BBL IN HIGHER HEATING VALUE. BOTH FOR FUEL OIL.

EQUIPMENT SIZES*

Capacity	Traveling Grate	Rotary Kiln	Air-Quenching Cooler
Bbls. per Day	Wdth. x Lgth.	Dia. x Lgth.	Wdth. x Lgth.
4,000	12½' x 82'	13' x 175'	6' x 100'
3,500	12½' x 72'	12½' x 160'	6' x 85'
3,000	12½' x 65'	12' x 150'	4½' x 100'
2,500	12½' x 55'	11½' x 130'	4½' x 85'

*The above are average . . . actual sizes may vary according to raw materials and local conditions.

Eight Other Advantages of the

No Segregation of Raw Materials Once the proper blend of raw materials has been established, it makes little or no difference in the ACL system whether individual raw material particles differ in shape or specific gravity. Pelletizing the raw mix locks in and maintains the original proportions of the various components.

Regulated Feed In the ACL system, the traveling grate provides definite control of pelletized feed. Feed volume is constant — kiln operation is uniform and more efficient. The six to nine inch layer of feed protects grate castings.

No "Flushing" Because feed is pelletized into marble-like shapes of a definite size, segregation of mix is prevented . . . the tendency toward "flushing" of material down kiln is eliminated . . . biggest reason for "ringing" is minimized.

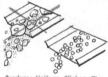

Pelletizing Avoids Fluidization Voids between pellets permit escape of moisture and gases from material in kiln without fluidization of bed.

Produces Uniform Clinker The ACL operation is a controlled method of burning cement clinkers. This means that clinker is uniform and meets required specifications. Because the clinker retains its pelletized characteristics, it travels through the kiln uniformly and burns easily.

Saves Manpower Only one man is required at feed end of ACL system. If installation is multiple unit, this one man can handle two or three pelletizers. The positive flow of pelletized materials eliminates blocked passages. Manpower for cleanup is avoided.

Uses Any Type of Fuel Powdered coal, fuel oil, natural or coke oven gas can be used to fire ACL kiln.

Dependable Operation Careful survey of existing installations indicates that maintenance of the ACL system is unusually low.

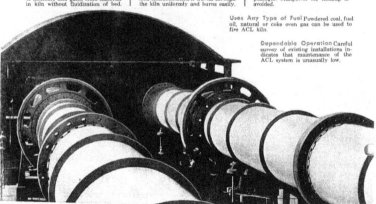

Kiln System for producing Cement Clinker

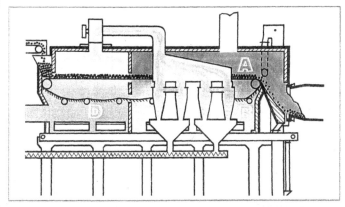

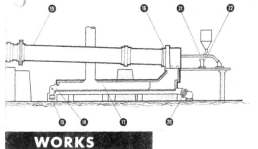

1	Feed bin
2	Feed elevator
3	Feeder
4	Pan type pelletizer
5	Grate feed hopper
6	Fan No. 1
7	ACL traveling grate
8	Baffle
9	Cyclone dust collectors
10	Screw conveyor for dust
11	Drag for returning grate spillage
12	Elevator for returning grate spillage to kiln
13	Fan No. 2
14	Air-cooled feed end
15	ACL kiln
16	Air-cooled discharge end
17	Air-quenching cooler
18	Hammermill clinker breaker
19	Product conveyor
20	Pulsating damper
21	Kiln firing system
22	Master kiln control panel

WORKS

Kiln Exhaust Gas Specially Treated

First Pass — Hottest gas direct from the kiln is first drawn through the bed of pellets on the traveling grate from A to B. In this first pass, pellets are partially calcined and kiln gas temperatures are reduced from approximately 1800° to 500° F. Dust filtering action also begins as the gas passes through the bed of pellets.

Next, (all gases pass through cyclone dust collectors where the larger dust particles are removed and alkalis, if present,

can be isolated and removed from the system. Normally these reclaimed dust particles are carried back to the pelletizer.

Second Pass — Gases from the cyclones at B are channeled to C. Final dust filtering takes place as the gases pass through the bed of moist pellets on the traveling grate from C to D. In this second pass through the bed of pellets gas temperatures are reduced from 500° to about 200° F.

58

installations by

Leliep Licensees

since 1950

3

381

The Carl Lueg Memorial
Medal Invitation

German Society of Iron and Steel Engineers—VDEH

Dr. Ing. Otto Lellep

5o8 North 115th Street
Wauwatosa 13, Wisc./USA

Düsseldorf, Sept. 8, 1960
Breite Strasse 27

Dear Dr. Lellep,

We have already cordially invited you, in
our letter of April 4 this year, to participate
in our yearly general meeting. This meeting has
a special significance for on this occasion we
can look back on the hundred year history of
our society.

Please permit us to repeat this invitation
in the name of our directors and, at the same
time, to inform you that our committee has decided, in recognition of your farreaching and

trailblazing work in the field of the application of oxygen to the production of steel, to
award you the Carl-Lueg Memorial Medal. This is
the highest distinction that the German Society
of Iron and Steel Engineers has to bestow in recognition of such merit. The ceremonial presentations will follow the grand assembly that takes
place in Düsseldorf the 4th of November. At this
reunion we expect more than four thousand
visitors, among which will be prominent representatives of science and industry from this
country and abroad.

cond.

You can well imagine how important it is
to us that you participate at this year's Steel
Engineer's day. To make sure, we have already
reserved a corresponding room so that you yourself need not be bothered with such matters.
In case we can be of help to you in any respect
we ask you to please let us know. We will
attempt to assist you in any possible way.

In the hopes of having from you a positive
answer we send you cordial greetings.

With best wishes,

German Society of Iron and Steel
Engineers

Schenk   Thomas
(President)   (Manager)

Medal Presentation Speech in English

Speech by Dr. Hermann Schenck
Chairman, Vereins Deutscher Eisenhüttenleute
(German Iron and Steel Association) On the presentation of the
Carl Lueg Medal to Dr. Robert Durrer and Dr. Otto Lellep

November 4, 1960

When announcement was made of the donation by the Thyssen family [for research by young scientists], we were grateful to acknowledge that these great benefactors now also support the sciences.

In expert circles today, as it was one hundred years ago, it is up to the businessman to decide whether the risk of introducing a new production method is worth the effort. This decision is now somewhat easier than it was in the past. One can rely on suggestions that come from creative spirits supported by scientific concepts.

The most recent development in metallurgy involves the processing of an essential ingredient, air, by the separation of oxygen from nitrogen. Here we should mention a name that has already been forgotten, even among metallurgists. In 1925, Dr. Matthias Frankl found a method for producing pure oxygen so cheaply that for the first time the application of oxygen in steel and iron production could be considered. In spite of this, it took a long time and many careful experiments in the laboratory and pre-production tests before the basis for the use of oxygen was firm enough that industrial production could be undertaken. We want to recognize important accomplishments along the way and to express our gratitude by means of awarding the Carl Lueg Memorial Medal.

We need to mention three men today: Robert Durrer, Otto Lellep, and Carl V. Schwarz. We are sad to note that Carl Schwarz is no longer among us. He passed away in November of last year. Having acknowledged him, I turn to you, very honored Professor Durrer, and to you, very honored Professor Lellep. Both of you aimed for the same goal in different ways.

You, Dr. Lellep, were grounded in your intuition and obsessed with a thought that seemed so evident but that was difficult to realize. The more you got into it, the harder it became. In you, we honor an engineer who dedicated himself to a great task with his whole heart and energy.

From the first, you, Professor Durrer, aimed for the broad utilization of oxygen. Your wide-ranging thinking has benefited not only your students, whom you taught as a professor of mining technology in Berlin. Over numerous years, your theoretical considerations have given us in the steel industry many insights regarding the processing of iron outside the furnace, providing a source for modern developments. You have not shied away from sacrifice in order to work on the theoretical foundation of the process. Based on this foundation, our Austrian friends and colleagues developed the [oxygen-blown process]. To successfully bring that process to production is an accomplishment recognized over the entire world, and particularly by us.

Based on the unanimous decision of our committee, I now have the honor and the joy to award to you, Dr. Lellep and Professor Durrer, the highest recognition that our association can give: the Carl Lueg Memorial Medal. I am glad that I am the first to offer you our congratulations.. I am convinced that in the great applause that is ringing in this hall now, the good wishes of our Austrian friends also sound, because you, Professor Durrer, have been exchanging ideas with them for more than two decades.

Good luck!

The Presentation Speech
in German

THE UNSHAKEABLE FAITH OF AN INVENTOR

Ansprache

Professor Dr.-Ing. Dr.-Ing. E. h. Hermann Schenck
Vorsitzender des Vereins Deutscher Eisenhüttenleute
zur Verleihung der Carl - Lueg - Denkmünze
an Professor Dr.-Ing. Dr. mont. h. c. Senator E. h. Robert Durrer und Dr.-Ing. Otto Lellep

in der Hauptsitzung des Eisenhüttentages am 4. November 1960

„Meine Damen und Herren!

Daß große Mäzene jetzt auch in Deutschland der Wissenschaft vorbehaltlos helfen, haben wir mit freudigem Dank registriert, als die große Stiftung der Familie Thyssen bekannt gemacht wurde. Im engeren Fachbereich bleibt es — wie vor hundert Jahren — so auch heute der unternehmerischen Verantwortung vorbehalten, abzuwägen, ob das Risiko der Einführung eines neuen Verfahrens getragen

haben beide das gleiche Ziel angesteuert — auf verschiedenen Wegen. Sie, Herr Dr. Lellep, von der Intuitive her und besessen von einem Gedanken, nicht zu liegen schien und die Schwierigkeiten seiner Verwirklichung um so schwerer preisgab, je weiter Sie sich hineinarbeiteten. Wir ehren in Ihnen den Ingenieur, der sich einer großen Aufgabe mit ganzem Herzen, mit aller Tatkraft hingab.

Verleihung der Carl-Lueg-Denkmünze an Professor Dr. Durrer und Dr. Lellep

werden kann. Die Entscheidung hierüber ist heute etwas leichter als in der Vergangenheit; sie kann sich auf Vorschläge stützen, die der kritischen Intuitive des schöpferischen Geistes entspringen und durch wissenschaftliche Vorstellungen mehr oder weniger gefestigt sind.

Das Kennzeichen der jüngsten Entwicklung der Metallurgie ist die Aufbereitung eines unerläßlichen Rohstoffes, nämlich der Luft, durch Abtrennung des Sauerstoffs vom Stickstoff. Wir wollen hier einen Namen nennen, der auch bei uns Metallurgen schon beinahe vergessen ist: der Name des schon vor 13 Jahren verstorbenen Dr. Matthias Fränkl, der im Jahre 1925 den Weg fand, den reinen Sauerstoff so billig herzustellen, daß seine Verwendung bei den Hüttenerzeugnissen überhaupt erst in Betracht gezogen werden konnte. Trotzdem hat es noch lange gedauert, bis nach vielen tastenden Versuchen im Laboratorium und im halbbetrieblichen Maßstabe die Grundlagen so weit gefestigt waren, daß die unternehmerische Initiative einsetzen und sich auswirken konnte. Entscheidende Verdienste auf diesem Wege wollen wir heute herausheben und ihnen durch Verleihung der Carl-Lueg-Denkmünze Ausdruck geben. Drei Männer sind es, deren Namen wir nennen wollen: Robert Durrer, Otto Lellep und Carl Schwarz.

Mit Trauer stellen wir fest, daß wir Carl V. Schwarz heute nicht mehr die ihm zugedachte Anerkennung aussprechen können; er ist im November vorigen Jahres für immer von uns gegangen. So möchte ich mich nach diesem Gedenken an Sie wenden, sehr verehrter Herr Professor **Durrer**, und an Sie, sehr verehrter Herr Dr. **Lellep**. Sie

Sie, Herr Professor Durrer, haben das Ziel der Sauerstoffnutzung zunächst in ganz breiter Front angesteuert, und Ihre weit gespannten Gedanken haben uns Hüttenleuten viele Anregungen gegeben, nicht nur Ihren Schülern, denen Sie als Professor der Eisenhüttenkunde in Berlin unmittelbar Lehrmeister waren. Die Verhüttung des Eisens außerhalb des Hochofens bleibt über lange Jahre hinaus eine Fundgrube und Quelle für die neuzeitliche Entwicklung der Eisenhüttentechnik. Sie haben auch keine Opfer gescheut, um zusammen mit Ihrem Mitarbeiter Dr. Hellbrügge die verfahrensmäßigen Grundlagen zu festigen, auf denen aufbauend unsere österreichischen Kollegen und Freunde das Sauerstoff-Aufblasverfahren zur Betriebsreife entwickeln und seinen großen Erfolgen zuführen konnten. Diese Leistung findet in aller Welt und erst recht bei uns vorbehaltlose Anerkennung.

So habe ich nun die Ehre und die besondere Freude, Ihnen, Herr Dr. Lellep und Herr Professor Durrer, auf einstimmigen Beschluß unseres Vorstandes die höchste Auszeichnung zu verleihen, die unser Verein zu vergeben hat, die Carl-Lueg-Denkmünze.

Ich freue mich, daß ich Ihnen als erster die Glückwünsche unseres Vereins aussprechen kann; ich bin überzeugt, daß in den großen Beifall dieses Hauses besonders stark die Glückwünsche der österreichischen Freunde durchklingen, mit denen Sie schon vor mehr als zwei Jahrzehnten in Gedankenaustausch gestanden haben.

Glück auf!"

APPENDIX 12

Jüri Lellep Scholarship

In his memoir, Otto mentions a scholarship he created in his father's name. He established the fund—the Jüri Lellep Scholarship—through the Eesti Üliõpilaste Toetusfond USAs: the Estonian Students Fund in USA, Inc. (ESF). After Otto's death, 60 percent of the funds from his estate were divided between the ESF (70 percent) and the Federation of Associations for the Advancement of Estonian Youth in Lakewood (30 percent). The latter was perhaps the vehicle for his support of Estonian Boy Scouts, to which he also alludes.

The ESF has awarded scholarships from the Jüri Lellep Scholarship Trust continuously since 1968. In distributing Otto's funds, it is required to aid Estonian students studying in institutions of higher learning in the "free world." According to an email received from the ESF (March 9, 2018):

> Until the mid-1980s, recipients of a scholarship from the Jüri Lellep [Fund] were primarily Estonian students from the United States with a sprinkling of candidates from Canada and Sweden. With Glasnost, a small number of students from Estonia were accepted to study at colleges and universities in the United States. Some applied for and were granted scholarships from the Lellep Trust. When Estonia regained its independence in 1991, the number of students from Estonia applying for financial aid to study in the United States and in colleges and universities throughout Europe increased dramatically. We now generally have an equal number of

Estonian students from the USA and from Estonia receiving scholarships from the Lellep Trust.

The amount of moneys received from the Jüri Lellep Scholarship Trust for distribution has varied . . . depending on the Trust's financial results in a particular year . . . but usually three to four [students] receive a scholarship each year . . . . . The amounts are determined [using] as criteria: academic excellence, financial need and the student's commitment and participation in their Estonian culture and community.

In an article on Estonians in the diaspora ("Claiming Ethnicity in Overlapping Diasporic Conditions: Estonian Americans and Academic Mobility During the Cold War"), Maarja Merivoo-Parro describes Otto's influence:

It was in fact Jüri Lellep's son, the inventive engineer and venerable representative of old American Estonians within the largely DP-dominated Estonian community in Milwaukee, who donated the money and suggested the [scholarship's] name in 1968.

Even before this grand gesture Otto G. Lellep had been a generous donor for years and had taken the initiative of paving the legal path towards a major contribution already before the EstfUSA's incorporation. Due to various legal obstacles he wasn't at first able to give as much as he had wanted to, but the "little" that he did give was still hugely influential. In 1965 his donation was the single largest amount among gifts from both individuals and organizations. With the Jüri Lellep Memorial Fund's emergence in 1968, a whole new era in the work of the EstfUSA began and one can also claim that to be true about the young Estonians it was directed toward.

Otto would surely have been pleased by Merivoo-Parro's praise and by the figures the ESF released to his daughter: from 2008 to 2017 the group distributed $117,000 from the Jüri Lellep Trust, and in the past fifty years, it has helped more than two hundred students.

APPENDIX 13

Life in Wauwatosa

1949-1965

Renate Lellep Fernandez

A fter his several years of struggle to find any regular employment or income-earning activities, Otto was elated to have been hired by Allis Chalmers. Mutti prepared the move from our Berkeley home to a very modest—in Mutti's words "unhappily designed" (*unglücklich gestaltet*)—tract home in Milwaukee's outlying suburbs. My parents chose Wauwatosa for the same reason they had chosen Berkeley: its good schools.

My sister Lee remained in Berkeley in order to enter the University of California as a freshman. I, too, remained in Berkeley on the West Coast to take a summer chemistry course in preparation for what we supposed would be more demanding in Midwestern Wauwatosa—"such an eastern school." Therefore, we lived as a threesome—Mutti and I and Opa, as we called him—while I took my senior year in "Tosa" High School, a school intensely bent on winning the state basketball championship in Madison, the state capitol and site of the University of Wisconsin.

Mutti had to do some hard persuading to have Otto support my going on to college. By the late 1940s, our family's dear friend Elfriede

Friese had managed to obtain an advanced social work degree from Bryn Mawr College, an Ivy League women's college. This college, though elite, was do-able with scholarships. It was there, or to Oberlin (marked in her view by Quaker values), that Elfriede thought I ought to apply.

I, however, conditioned by my father's reasonable but constant concern with practicality and employability, applied instead to the University of Wisconsin, the primary and local college destination of "Tosa" students—especially its athletes. For me, the attraction was the program in occupational therapy. Completion of its associated internships and required courses in art, human services, biology, and human anatomy assured me of a sure career, indeed a career for which demand was growing. Moreover, my state scholarship eased Otto's concern about any costs for my studying.

The pros and cons of my own future were, during my senior year in high school, much under consideration around our Wauwatosa kitchen table. Our table was at one end laden with Mutti's Remington typewriter and her stack of paperwork: forms, certificates, and documents needed to apply for social security reimbursement to be accorded by the post-war German state. These monies were legally and historically owed to her for her more than two decades of work in German institutions of welfare. The pile consisted mostly of references and professional certifications attesting to her service. I realized years later that Mutti must have carefully stashed these papers in the trunk accompanying us out of Germany, over the Brenner Pass, and into Mussolini's Italy, in the spring of 1940. Mutti must have thought that the documentation would support her right—however stateless she may have thought herself to be—to exit out of Hitler-dominated Europe.

During those Wisconsin years, Otto, though physically present, was generally preoccupied with what he was cooking—only for himself—given his lifelong dietary concerns. He sat at the opposite end of our kitchen table, close to the stove, so that he could quickly attend to whatever he had on the gas burner. This was always something in his pressure cooker, though occasionally he tended to an additional pot.

I vividly remember once thinking there was something of Mutti's in a pot—perhaps a soup, simmering on our stove. Upon lifting the lid to peep in, I saw something distinctly non-food-like: pellets of gray taconite. Everywhere and always, at the kitchen table and in the laboratory, it seemed Otto was aspiring to become and realize himself as an inventor.

Tribute to Elfriede Friese

In the United States, Elfriede Friese served in the Philadelphia projects as a social worker, though in 1940, when Otto
first arrived in New York and looked for her, he found her
barely making a living at jobs "far below her capabilities."
Later, she traveled abroad as a consultant to heads of state
in both Thailand and Iran. Close to retirement age, Elfriede
entered Medford Leas, a Quaker Continuing Care Residence
Community near Philadelphia, where she helped establish a
pre-school for the children of staff members.

April 2002

Memorial Tribute to Elfriede Friese
Renate Lellep Fernandez
(Written by Renate on behalf of sisters Lee and Renate)

Elfriede told us once, many years ago, that it was her father's
example that made her appreciate laughter but that she really
only began herself, to practice laughing after she left her parents'
home. She never stopped that practice. Four years ago, she gave us—
our shy, two-year-old grandchild Will, his mother (our daughter
Lisa), and me—a goodbye example of that laugh. By that time, her
speech was much impeded but not her perception. The little boy was
carrying a beloved Pooh-Bear, thin and losing his stuffing, handed
down through the generations in our family—a bear Elfriede had

known when our own grown kids were small. She greeted that bear, took him in her arms. Lying down on her bed, she set him on her belly and looking into his cataract eyes (embroidered in black yarn, the black shiny buttons long gone), she gave us the best, uplifting laugh of her life. We still hear it.

We are one of Elfriede's many families. She knew me first as a newborn in Germany, in 1932. The following year, she spent some weeks or months in our semi-rural home not far from the Düsseldorf/Essen industrial zone, helped by our parents to "keep a low profile." Having sensed that she was being "watched" by the rising Nazi authorities, Elfriede—to protect her colleagues *im Widerstand* (Resistance Movement) from her possibly coerced betrayal—was my nanny, awaiting the best moment to slip out of the country. In doing so, she was also giving up marriage to her fiancé.

By spring 1940, she was living in Manhattan, her street address (she had no telephone) offered as a possible lifeline to my mother should she, with me and my sister (Lee Maher) manage to get out of Europe. When, well after the US had joined the Allies against the Axis powers, Elfriede did meet up with us, I—then ten or twelve— was putting all my efforts into passing as an American girl. I was discomfited by Elfriede's German accent (that of the enemy), her physical departure from the ideal womanly type of the time, and her conspicuously vigorous laughter—especially when audible in the streetcar taking us to our home in the Berkeley hills. It was I who wanted the low profile, while she had long ago learned to cheerfully live with hers—whatever shape—and to share her cheer and willed optimism with others. That attitude and style, along with her intelligence, may have been credited and reinforced by Bryn Mawr when the college accepted her for graduate education in social work despite her lacking any prior college experience.

That training brought Elfriede into ever widening social circles in Philadelphia and New Jersey, where she practiced her profession and added to her ever-increasing number of "families." Her reputation made it possible in the early, computer-less sixties, without any address book for a clue, for me to locate her in that two-state area. This was when my husband and I (pregnant with our eldest, Lisa) and somewhat at loose ends returning from anthropological field work in the villages of Equatorial Africa, needed shelter and re-accommodation to this country. She gave us all that and more in her log cabin home in the Rancocas Woods of New Jersey.

By the late sixties, she had become a regular holiday visitor to our home in the New Hampshire (Hanover) woods. My kids' high expectations—as well as my sister's kids when Elfriede visited them in Kalamazoo—were always rewarded when, from out of her bags, she pulled, say, a "wooly" coconut-coated lamb for Easter or ornaments for the Christmas tree—ornaments beaded or woven by herself. By the late seventies, our little, tan mongrel dog Happy raced around the circle of our family embracing Elfriede. In that dizzy, run-around, Happy vocalized strange sounds, striving to express the joy of reunion with this larger family. Elfriede must have received such greetings wherever she came as a guest.

In the eighties, Elfriede visited us in the Rocky Mountains, where we put her up in a cabin by a swift flowing stream. When, at our home, Canadian camp-robber jays would swoop down from the Ponderosa trees surrounding our deck, trying to seize a bright bead from Elfriede's active, craftswoman hands, she laughed at the birds' "mischievousness" and tempted them some more.

Carpal tunnel syndrome soon slowed down her work with threads of yarn. Social threads, however, she kept weaving. Who could forget the eightieth birthday party she organized around herself at Medford Leas, so that she might be present as her diverse friends—who, as she said, "might never get to know each other except at my memorial service"—were celebrating her life?

The threads remain. I think of Elfriede whenever I wind a soft, winter scarf around my neck, she having combined just for me threads of grey and subtle periwinkle with flecks of sliver highlight—like good cheer and laughter. I think of Elfriede whenever I look at the framed Miró print ("Constellation Series: *Chiffres et constellations amoureux d'une femme*) hanging over our dresser. She had recognized its spirit and rescued it when it was about to be discarded from the apartment of a just-deceased Medford neighbor. And she passed it on to me years before she herself passed away. I see André Breton's surrealist prose on the backside of the print as especially fitting, reminding me of disparate words haltingly spoken by Elfriede in these last years. Much remains to be remembered and, perhaps, deciphered as from many parts of the world, we put together and reflect upon these many memories of Our Dear Elfriede.

GLOSSARY

Charge: To load materials into a furnace (verb) or the materials that have been loaded into a furnace (noun).

Cinter ("sinter"): To cause a material to become a solid or porous mass through the application of heat (and usually also by compression) without melting it during the process.

Clinker: "Portland cement clinker is a dark grey nodular material made by heating ground limestone and clay at a temperature of about 1400 °C–1500 °C." On occasion, Otto refers to "clinker pellets." (Definition from *Understanding Cement*, https://www.understanding-cement.com/about.html. Accessed June 10, 2018).

Matte: "A crude mixture of molten sulfides formed as an intermediate product of the smelting of sulfide ores of metals, especially copper, nickel, and lead. Instead of being smelted directly to metal, copper ores are usually smelted to matte, preferably containing 40–45 percent copper along with iron and sulfur, which is then treated by converting it in a Bessemer-type converter." (*Encyclopedia Britannica*)

Monel metal: An alloy of nickel (present to a high degree), copper, and other metals.

Refractory: A non-combustible material used, for example, to line furnaces.

Regenerators: Open brickwork heated by a furnace's exhaust gases. The brickwork is used in turn to preheat the incoming gases passing through them before they are used for fuel. (See Introduction regarding open-hearth furnaces.)

Smelt: "The process by which a metal is obtained, either as the element or as a simple compound, from its ore by heating beyond the melting point, ordinarily in the presence of oxidizing agents, such as air, or reducing agents, such as coke." (*Encyclopedia Britannica*)

Theoretical mixture: As explained by B.J. Bernard, "A theoretical mixture of gas and combustible air is the mixture required to fully combust the gas (e.g. convert the gas and air to nitrogen, carbon dioxide, water vapor and heat) based on stoichiometry. For example, for methane (the principal component of natural gas), the theoretical mixture is approximately 1 part methane to 10 parts air. The theoretical mixture is different for different types of gas." [Stoichiometry: "The relationship between the relative quantities of substances taking part in a reaction or forming a compound, typically a ratio of whole integers." (Oxford English Dictionaries)

A SELECTION
OF RECURRING NAMES

General Chrabrof: A general in New York City who was managing the purchase of war supplies for Russia when Otto traveled there in 1917. (Chapters 16, 17)

Dr. Duschak: Professor of metallurgy at the University of California, Berkeley, who, in the early 1940s, helped Otto find work at the Kaiser Company, then let Otto use his laboratory for his research on a new method for producing steel. (Chapters 21, 29 and 31)

Bernard Helming: An engineer who first worked with Otto in 1926, trying to fix the problems with the first commercially sold Lellep kilns. A "lifelong friend," he became chief engineer at the Polysius Company in Neubeckum and worked with Otto again after the end of World War II, when the Allis Chalmers Company began to modify the kiln for use in the West. (Chapters 21, 29 and 31)

Gustav Klaas: Otto describes Klaas as "my dear old friend," "my Estonian friend," and "my best friend." Their friendship spanned their time in Germany (at Clausthal), Russia, and the United States. They took vacations together in the Harz Mountains, Maine, and Cuba and were together in New York City in the 1920s. They stayed in touch throughout their lives. (Chapters 13, 14, 17, 18, 23, and 26)

Doctor Köhler (Köler): Otto lived with Doctor Köhler from 1904—1905 during his last year in the real school in Tallinn. (Chapter 11)

Professor Köhler (Köler): In Otto's words, a famous painter living in "Petrograd" who was close to the court of the Tsar. (Chapters 1 and 11)

Endel [Lellep]: Son of Otto's brother Willem Lellep. Endel turned the crank on the experimental rotating drum that Otto first used to create cement pellets in Estonia (Chapter 20). Otto and Aina sent money to help him out of a prisoner-of-war camp during and after World War II (Letters, Lellep Family Archive).

Willem Lellep: Separated from Otto (the youngest) only by the next youngest brother, Peter. Willem was Otto's occasional playmate, operated a sawmill in Tallinn where Otto briefly worked, and provided space in his house in Tallinn for the laboratory where Otto invented the prototype for the first Lellep kiln. (Chapters 5, 14, 20, 21)

Mr. [Robert W.] Lesley: One of the founders of the Giant Cement Company of Egypt, Pennsylvania, where Otto worked during the early 1920s. (Chapters 18, 20)

Mary Lichty: A US high school teacher initially hired by Frieda Aina to teach Liisa and Renate English after they arrived in New York, in 1940. Mary Lichty became a close friend. (Chapters 25 and 26)

Mr. Maier: A "graduate engineer" who helped Otto test, improve, and demonstrate the Lellep kiln in Rudersdorf, Germany, in the late 1920s. Otto later met him again in the mid-1940s, in Argentina, where Maier worked as manager of a cement plant. (Chapters 21 and 29)

Dr. Merica: Director of Research at the International Nickel Company (INCO). (Chapters 18 and 19)

Mutti: "Mother"—an affectionate form of address or reference in German, always used by Renate for Frieda Aina.

Karl Otto Polysius: Owner of the Polysius Company, who greeted Otto when he traveled to Neubeckum to see the company a few years after the end of World War II. (Chapter 32)

Professor [Joseph W.] Richards: A professor of metallurgy and minerology at Lehigh University, whose *Metallurgical Calculations* Otto read while he was at Clausthal. During his first trip to the US to investigate the possibilities for nickel production in Russia, Otto met Professor Richards and received from him an introduction to people at INCO. (Chapters 13, 18)

Watto: The father was employed as an electrician by the Russian navy; the son, Jon, became Otto's friend. Later, when Jon was a student in "Petrograd's" electrotechnical institute, he showed Otto around the city. (Chapters 7 and 11) nickel production in Russia, Otto met Professor Richards and received from him an introduction to people at INCO. (Chapters 7 and 11)

RECOMMENDED READINGS

Renate Lellep Fernandez

Agricola, Georgius {Georgius Bauer} *De re Metallica*; [in Special Collections, University of Chicago, translated by Herbert and Lou Hoover, 1912. Regenstein, B Level Science Microform Q111.L363 1980.] This 16th century work, translated back into German, and edited many times over, must have in some form come to Otto's attention in his youth as he was nicknamed "the Chemist" by his schoolmates, and was already doing meticulous technical drawings, probably modeled or inspired on the woodcut illustrations of Agricola's adapted editions.

Fermi, Laura. *Atoms in the Family: My Life with Enrico Fermi.* Chicago: University of Chicago Press, 1954.

Fittko, Lisa. *Escape Through the Pyrenees.* Translated by David Koblick. Evanston, Illinois: Northwestern University Press, 1991.

Gessen Masha, and Misha Friedman. *Never Remember: Searching for Stalin's Gulags in Putin's Russia.* New York: Columbia Global Reports, 2018.
I had Misha Friedman inscribe a copy of the book for me—"To Juri Lellep"—meaning "To the descendants of Juri Lellep." Not because Otto or any of us experienced a gulag but because, apparently, many Lelleps were deported, and their home base, the Ripsi farm near Viljandi, seemed to have vanished, to have not been remembered. When I looked for it during a recent visit to Estonia, no one could tell me where it was.

Kross, Jaan.
The Conspiracy & Other Stories (Silmade avamise päeve). London: Harvill Press, 1991.
How few, if not many, of the deported survived. Kross was able to return.

Professor Martens' Departure (Professor Martensi ärasõit). Translated by Anselm Hollo. London: Harvill, 1994.
The professor is the elite Estonian political/historical protagonist whose tsarist lifetime largely overlaps with Otto's. It is Martens' interior monologue remembering his life as he makes his last train ride from Pärnu toward St. Petersburg, dying along the way in borderline Valga, some years before the Bolshevik Revolution.

The Ropewalker: Between Three Plagues, Volume One (Kolme katku vahei). Translated by Merike Lepaaar Beecher. London: MacLehose Press, 2016.
In her introduction, the translator explains the trilogy's writing and emergence, and the symbolic paralleling of the time of Balthasar Russo (the protagonist) with Jaan Kross' time. The book includes interior monologues that I can imagine Otto mumbling to himself. It was published in Estonian in 1970, just as Otto was writing his memoir under the care and attentions of his Estonian niece Alice Veinbergs, also his typist. She never lost touch with the Estonian expatriate community and may well have been aware of it, even as Otto was writing his own.

Sailing Against the Wind (Vastutuulelaev). Translated by Eric Dickens. Evanston, Illinois: Northwestern University Press, 2012.
There are uncanny parallels with Otto's life in this story of a brilliant Estonian inventor who is independent of institutions, limited in his personal relationships with women, and seen by others as "tainted" by his connection with the "enemy." The protagonist has only one hand—as did the farmer for whom Mutti worked and with whom we lived while Otto was in Mexico.

Treading Air (Paigallend). Translated by Eric Dickens. London: Harvill, 2003.
The life of Ullo, the protagonist, as interviewed and intersecting with the fictional author/narrator—Kross himself. Both are about a generation younger than Otto. The book traces their journey through school years, and the Soviet, then German, then Soviet occupation and repression—years that Otto is likely to have glimpsed, imagined, and partially suppressed, most intensely, I suppose, while he was seeking employment in Pittsburgh. Only later, when receiving Estonian refugees in our Wauwatosa home was he in direct contact with any who had lived through those years of "treading air.")

Salumets, Thomas. *Unforced Flourishing: Understanding Jaan Kaplinski.* Montreal, Quebec, and Kingston: McGill-Queen's University Press, 2014.
Epigraph: "I have to build some bulwark for myself that this pain wouldn't crush me; that I'm even able to live. To some extent, I have managed to do that." (Jaan Kaplinski)

Taagepera, Rein. *Estonia: Return to Independence.* New York: Westview Press, 1993.
The descriptions of the Estonian National Awakening versus Russification (1860–1917) and Estonia's preparation for and achievement of independence (1917–1920) showed me how quickly events, people, and positions were moving—too rapidly to be remembered very clearly.

Wulf, Meike. *Shadowlands: Memory and History in Post-Soviet Estonia.* New York and Oxford: Berghan Books, 2016.
This book, and the others above, helped me to understand and better accept the discrepancies between Otto's memoir and my own memory, omissions from his story, and his many absences during signal periods and events for our family.

SELECTED BIBLIOGRAPHY

Kesaya E. Noda

For basic background regarding Estonia and its history and culture, as well as explanations of terms related to Otto's research and inventions, I consulted various websites (cited with other materials in the endnotes when they were significant to the text) and the *Encyclopedia Britannica* online. Sources upon which I depended most heavily are listed below. In cases where dates or details in the works of Raun and Miljan conflict, I have depended upon Raun. Please see, as well, Renate's recommended readings.

BIOGRAPHICAL MATERIALS RELATED TO OTTO G. LELLEP

Lellep Family Archive

ESTONIAN HISTORY AND CULTURE

Raun, Toivo U. *Estonia and the Estonians, Updated Second Edition (Studies of Nationalities)*. Stanford University: Hoover Institution Press, 2001.

Miljan, Toivo. *Historical Dictionary of Estonia (Historical Dictionaries, No. 43)*. Lanham, Maryland: Scarecrow Press, Inc., 2004.

THE ESTONIAN STUDENTS FUND IN USA, INC. (ESF)

Merivoo-Parro, Maarja. "Claiming Ethnicity in Overlapping Diasporic Conditions: Estonian Americans and Academic Mobility During the Cold War." *Acta Historica Tallinnensia, 21* (2015): 106-124.

Email from ESF, March 9, 2018.

OTTO'S RESEARCH AND INVENTIONS

Moore, Dylan. "Cement Plants and Kilns in Britain and Ireland." Accessed in 2016; still accessible in May 2018, but in an edited version as of 2017. http://www.cementkilns.co.uk/intro.html.

Spoerl, Joseph S. "A Brief History of Iron and Steel Production." Uploaded by Professor Joseph S. Spoerl, Saint Anselm College and last accessed May 3, 2018. http://www.academia.edu/31060927/A_Brief_History_of_Iron_and_Steel_Production.

Email correspondence (2016–2018) with Roger H. Soderberg (Professor Emeritus of Chemistry, Dartmouth College), Mr. Dylan Moore (environmental and industrial chemist), Eric Suuberg (Professor of Engineering, Brown University), and William J. Bernard, III (President, Surface Combustion, Inc.).

Photograph by Patricia Kalven

RENATE LELLEP FERNANDEZ

Born in 1932 in Heidelberg, Germany, Dr. Renate Lellep Fernandez is the youngest daughter of Otto G. Lellep and Frieda Brandt Lellep. Raised in the United States and originally trained as an occupational therapist, Dr. Fernandez earned a Ph.D. from Rutgers University as a biocultural anthropologist. Author of *A Simple Matter of Salt: An Ethnography of Nutritional Deficiency in Spain*, she is an independent scholar, writer, and consultant who has published in books and professional journals in the United States and abroad.

renate.l.fernandez@gmail.com

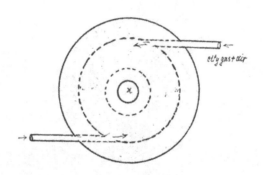

city gas + air

CPSIA information can be obtained
at www.ICGtesting.com
Printed in the USA
JSHW021950080722
27724JS00003B/11